12 ◆ LUDMILA

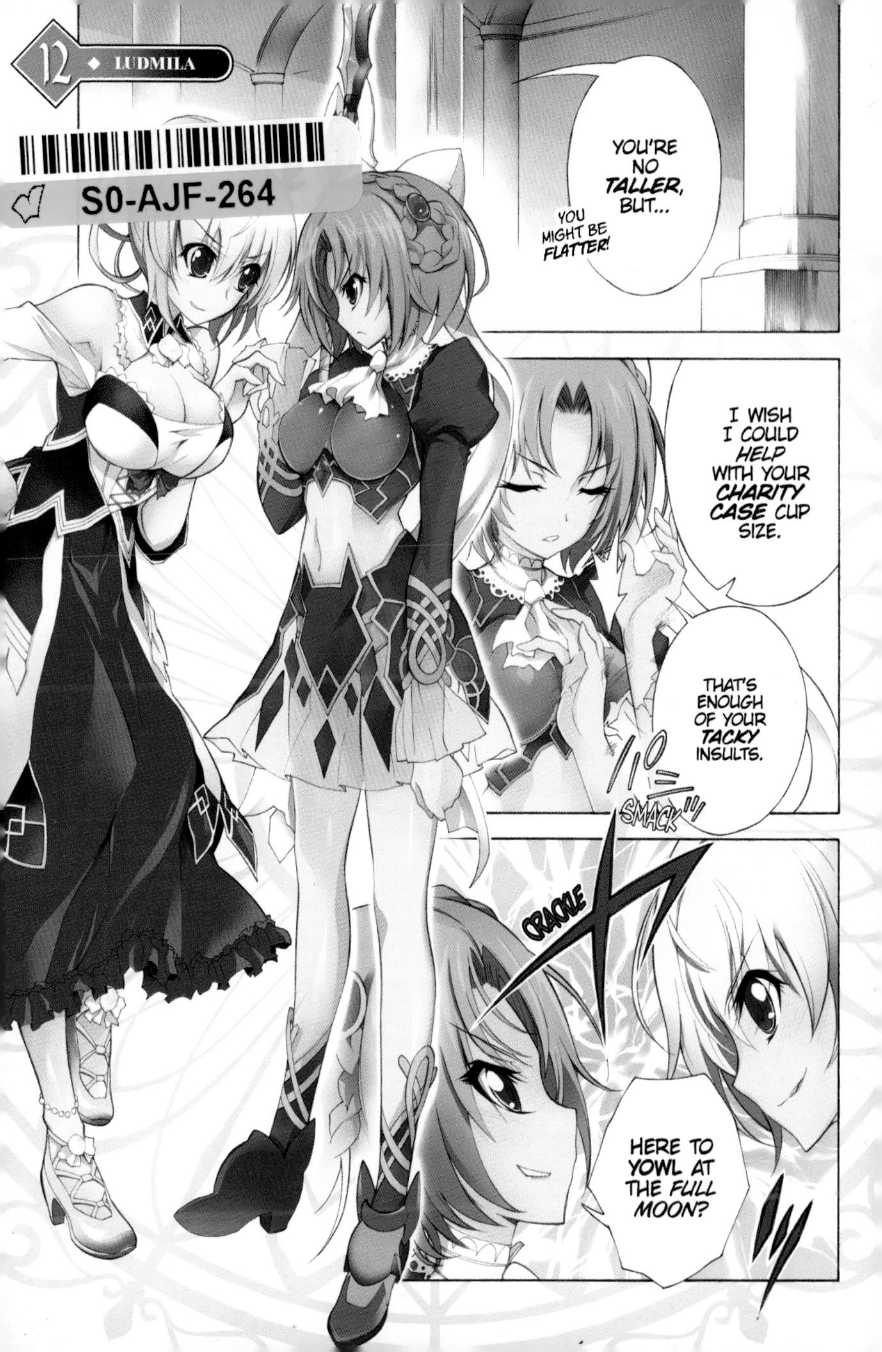
YOU'RE NO TALLER, BUT...
YOU MIGHT BE FLATTER!
I WISH I COULD HELP WITH YOUR CHARITY CASE CUP SIZE.
THAT'S ENOUGH OF YOUR TACKY INSULTS.
SMACK
CRACKLE
HERE TO YOWL AT THE FULL MOON?

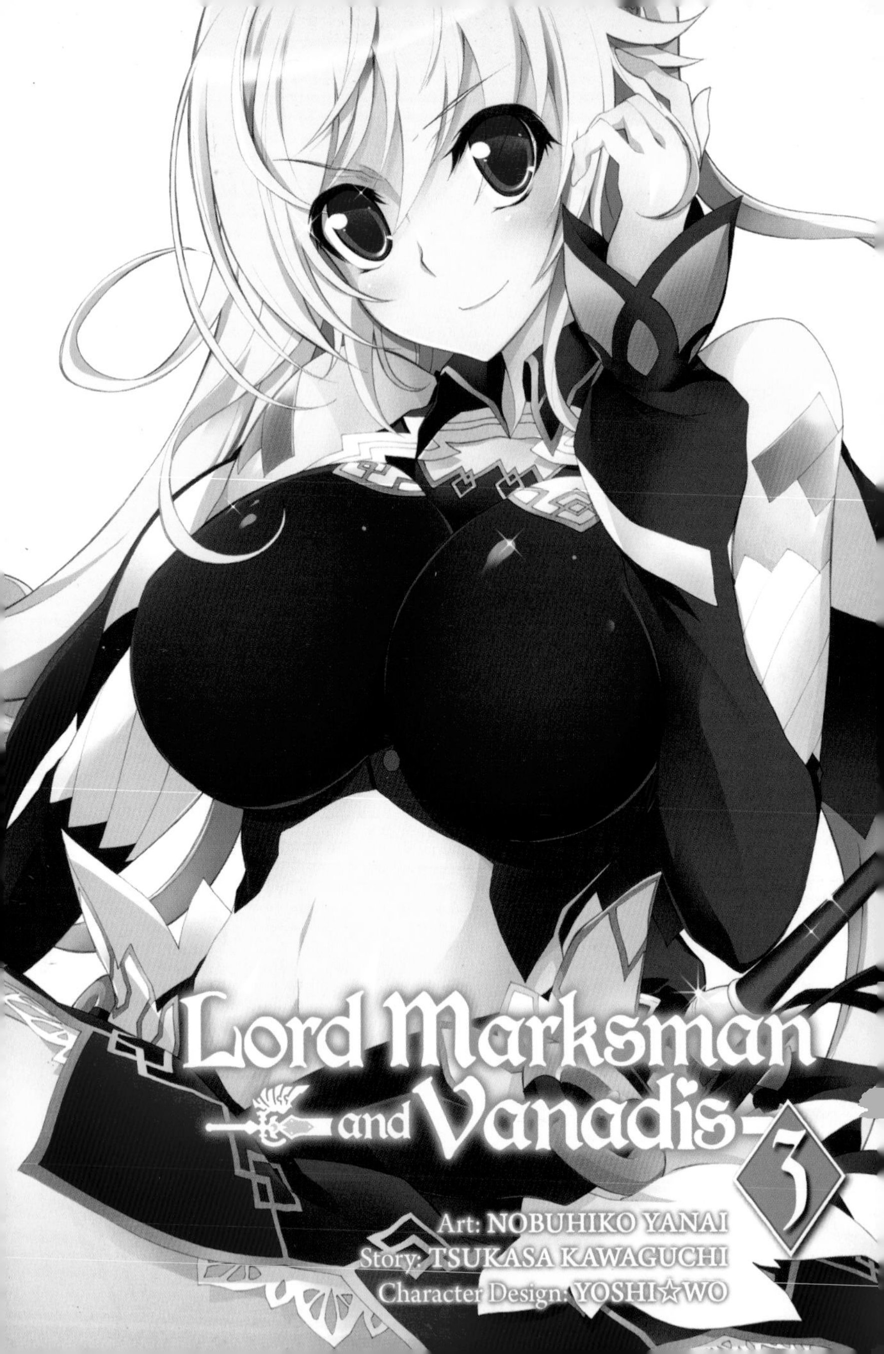
Lord Marksman and Vanadis
3
Art: NOBUHIKO YANAI
Story: TSUKASA KAWAGUCHI
Character Design: YOSHI☆WO

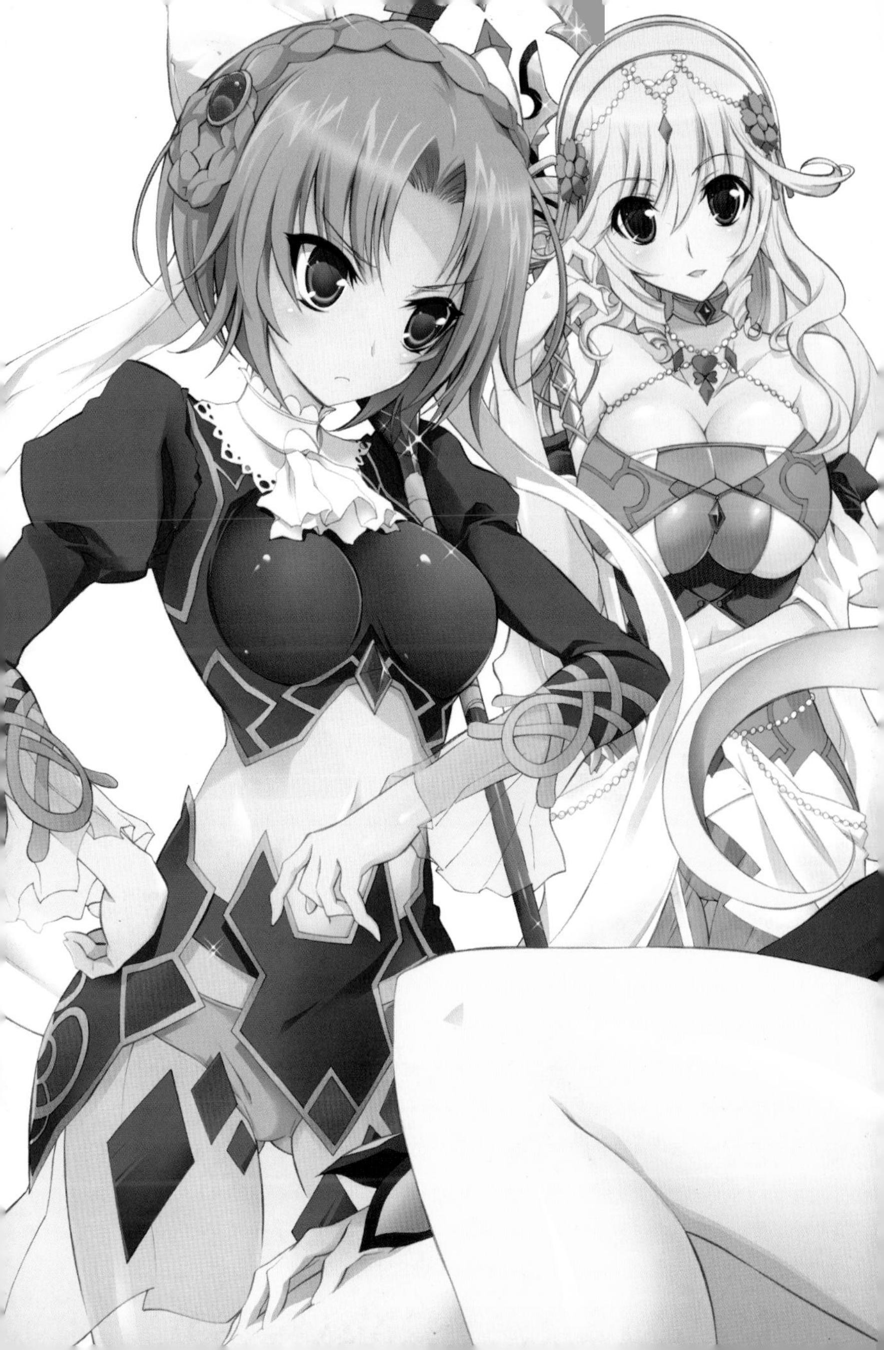

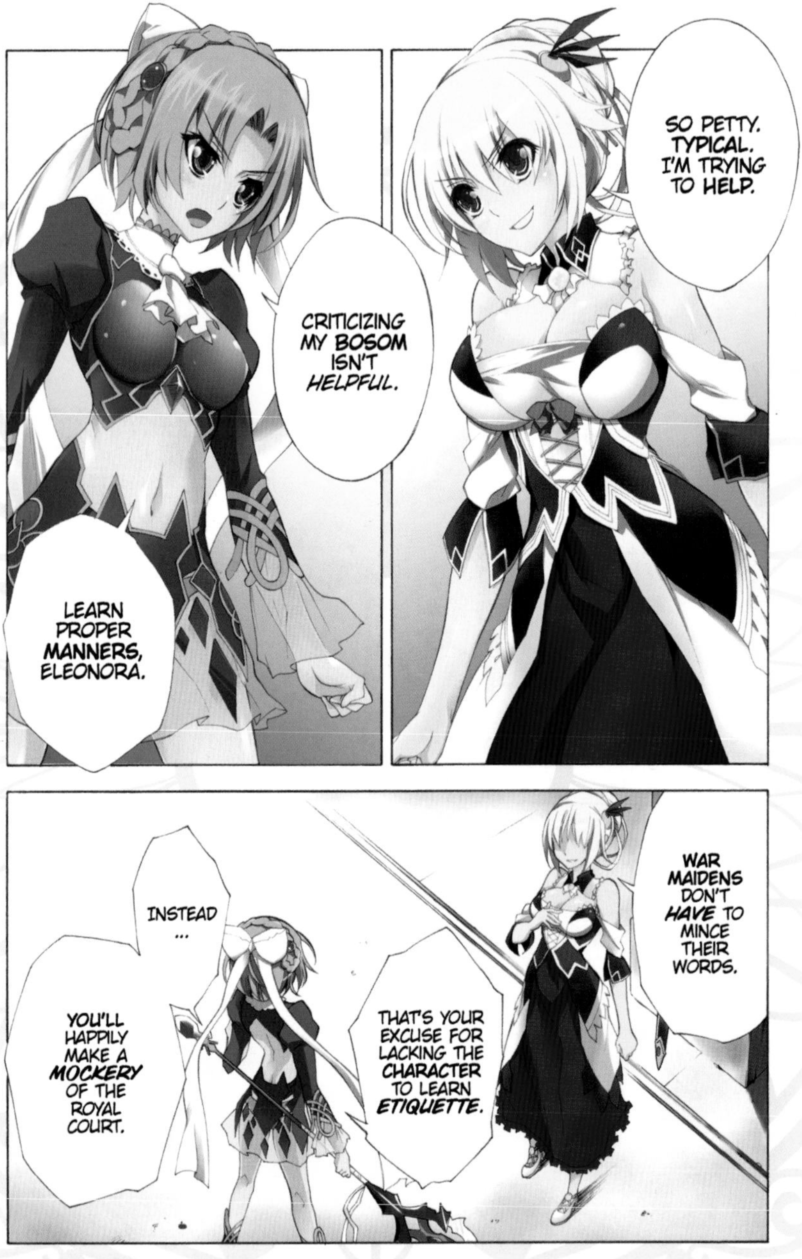
SO PETTY. TYPICAL. I'M TRYING TO HELP.
CRITICIZING MY BOSOM ISN'T HELPFUL.
LEARN PROPER MANNERS, ELEONORA.
WAR MAIDENS DON'T HAVE TO MINCE THEIR WORDS.
THAT'S YOUR EXCUSE FOR LACKING THE CHARACTER TO LEARN ETIQUETTE.
INSTEAD ...
YOU'LL HAPPILY MAKE A MOCKERY OF THE ROYAL COURT.

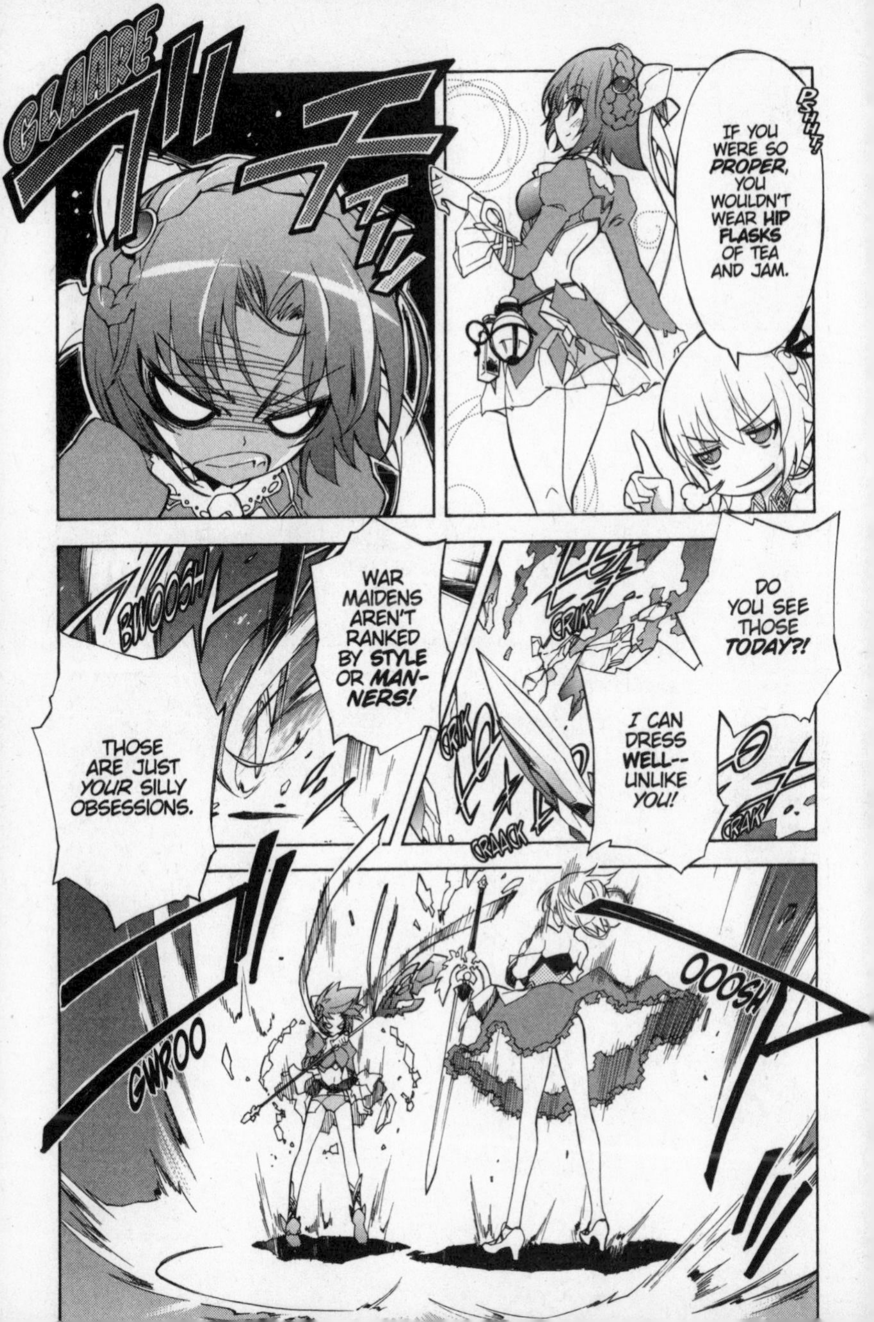
PSHHT
IF YOU WERE SO PROPER, YOU WOULDN'T WEAR HIP FLASKS OF TEA AND JAM.
GLAARE
DO YOU SEE THOSE TODAY?!
CRAK
I CAN DRESS WELL--UNLIKE YOU!
CRIK
CRIK
CRAACK
WAR MAIDENS AREN'T RANKED BY STYLE OR MAN-NERS!
BWOOSH
THOSE ARE JUST YOUR SILLY OBSESSIONS.
OOOSH
GWROO

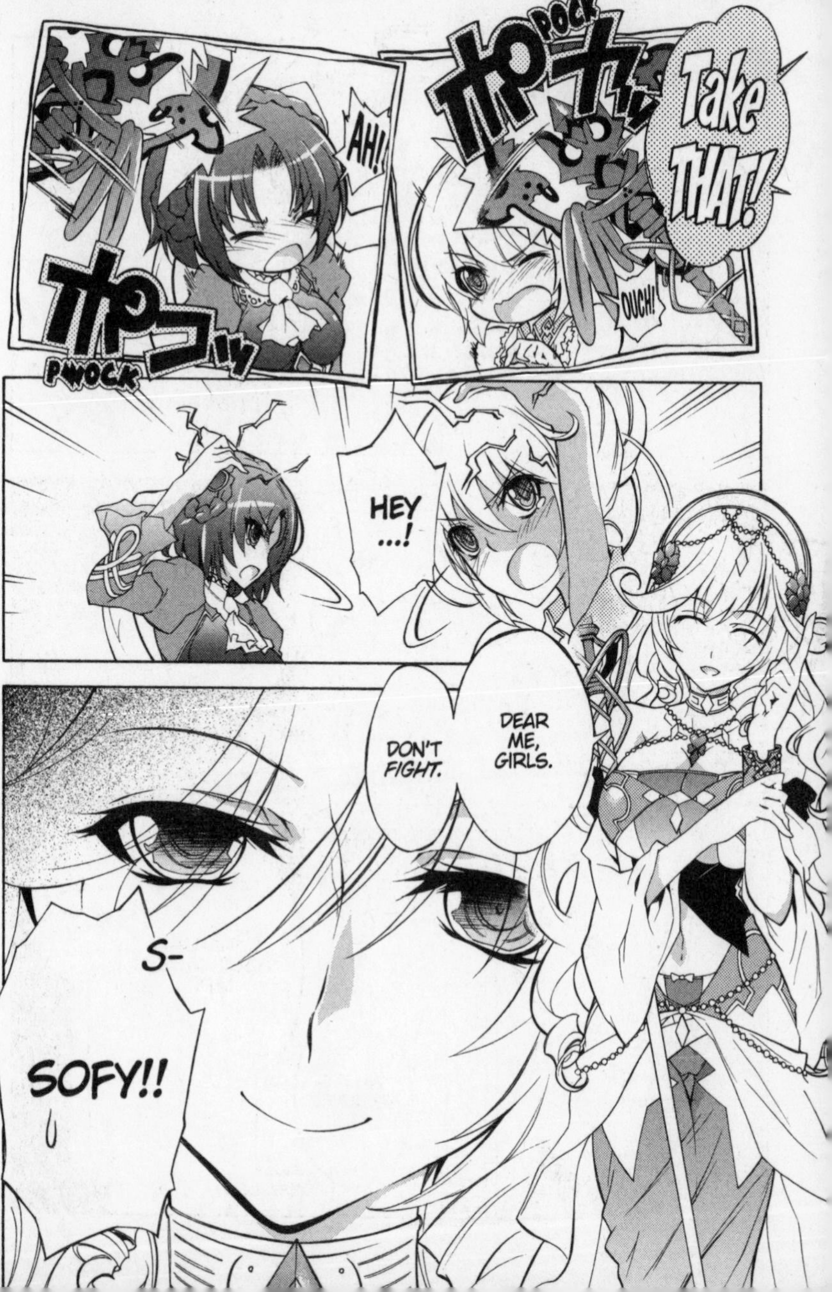
POCK
Take THAT!
OUCH!
AH!!
PWOCK
HEY ...!
DEAR ME, GIRLS.
DON'T FIGHT.
S-
SOFY!!

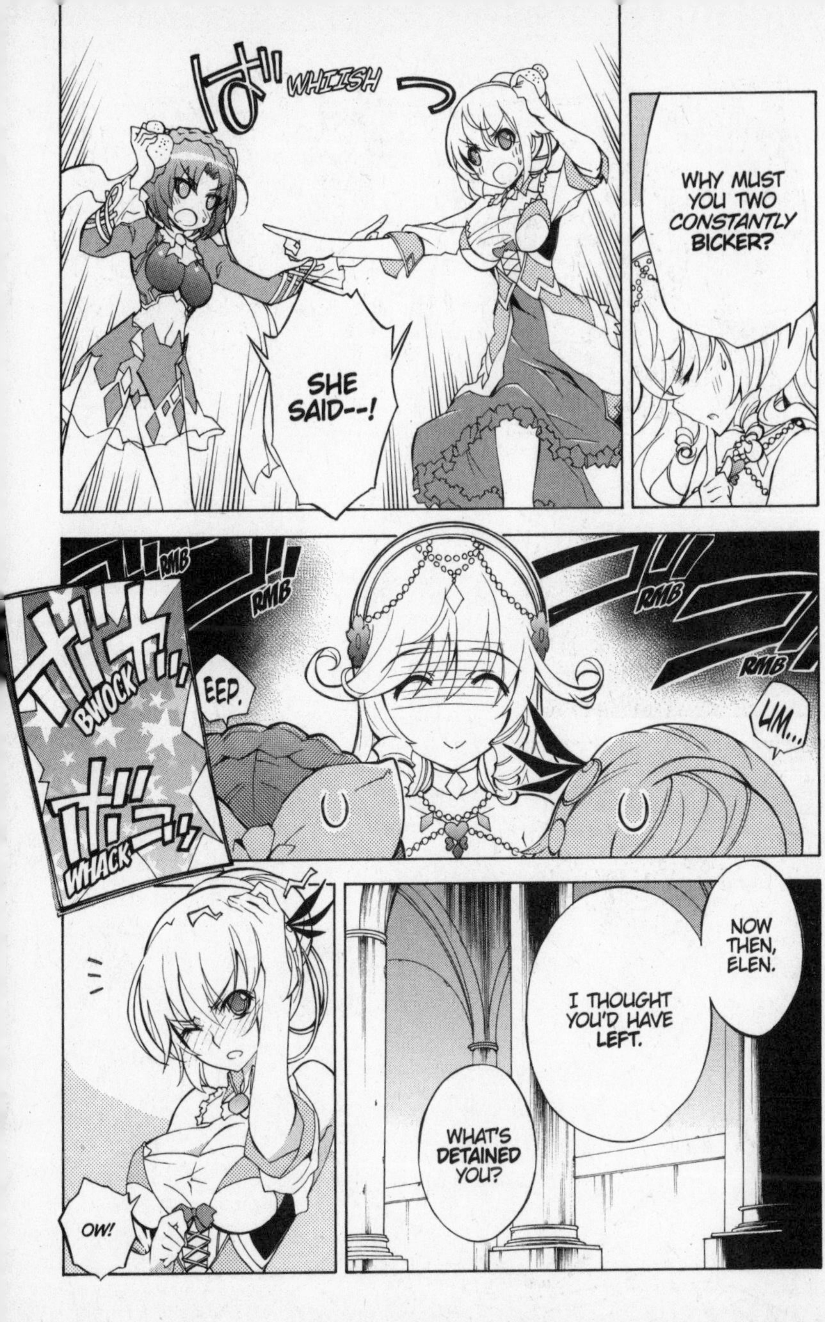
WHY MUST YOU TWO CONSTANTLY BICKER?
WHIISH
SHE SAID--!
RMB
RMB
UM...
EEP.
RMB
RMB
BWOCK
WHACK
NOW THEN, ELEN.
I THOUGHT YOU'D HAVE LEFT.
WHAT'S DETAINED YOU?
OW!

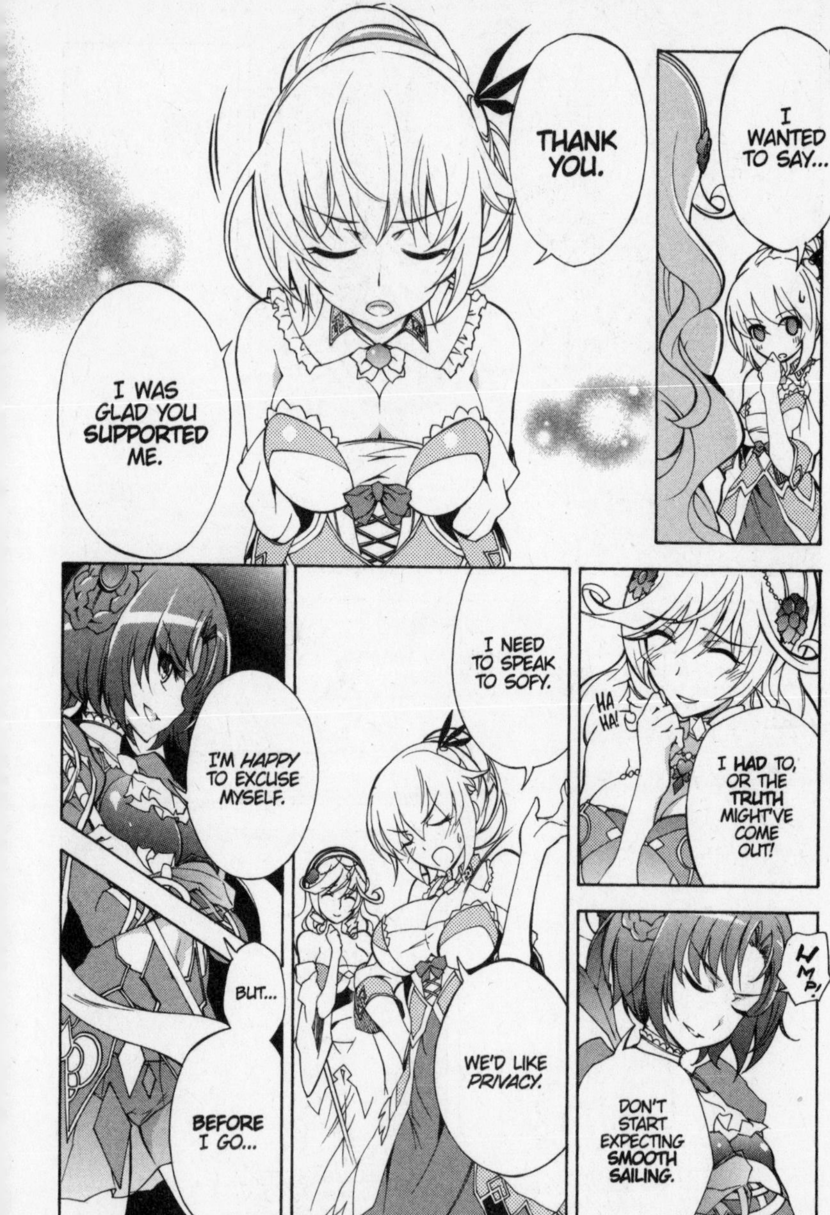
AHEM!
I WANTED TO SAY...
THANK YOU.
I WAS GLAD YOU SUPPORTED ME.
HA HA!
I HAD TO, OR THE TRUTH MIGHT'VE COME OUT!
HMP!
DON'T START EXPECTING SMOOTH SAILING.
I NEED TO SPEAK TO SOFY.
WE'D LIKE *PRIVACY.*
I'M *HAPPY* TO EXCUSE MYSELF.
BUT...
BEFORE I GO...

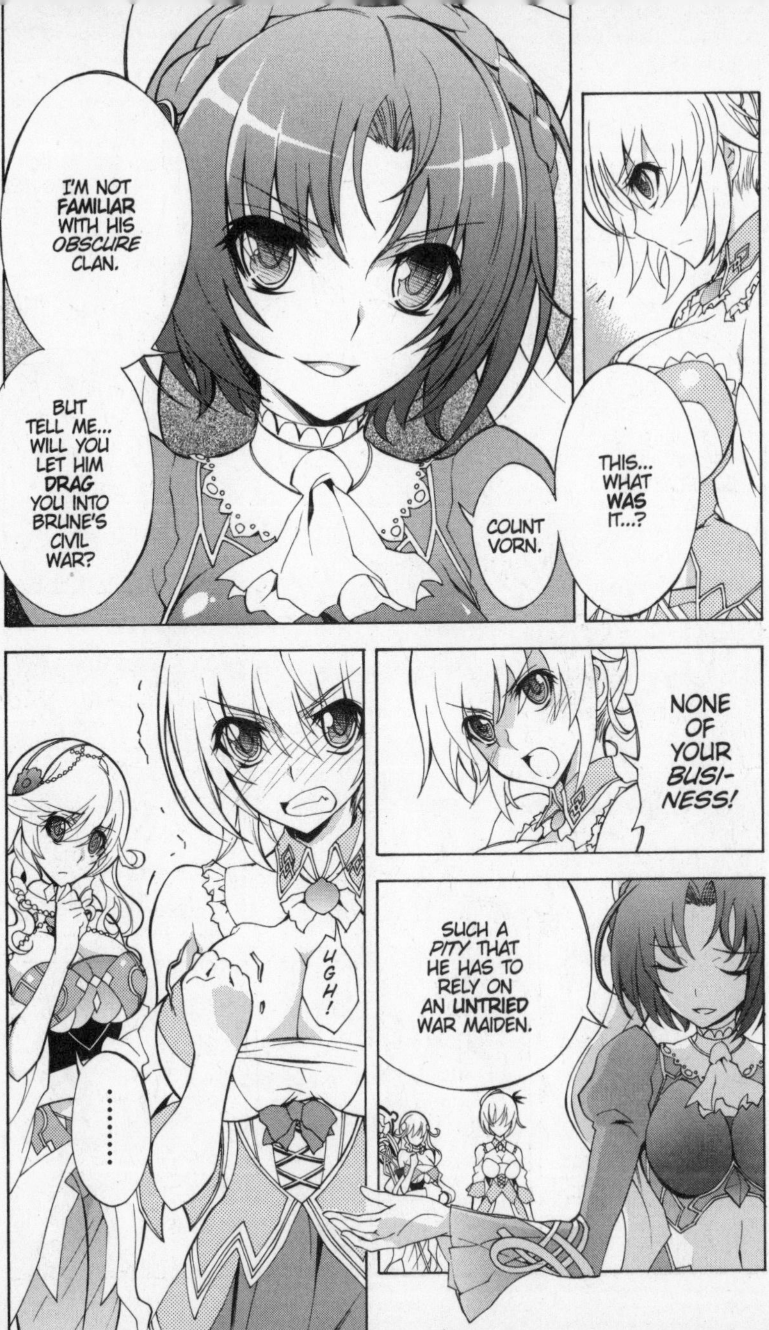
THIS... WHAT WAS IT...?
COUNT VORN.
I'M NOT FAMILIAR WITH HIS OBSCURE CLAN.
BUT TELL ME... WILL YOU LET HIM DRAG YOU INTO BRUNE'S CIVIL WAR?
NONE OF YOUR BUSINESS!
SUCH A PITY THAT HE HAS TO RELY ON AN UNTRIED WAR MAIDEN.
UGH!
......

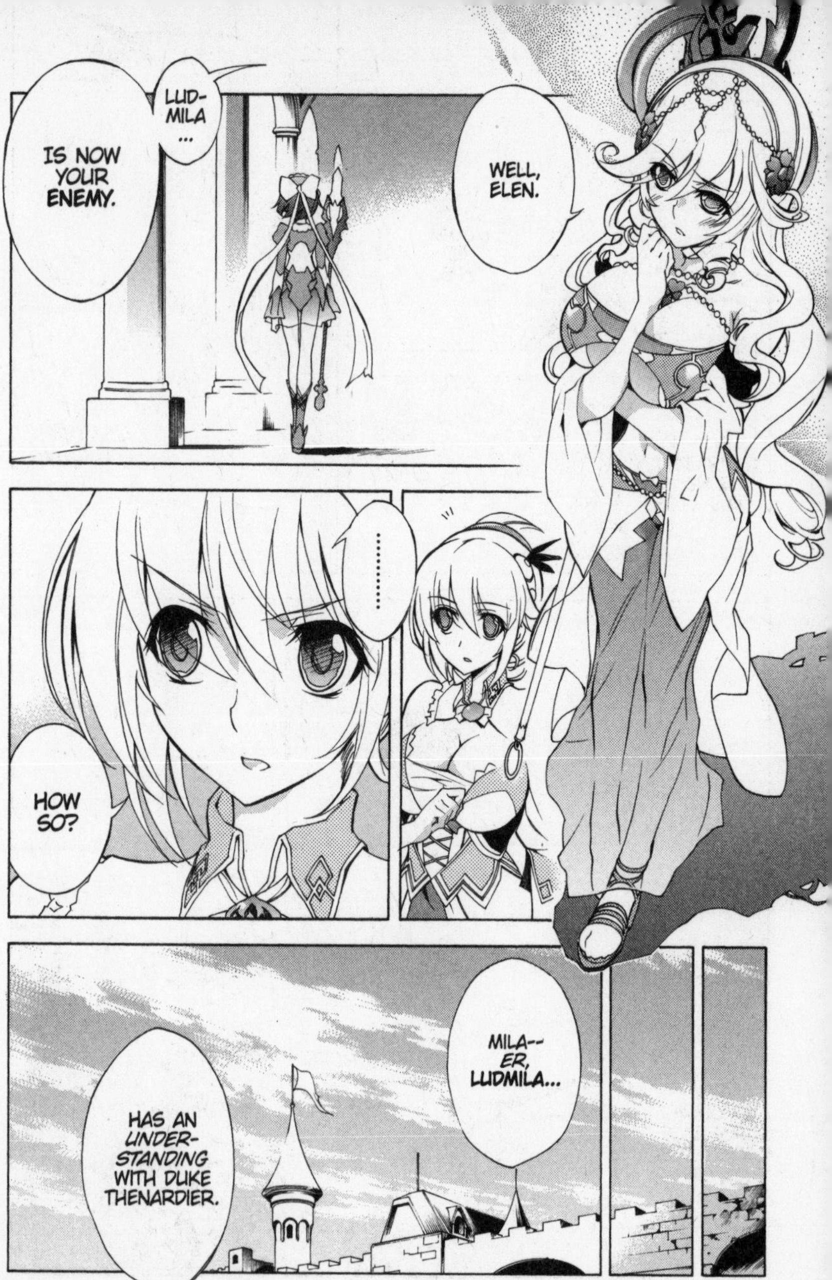
WELL, ELEN.
LUD-MILA ...
IS NOW YOUR ENEMY.
......
HOW SO?
MILA-- ER, LUDMILA...
HAS AN *UNDER-STANDING* WITH DUKE THENARDIER.

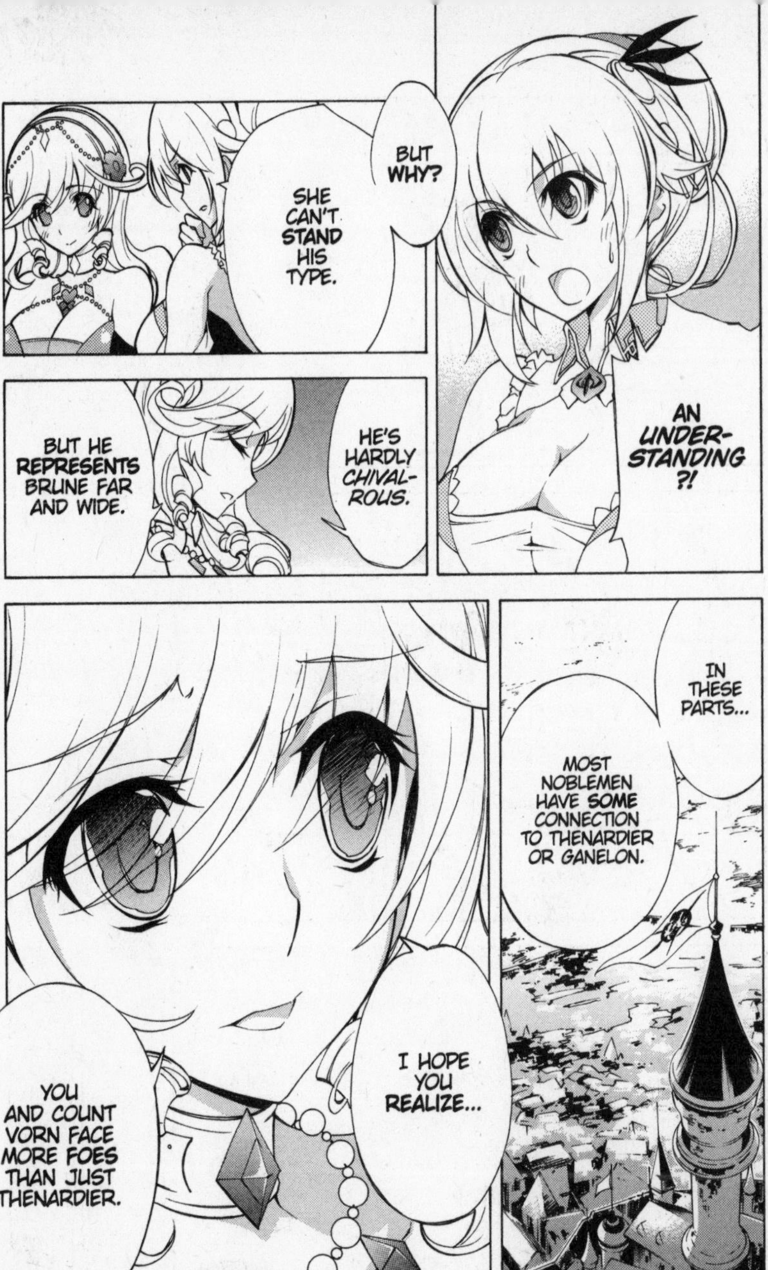
AN UNDER-STANDING?!
BUT WHY?
SHE CAN'T STAND HIS TYPE.
HE'S HARDLY CHIVAL-ROUS.
BUT HE REPRESENTS BRUNE FAR AND WIDE.
IN THESE PARTS...
MOST NOBLEMEN HAVE SOME CONNECTION TO THENARDIER OR GANELON.
I HOPE YOU REALIZE...
YOU AND COUNT VORN FACE MORE FOES THAN JUST THENARDIER.

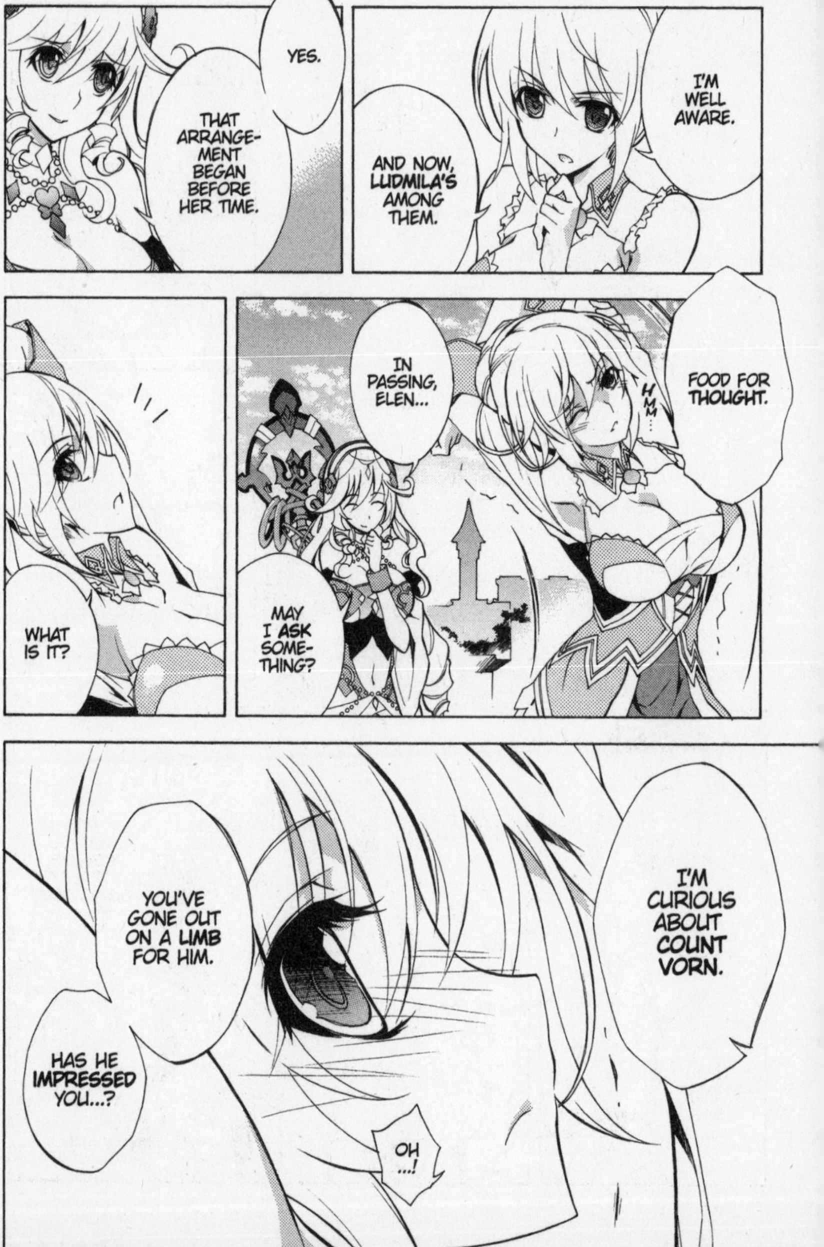
I'M WELL AWARE.
AND NOW, LUDMILA'S AMONG THEM.
YES.
THAT ARRANGEMENT BEGAN BEFORE HER TIME.
FOOD FOR THOUGHT.
HMM...
IN PASSING, ELEN...
MAY I ASK SOMETHING?
WHAT IS IT?
I'M CURIOUS ABOUT COUNT VORN.
OH...!
YOU'VE GONE OUT ON A LIMB FOR HIM.
HAS HE IMPRESSED YOU...?

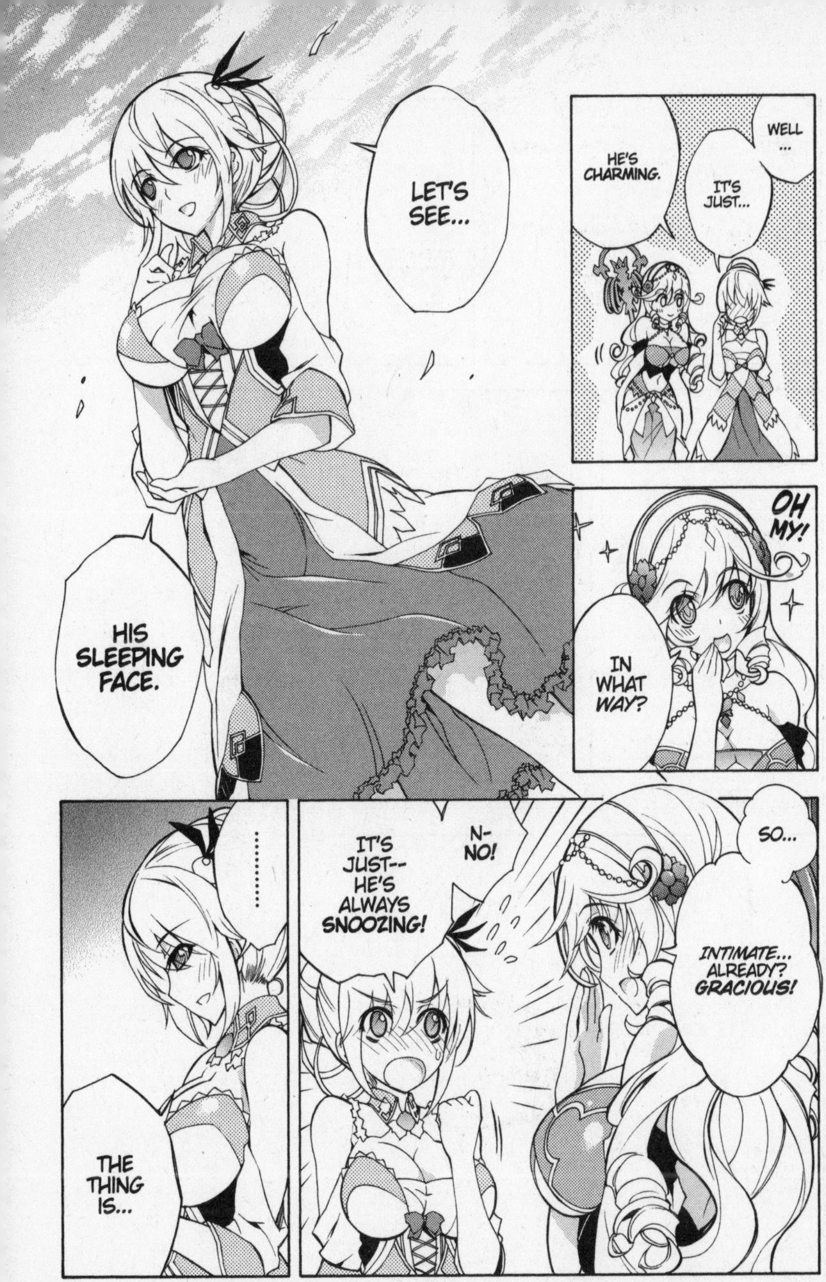
WELL...
IT'S JUST...
HE'S CHARMING.
OH MY!
IN WHAT WAY?
LET'S SEE...
HIS SLEEPING FACE.
SO...
INTIMATE... ALREADY? GRACIOUS!
N-NO!
IT'S JUST-- HE'S ALWAYS SNOOZING!
....
THE THING IS...

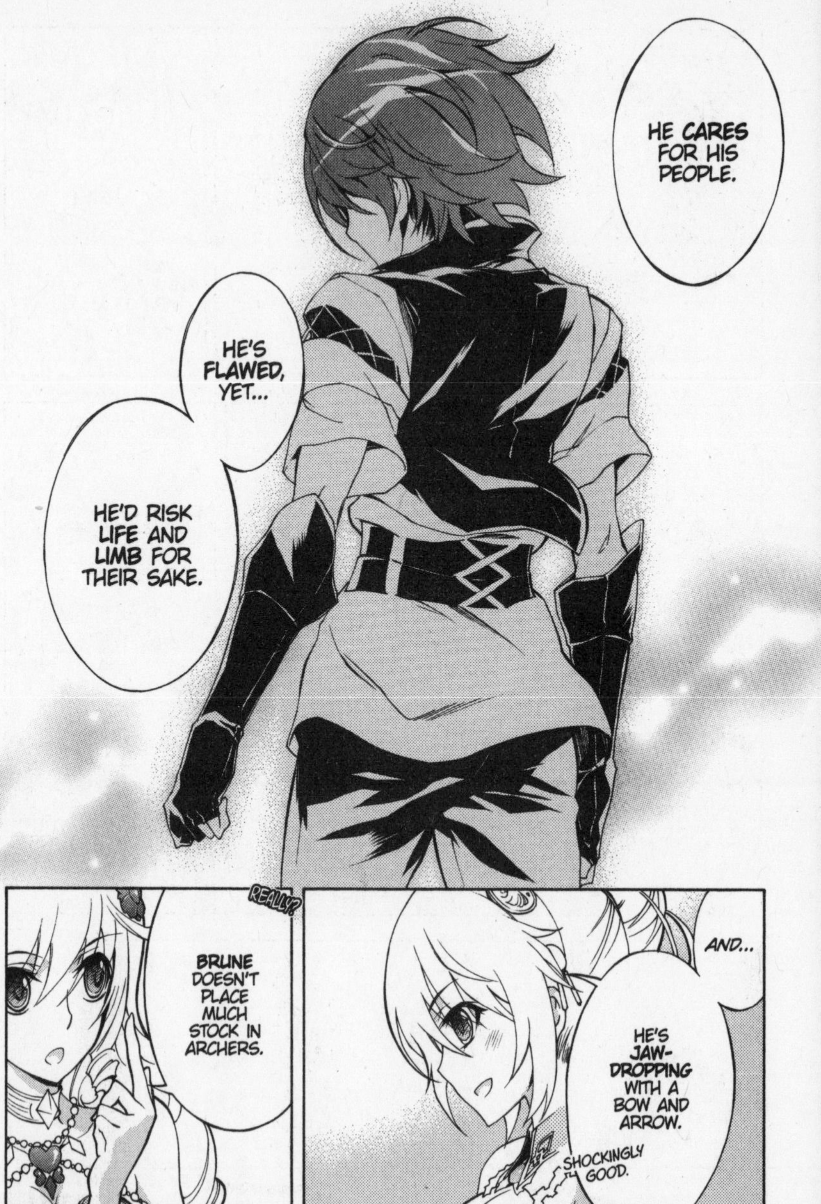
HE CARES FOR HIS PEOPLE.
HE'S FLAWED, YET...
HE'D RISK LIFE AND LIMB FOR THEIR SAKE.
AND...
HE'S JAW-DROPPING WITH A BOW AND ARROW.
SHOCKINGLY GOOD.
REALLY?
BRUNE DOESN'T PLACE MUCH STOCK IN ARCHERS.

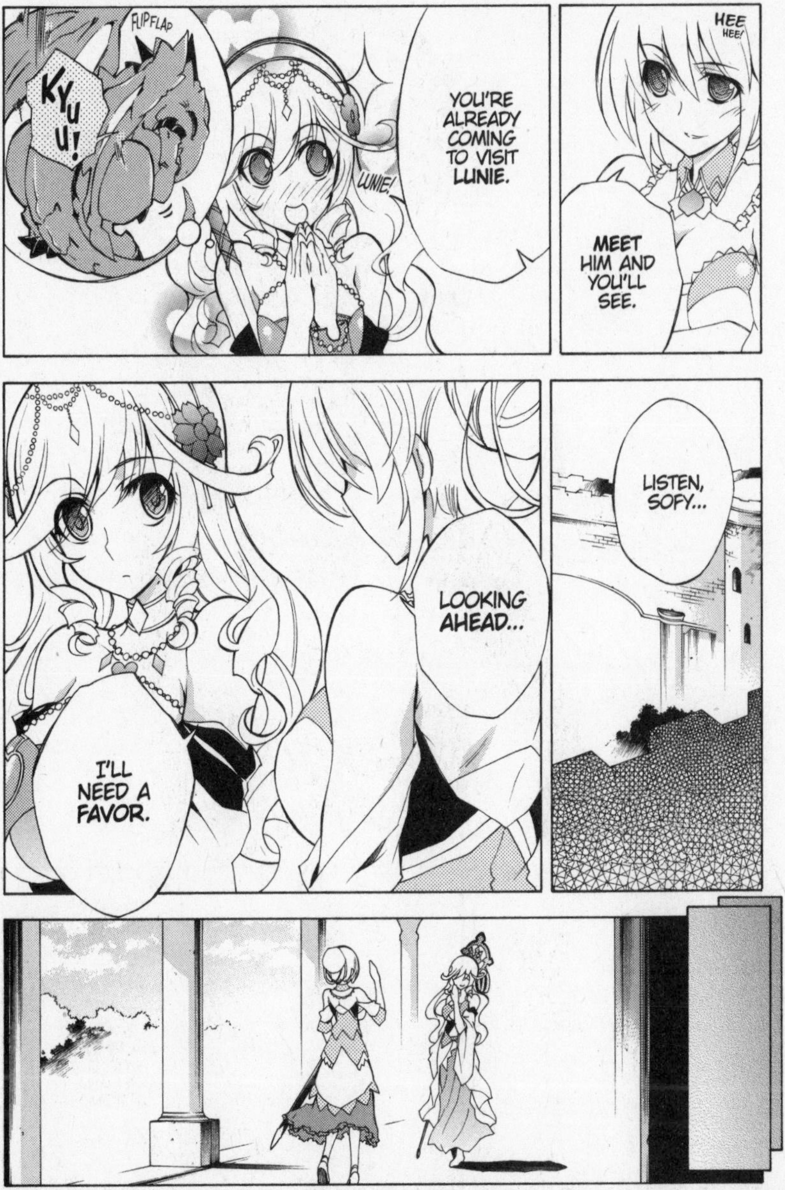
HEE HEE!
MEET HIM AND YOU'LL SEE.
YOU'RE ALREADY COMING TO VISIT LUNIE.
FLIPFLAP
LUNIE!
KYUU!
LISTEN, SOFY...
LOOKING AHEAD...
I'LL NEED A FAVOR.

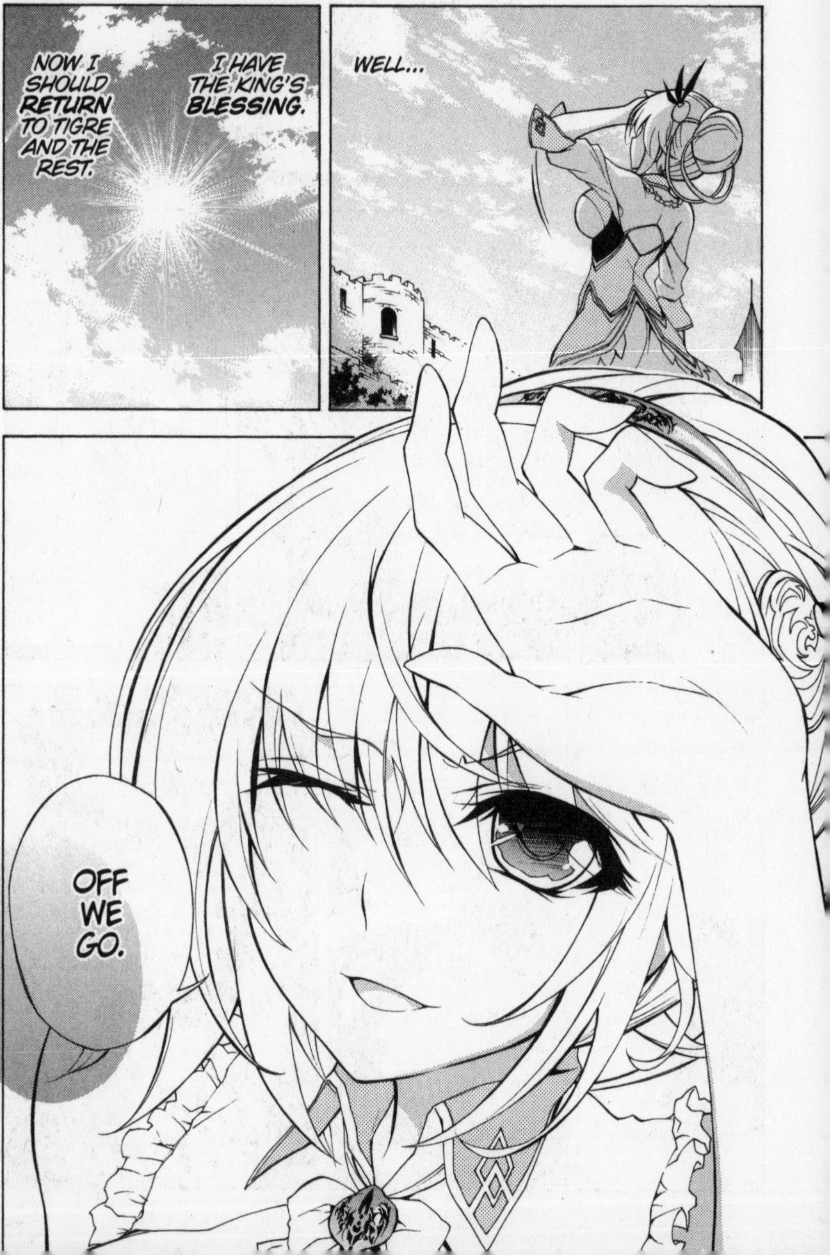
WELL...
I HAVE THE KING'S BLESSING.
NOW I SHOULD RETURN TO TIGRE AND THE REST.
OFF WE GO.

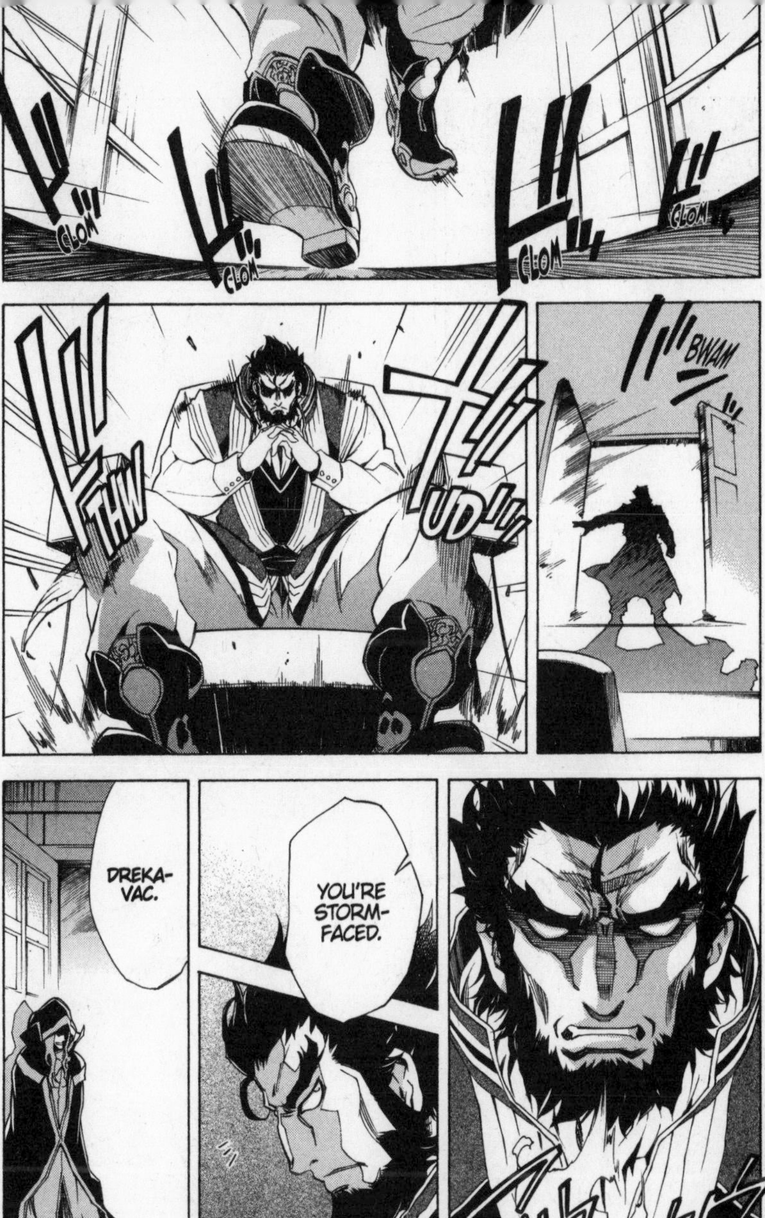
CLOM
CLOM
CLOM
CLOM
BWAM
THW
UD
HAA
AHHHH...
YOU'RE STORM-FACED.
DREKA-VAC.

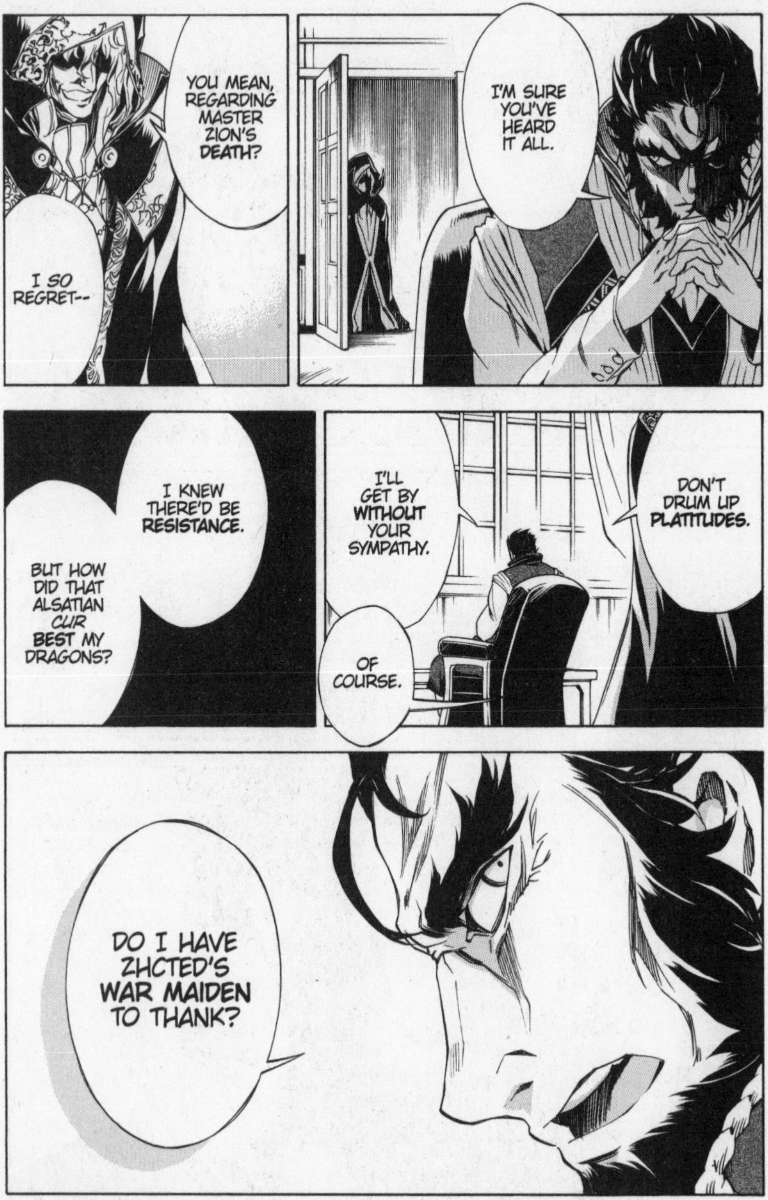
I'M SURE YOU'VE HEARD IT ALL.
YOU MEAN, REGARDING MASTER ZION'S DEATH?
I SO REGRET--
DON'T DRUM UP PLATITUDES.
I'LL GET BY WITHOUT YOUR SYMPATHY.
OF COURSE.
I KNEW THERE'D BE RESISTANCE.
BUT HOW DID THAT ALSATIAN CUR BEST MY DRAGONS?
DO I HAVE ZHCTED'S WAR MAIDEN TO THANK?

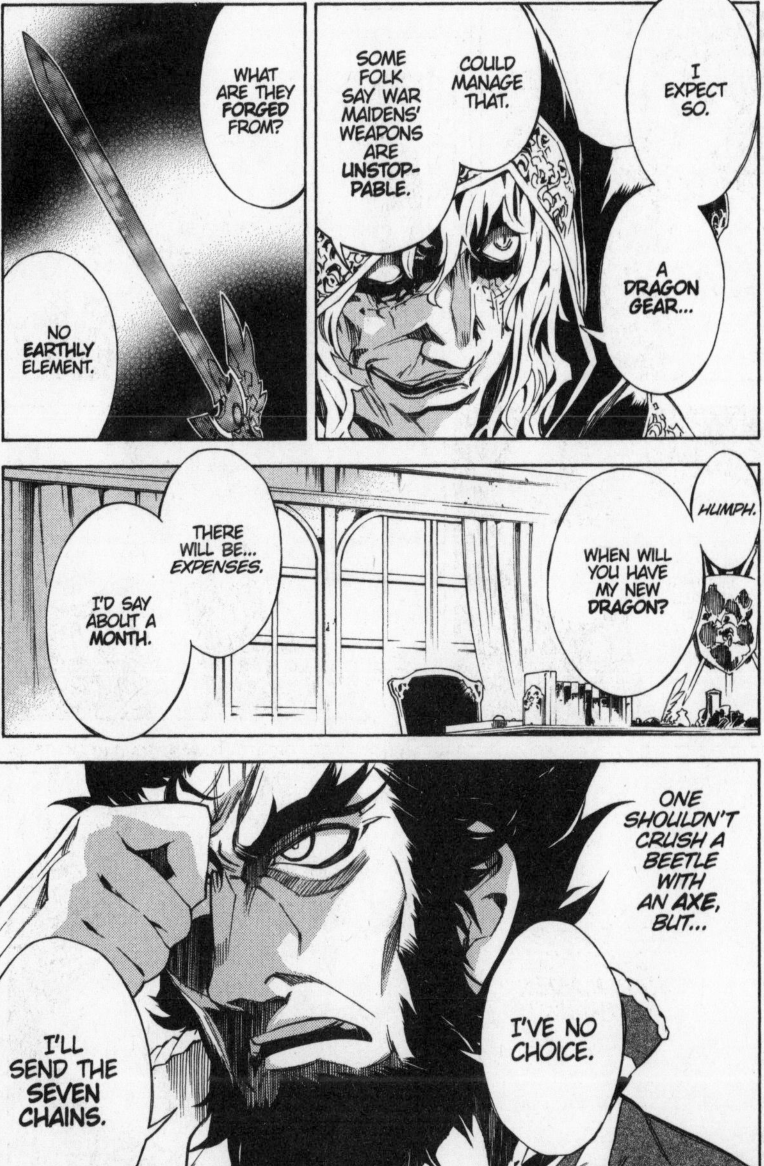
I EXPECT SO.
A DRAGON GEAR...
COULD MANAGE THAT.
SOME FOLK SAY WAR MAIDENS' WEAPONS ARE UNSTOP-PABLE.
WHAT ARE THEY FORGED FROM?
NO EARTHLY ELEMENT.
HUMPH.
WHEN WILL YOU HAVE MY NEW DRAGON?
THERE WILL BE... EXPENSES.
I'D SAY ABOUT A MONTH.
ONE SHOULDN'T CRUSH A BEETLE WITH AN AXE, BUT...
I'VE NO CHOICE.
I'LL SEND THE SEVEN CHAINS.

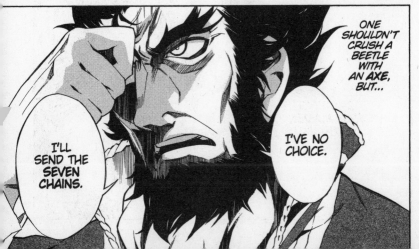

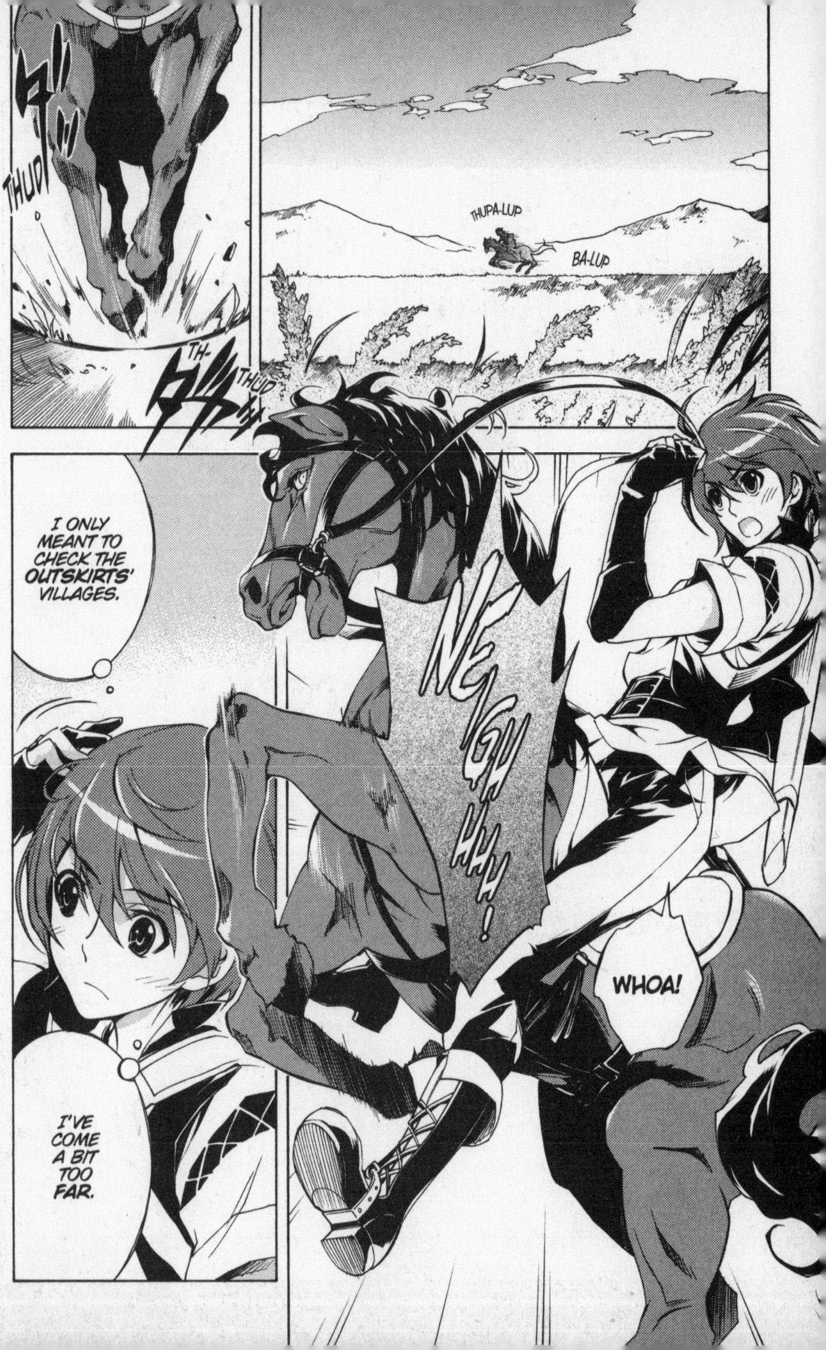
THUPA-LUP
BA-LUP
THUD!
TH-THUD
NEIGHHHH!
WHOA!
I ONLY MEANT TO CHECK THE OUTSKIRTS' VILLAGES.
I'VE COME A BIT TOO FAR.

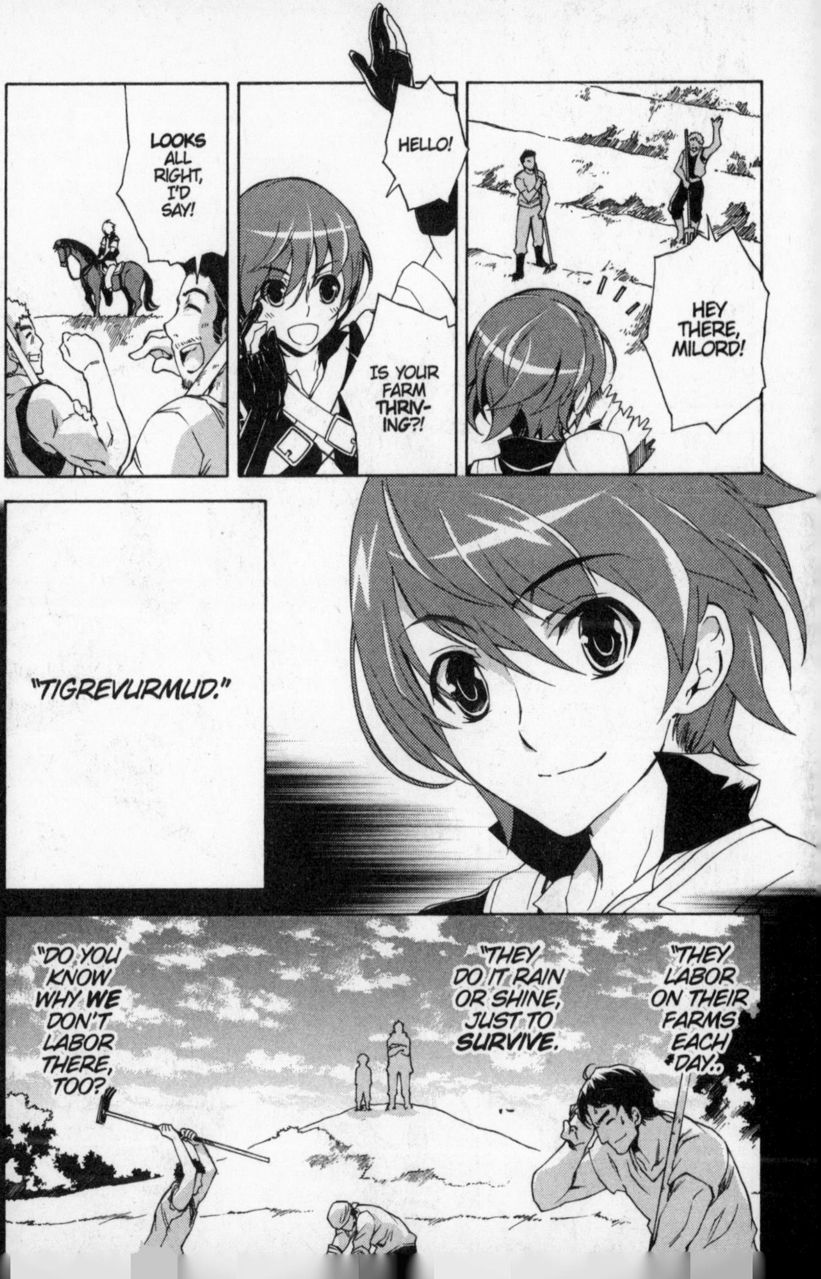
HEY THERE, MILORD!
HELLO!
IS YOUR FARM THRIVING?!
LOOKS ALL RIGHT, I'D SAY!
"TIGREVURMUD."
"THEY LABOR ON THEIR FARMS EACH DAY..
"THEY DO IT RAIN OR SHINE, JUST TO SURVIVE.
"DO YOU KNOW WHY WE DON'T LABOR THERE, TOO?

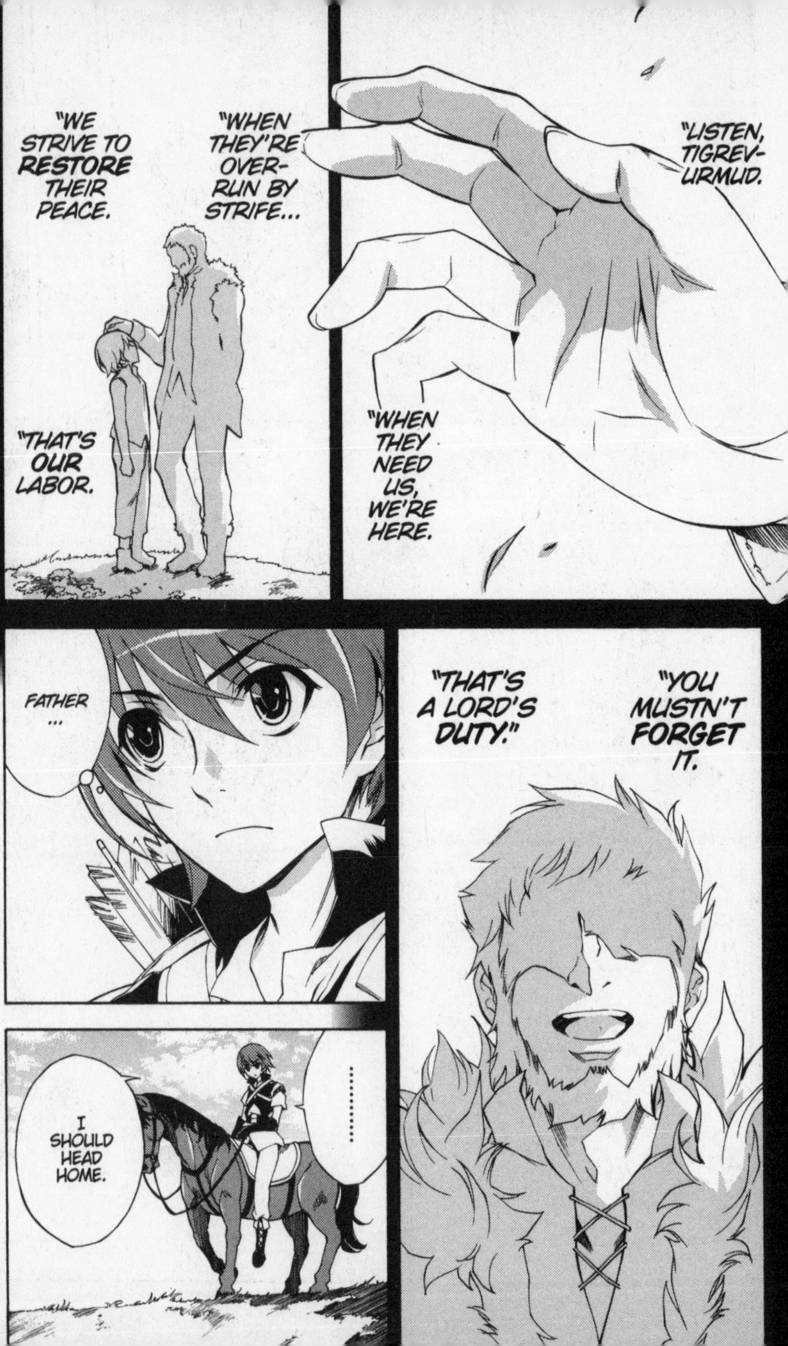
"LISTEN, TIGREVURMUD.
"WHEN THEY NEED US, WE'RE HERE.
"WHEN THEY'RE OVER-RUN BY STRIFE...
"WE STRIVE TO RESTORE THEIR PEACE.
"THAT'S OUR LABOR.
"YOU MUSTN'T FORGET IT.
"THAT'S A LORD'S DUTY."
FATHER ...
......
I SHOULD HEAD HOME.

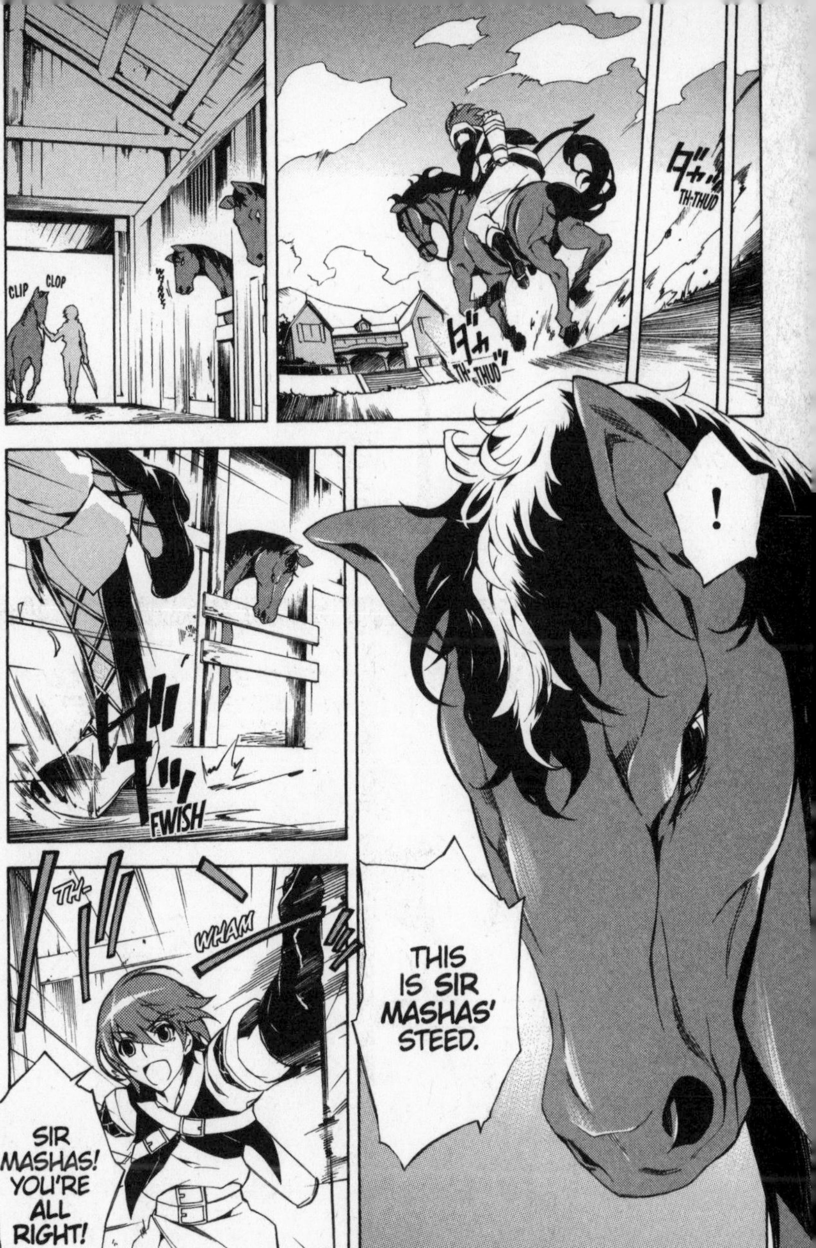
TH-THUD
TH-THUD
CLIP CLOP
!
THIS IS SIR MASHAS' STEED.
FWISH
TH-
WHAM
SIR MASHAS! YOU'RE ALL RIGHT!

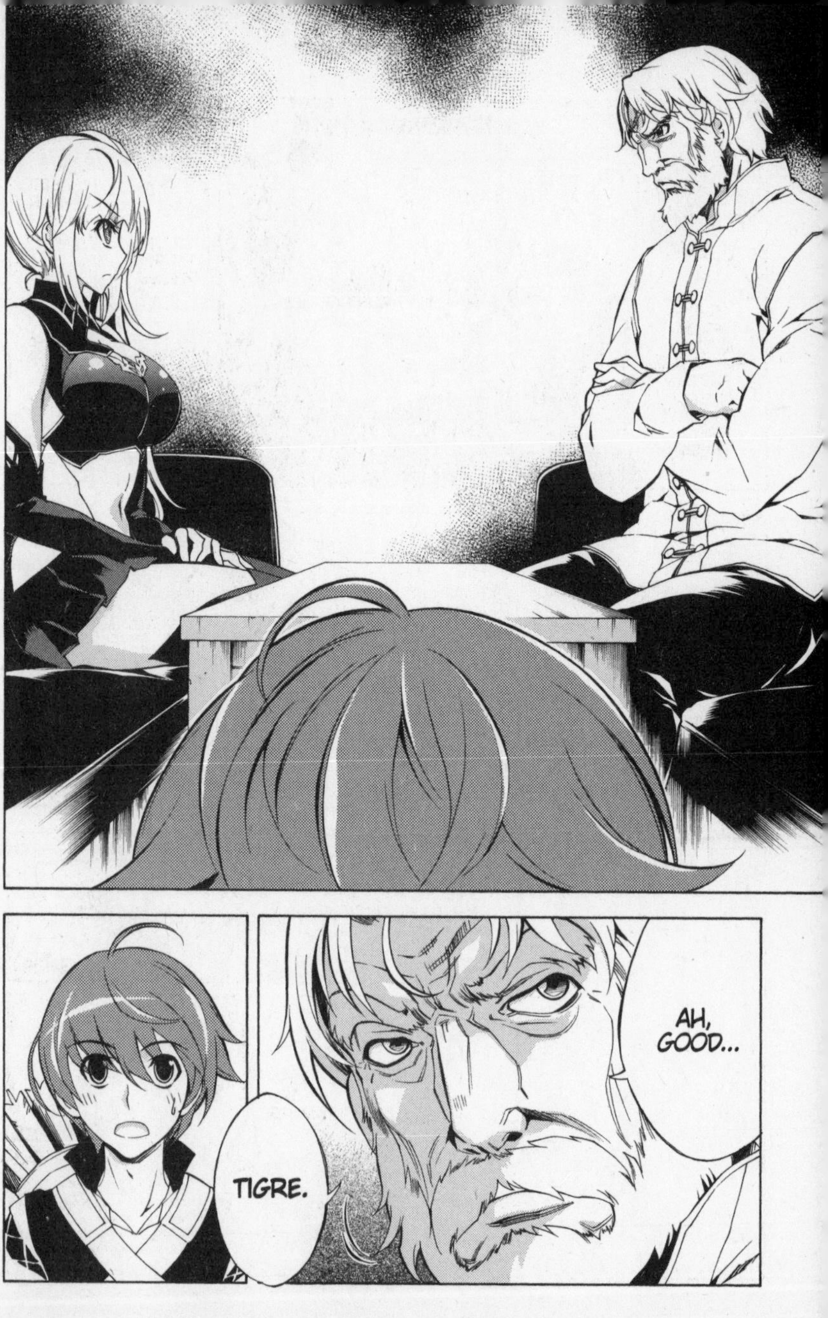
AH, GOOD...
TIGRE.

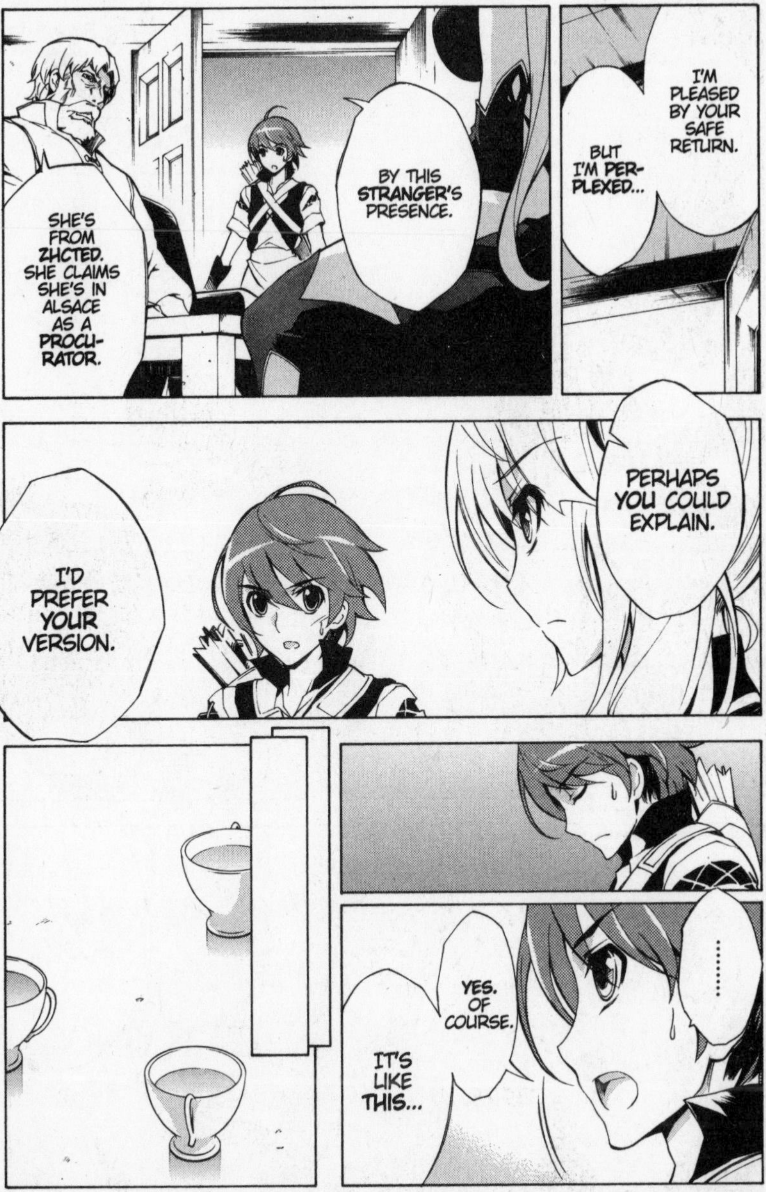
I'M PLEASED BY YOUR SAFE RETURN.
BUT I'M PERPLEXED...
BY THIS STRANGER'S PRESENCE.
SHE'S FROM ZHCTED. SHE CLAIMS SHE'S IN ALSACE AS A PROCURATOR.
PERHAPS YOU COULD EXPLAIN.
I'D PREFER YOUR VERSION.
....
YES. OF COURSE.
IT'S LIKE THIS...

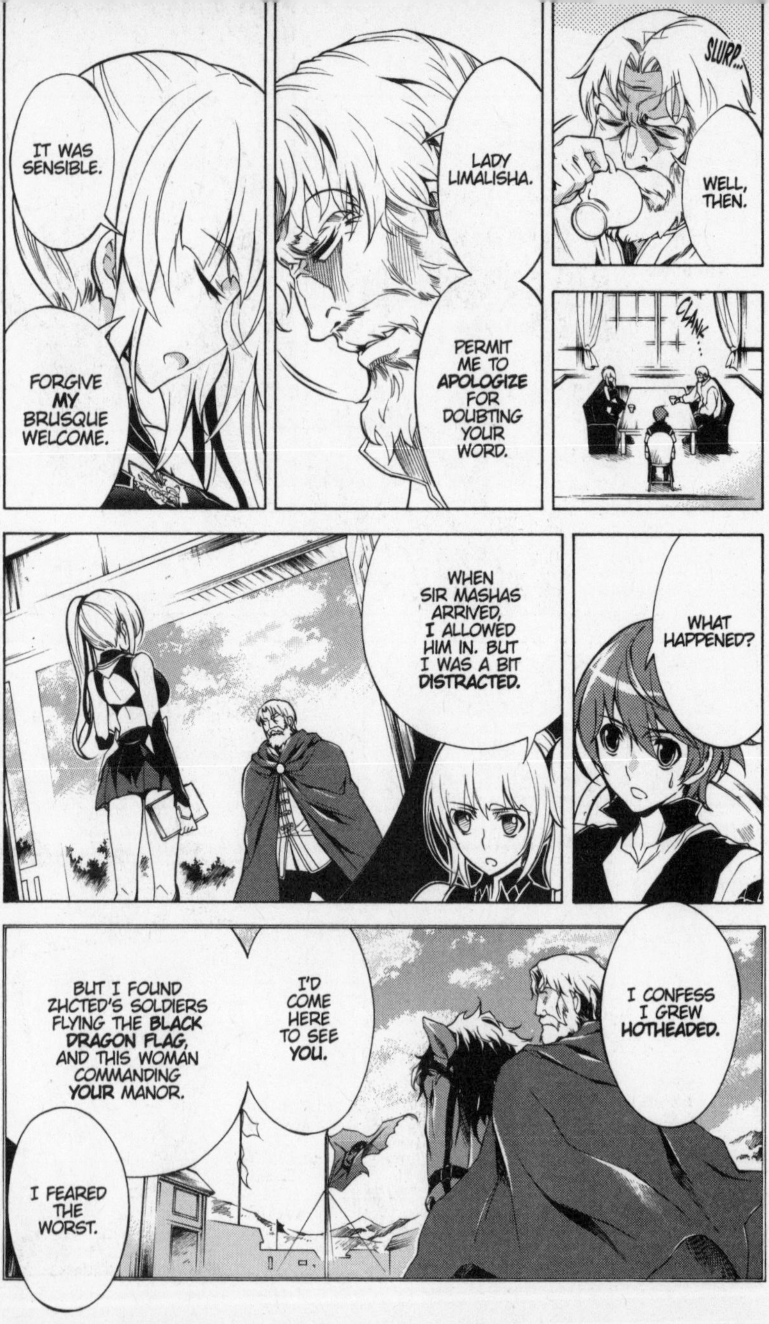
SLURP...
WELL, THEN.
CLANK...
LADY LIMALISHA.
PERMIT ME TO APOLOGIZE FOR DOUBTING YOUR WORD.
IT WAS SENSIBLE.
FORGIVE MY BRUSQUE WELCOME.
WHAT HAPPENED?
WHEN SIR MASHAS ARRIVED, I ALLOWED HIM IN. BUT I WAS A BIT DISTRACTED.
I CONFESS I GREW HOTHEADED.
I'D COME HERE TO SEE YOU.
BUT I FOUND ZHCTED'S SOLDIERS FLYING THE BLACK DRAGON FLAG, AND THIS WOMAN COMMANDING YOUR MANOR.
I FEARED THE WORST.

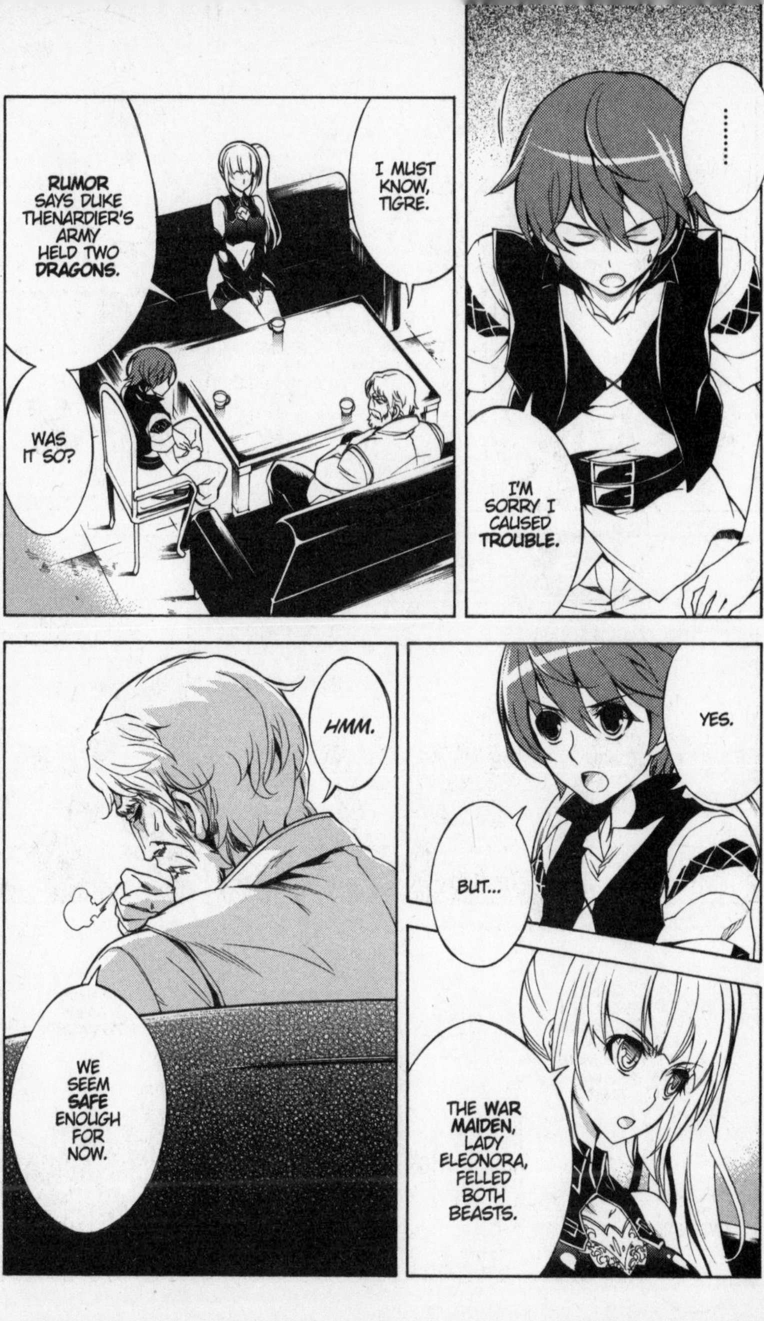
……
I'M SORRY I CAUSED TROUBLE.
I MUST KNOW, TIGRE.
RUMOR SAYS DUKE THENARDIER'S ARMY HELD TWO DRAGONS.
WAS IT SO?
YES.
BUT...
THE WAR MAIDEN, LADY ELEONORA, FELLED BOTH BEASTS.
HMM.
WE SEEM SAFE ENOUGH FOR NOW.

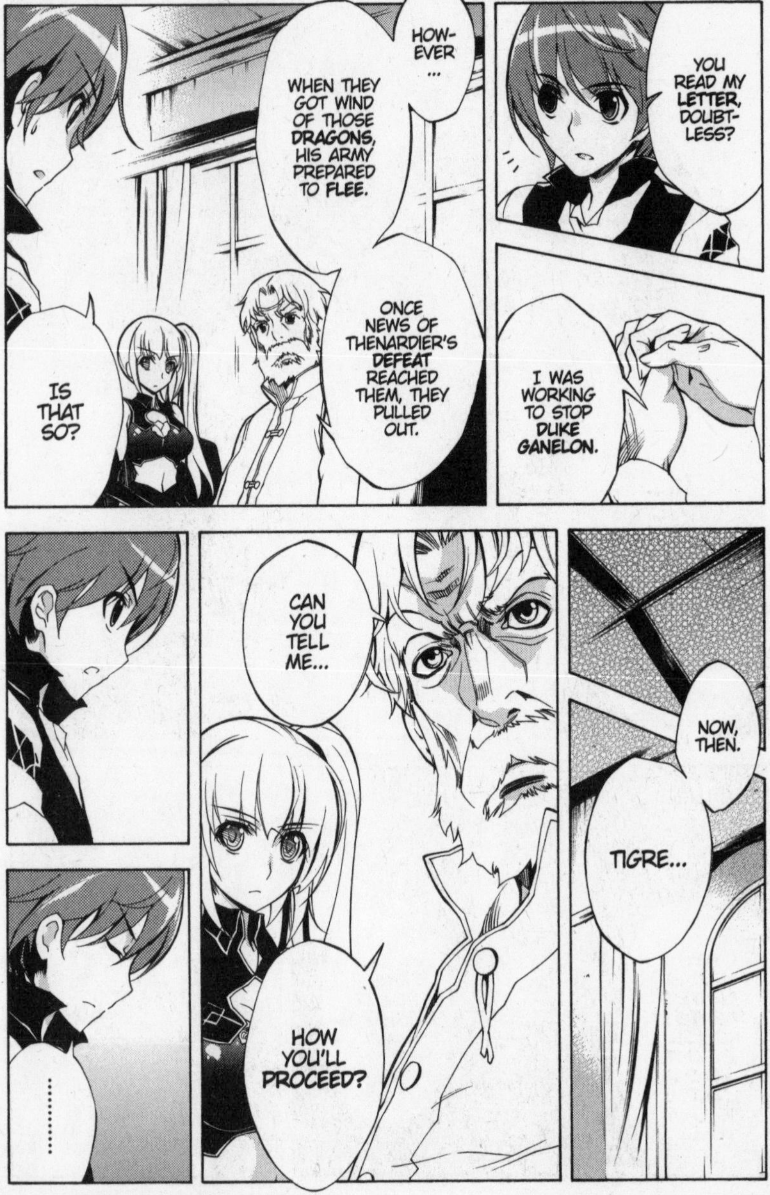
YOU READ MY LETTER, DOUBTLESS?
I WAS WORKING TO STOP DUKE GANELON.
HOW-EVER ...
WHEN THEY GOT WIND OF THOSE DRAGONS, HIS ARMY PREPARED TO FLEE.
ONCE NEWS OF THENARDIER'S DEFEAT REACHED THEM, THEY PULLED OUT.
IS THAT SO?
NOW, THEN.
TIGRE...
CAN YOU TELL ME...
HOW YOU'LL PROCEED?
....

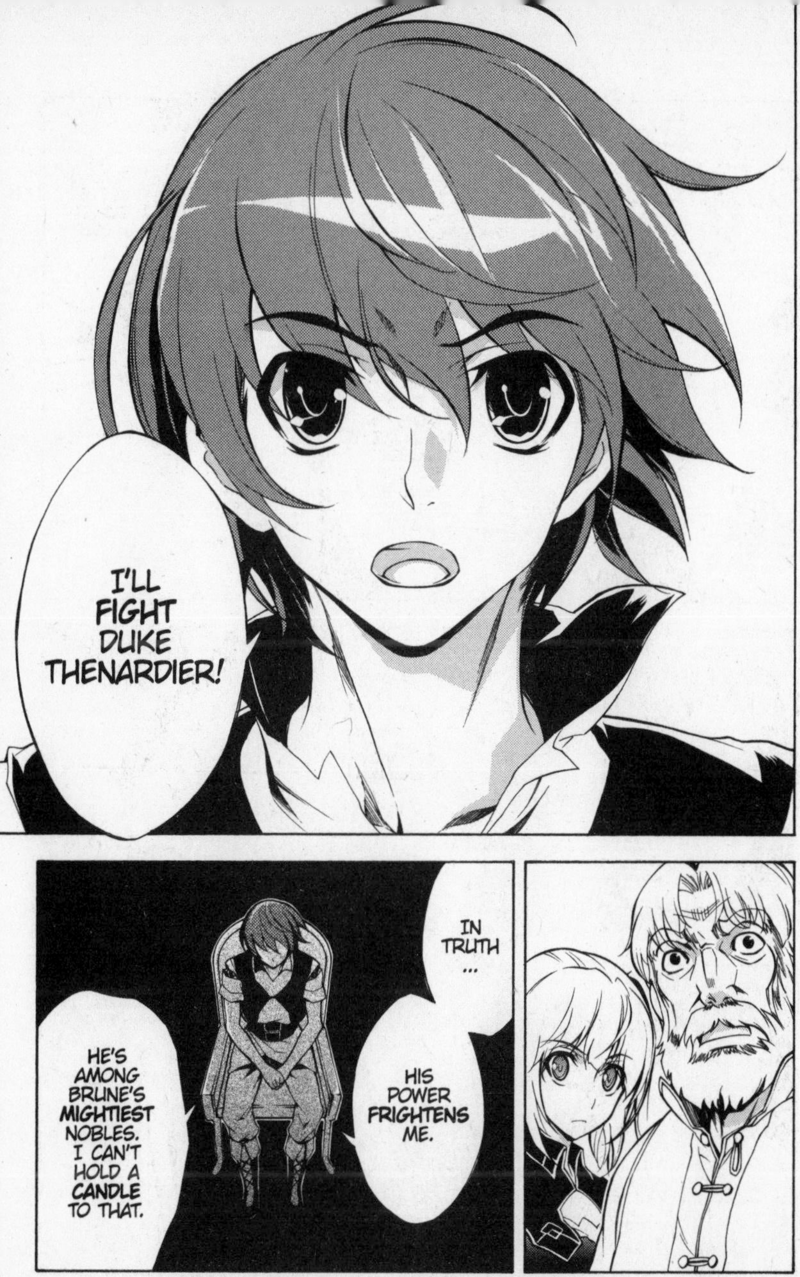
I'LL FIGHT DUKE THENARDIER!
IN TRUTH ...
HIS POWER FRIGHTENS ME.
HE'S AMONG BRUNE'S MIGHTIEST NOBLES. I CAN'T HOLD A CANDLE TO THAT.

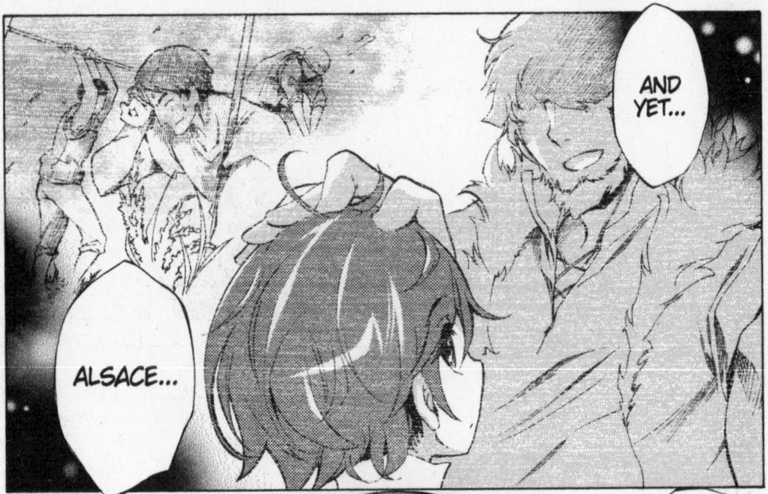
AND YET...
ALSACE...

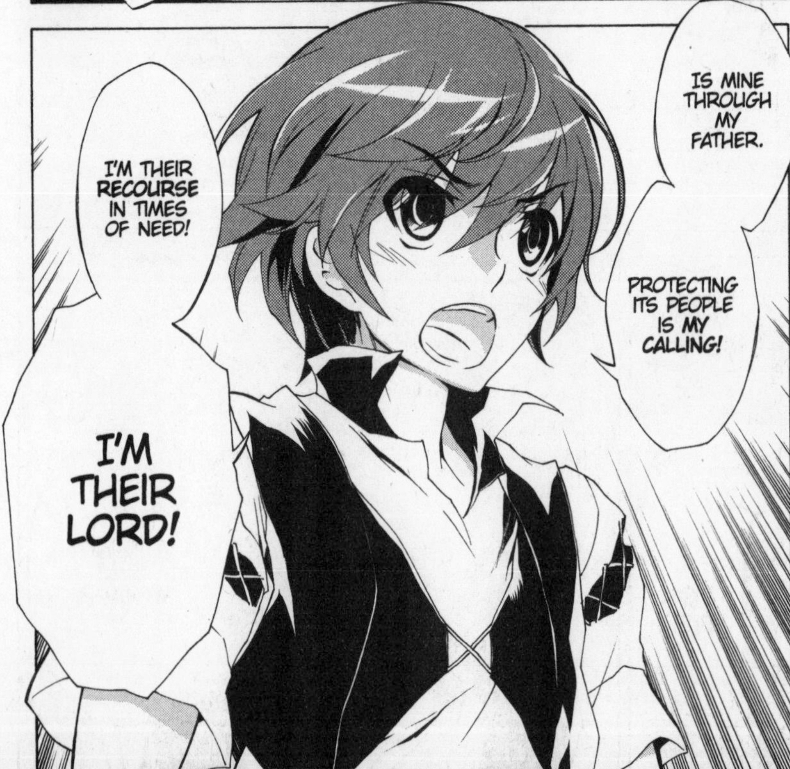
IS MINE THROUGH MY FATHER.
PROTECTING ITS PEOPLE IS MY CALLING!
I'M THEIR RECOURSE IN TIMES OF NEED!
I'M THEIR LORD!

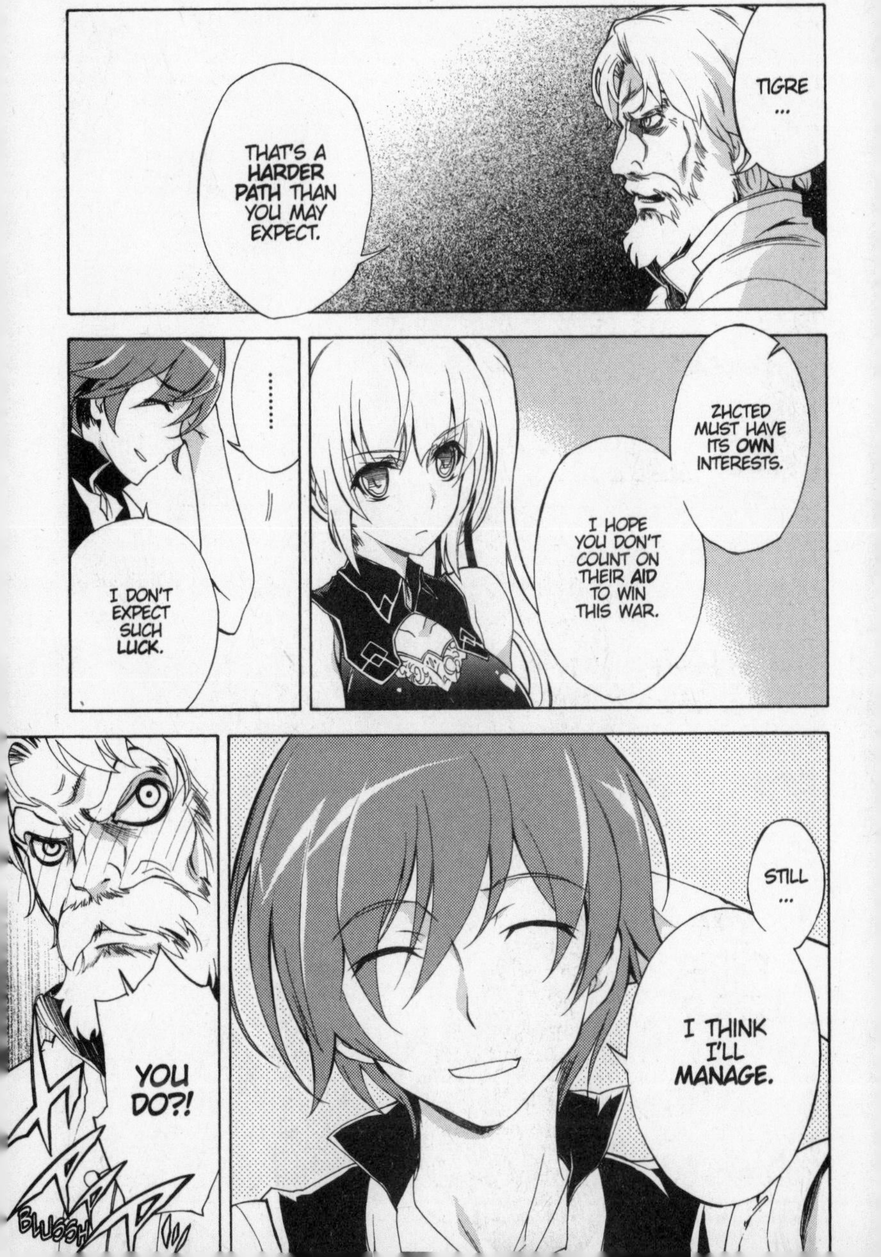
TIGRE ...
THAT'S A HARDER PATH THAN YOU MAY EXPECT.
ZHCTED MUST HAVE ITS OWN INTERESTS.
I HOPE YOU DON'T COUNT ON THEIR AID TO WIN THIS WAR.
......
I DON'T EXPECT SUCH LUCK.
STILL ...
I THINK I'LL MANAGE.
YOU DO?!
BLUSSH

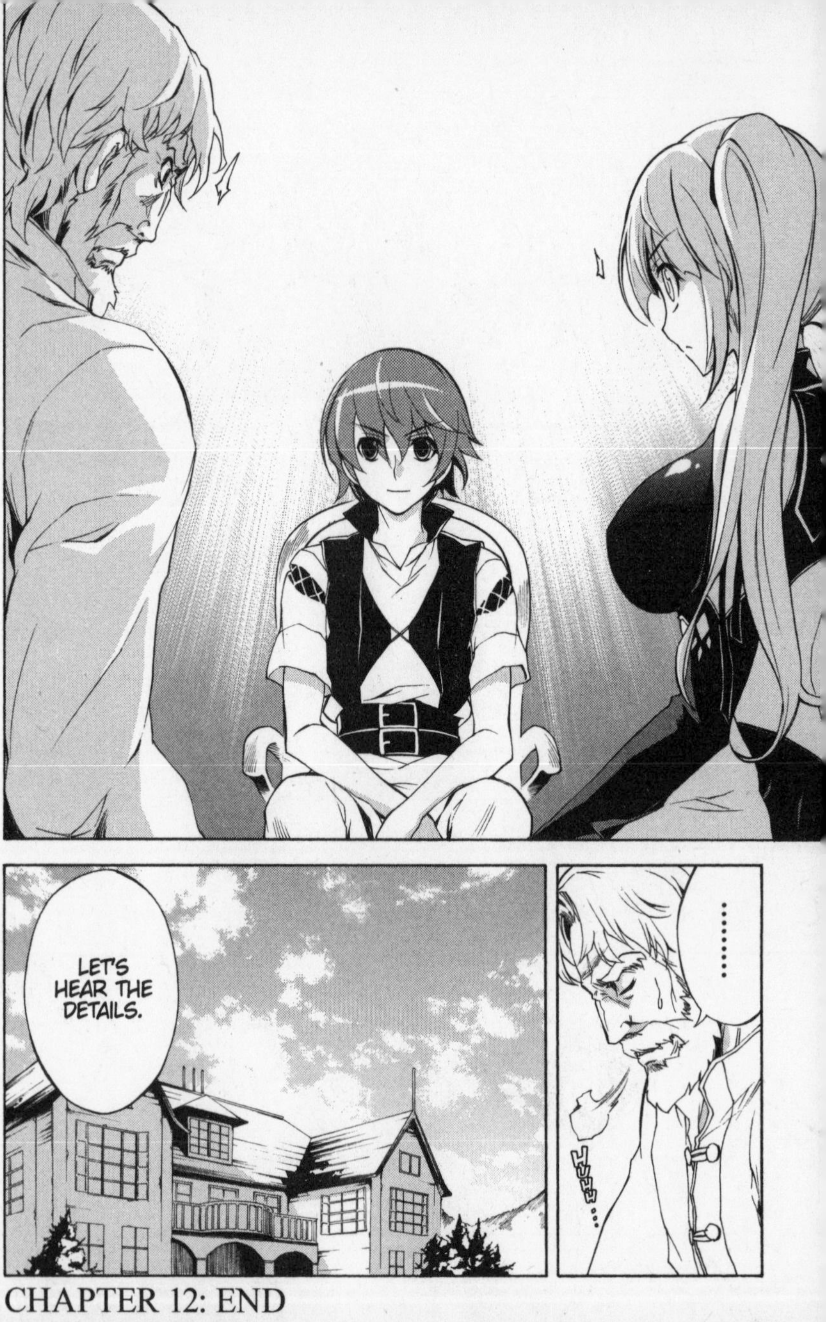
......
HUHH...
LET'S HEAR THE DETAILS.

CHAPTER 12: END

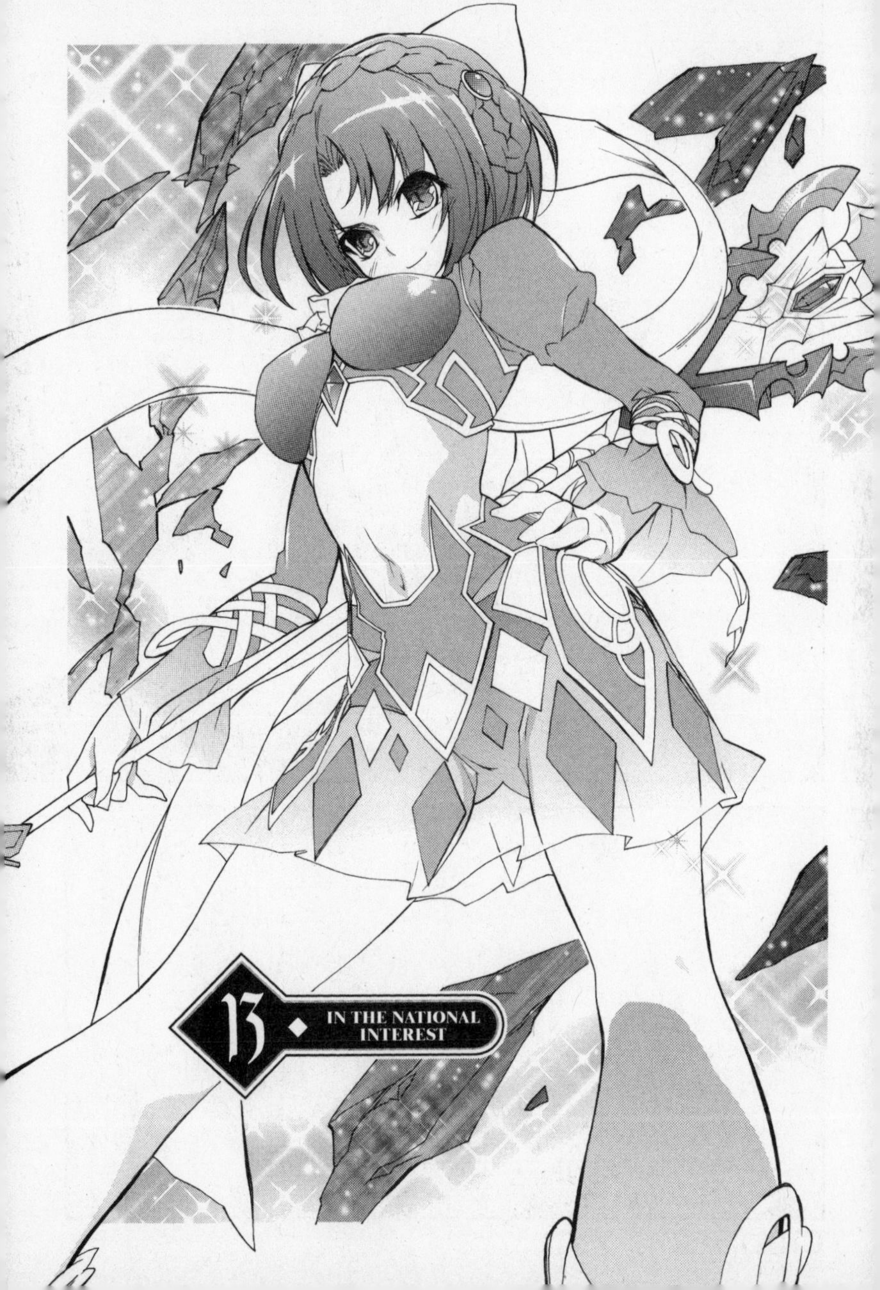
13
IN THE NATIONAL INTEREST

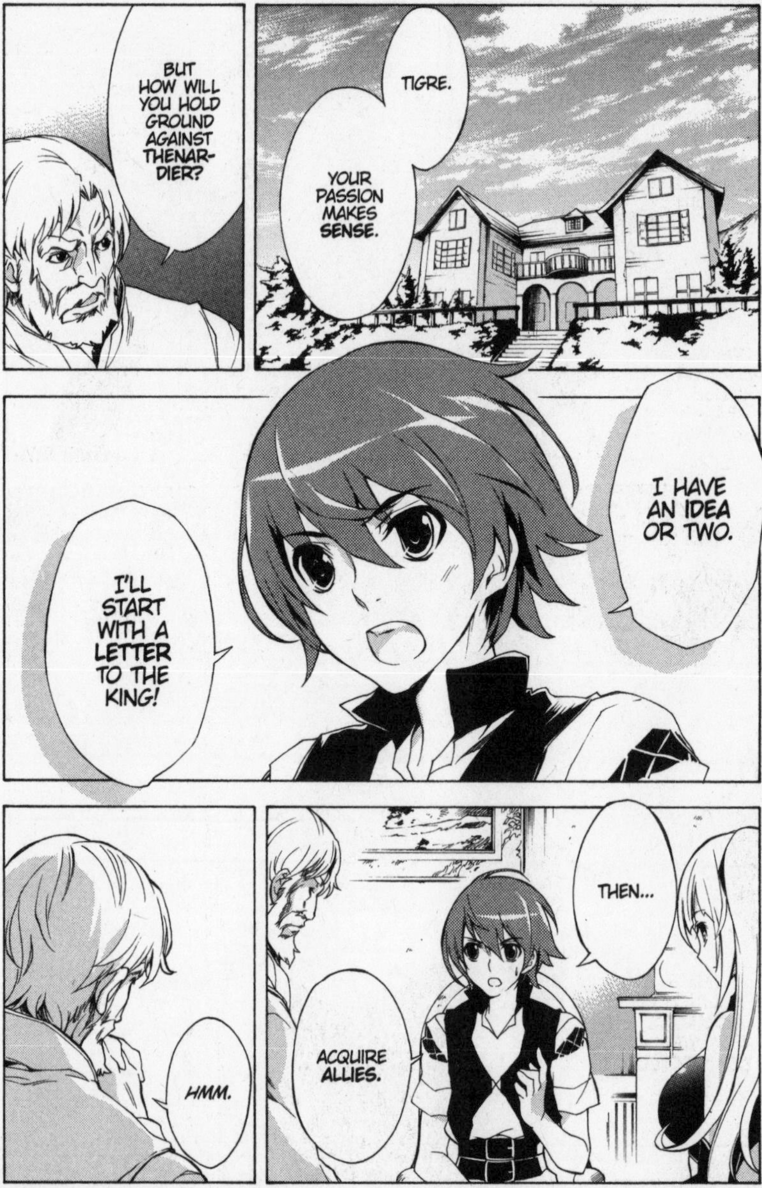
TIGRE.
YOUR PASSION MAKES SENSE.
BUT HOW WILL YOU HOLD GROUND AGAINST THENARDIER?
I HAVE AN IDEA OR TWO.
I'LL START WITH A LETTER TO THE KING!
THEN...
ACQUIRE ALLIES.
HMM.

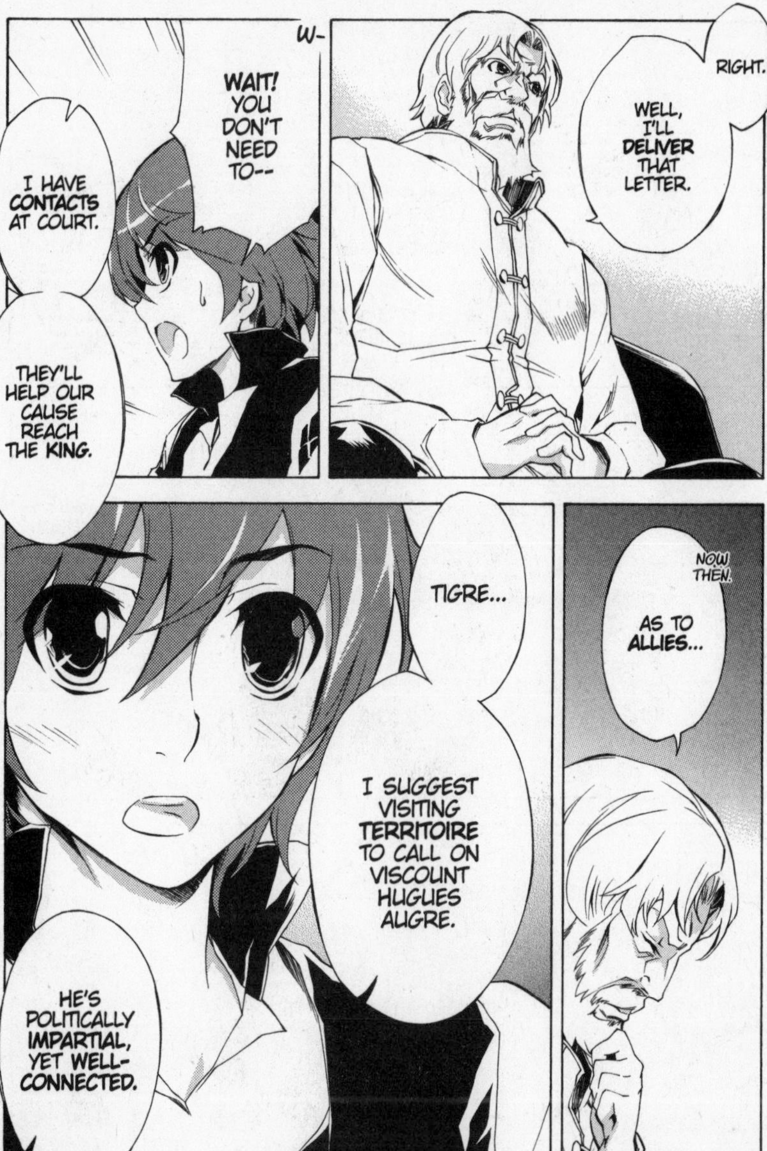
RIGHT.
WELL, I'LL DELIVER THAT LETTER.
W-
WAIT! YOU DON'T NEED TO--
I HAVE CONTACTS AT COURT.
THEY'LL HELP OUR CAUSE REACH THE KING.
NOW THEN.
AS TO ALLIES...
TIGRE...
I SUGGEST VISITING TERRITOIRE TO CALL ON VISCOUNT HUGUES AUGRE.
HE'S POLITICALLY IMPARTIAL, YET WELL-CONNECTED.

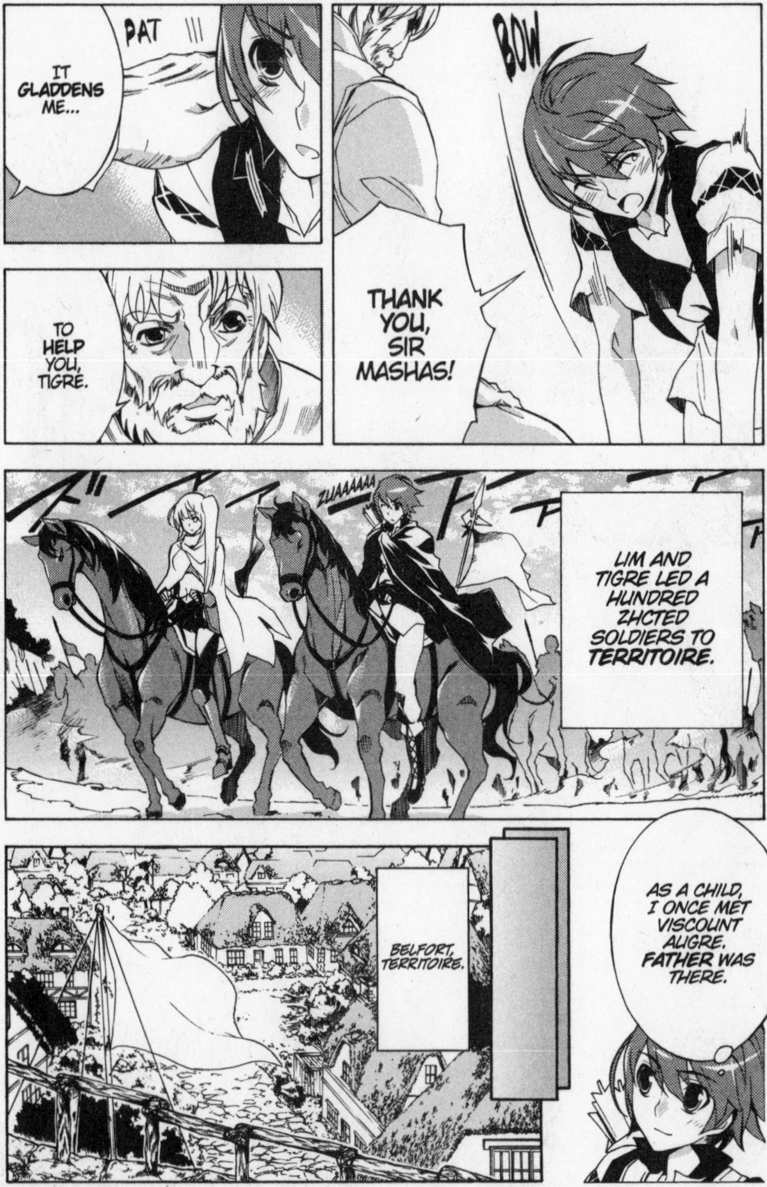
PAT
IT GLADDENS ME...
TO HELP YOU, TIGRE.
BOW
THANK YOU, SIR MASHAS!
ZUAAAAAA
LIM AND TIGRE LED A HUNDRED ZHCTED SOLDIERS TO TERRITOIRE.
BELFORT, TERRITOIRE.
AS A CHILD, I ONCE MET VISCOUNT AUGRE. FATHER WAS THERE.

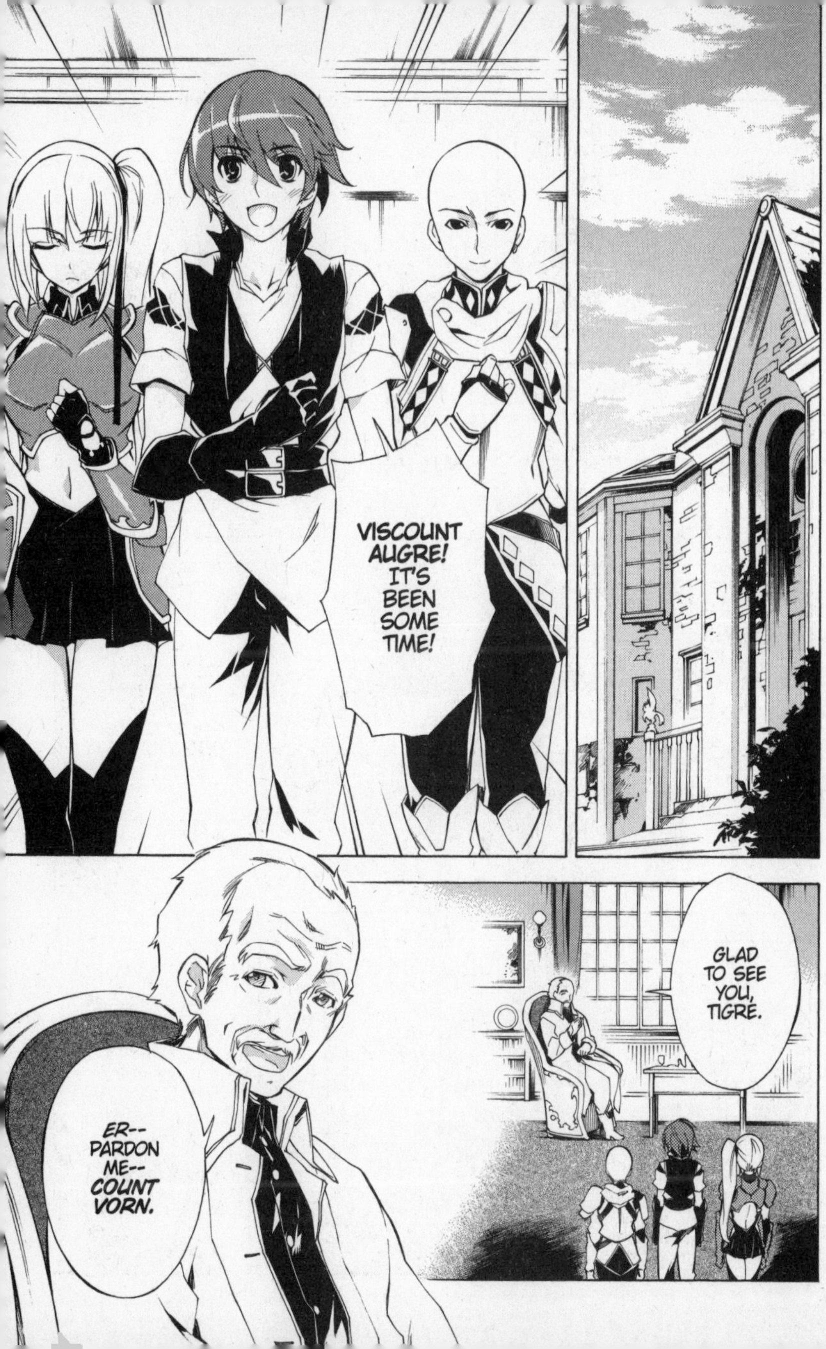
VISCOUNT AUGRE! IT'S BEEN SOME TIME!
GLAD TO SEE YOU, TIGRE.
ER-- PARDON ME-- COUNT VORN.

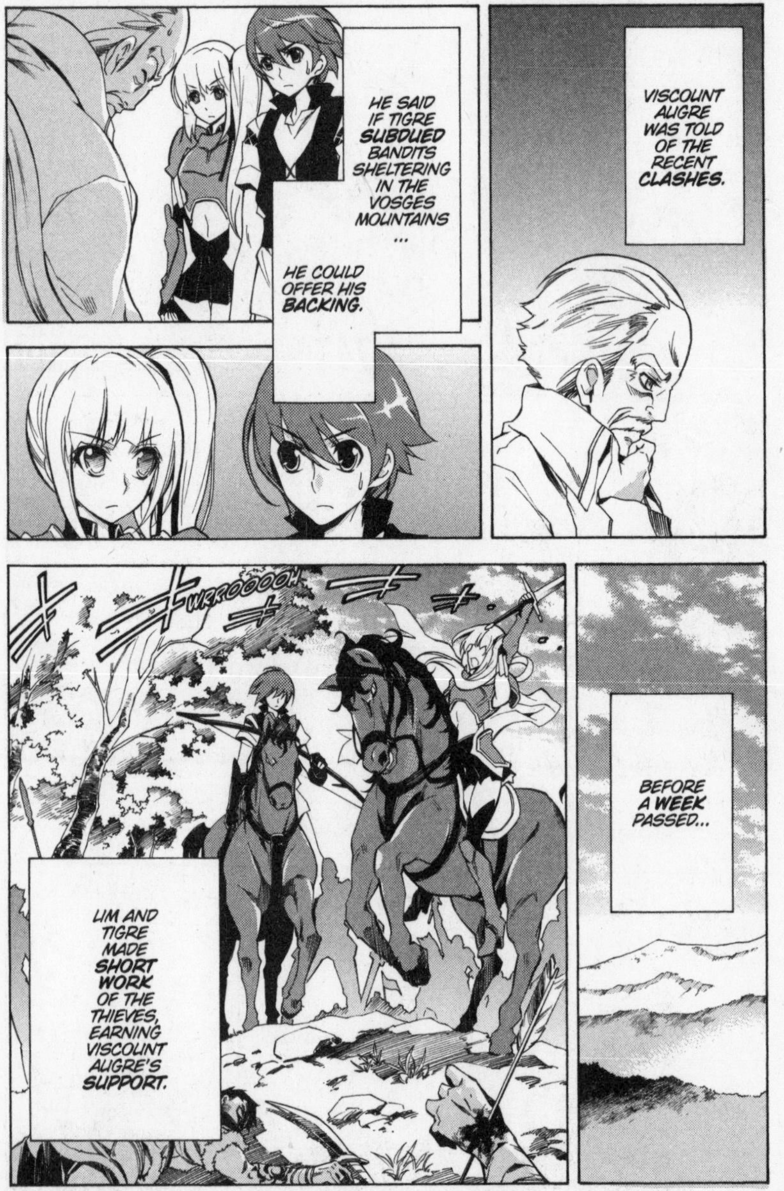
VISCOUNT AUGRE WAS TOLD OF THE RECENT CLASHES.
HE SAID IF TIGRE SUBDUED BANDITS SHELTERING IN THE VOSGES MOUNTAINS ...
HE COULD OFFER HIS BACKING.
BEFORE A WEEK PASSED...
WRROOOOH
LIM AND TIGRE MADE SHORT WORK OF THE THIEVES, EARNING VISCOUNT AUGRE'S SUPPORT.

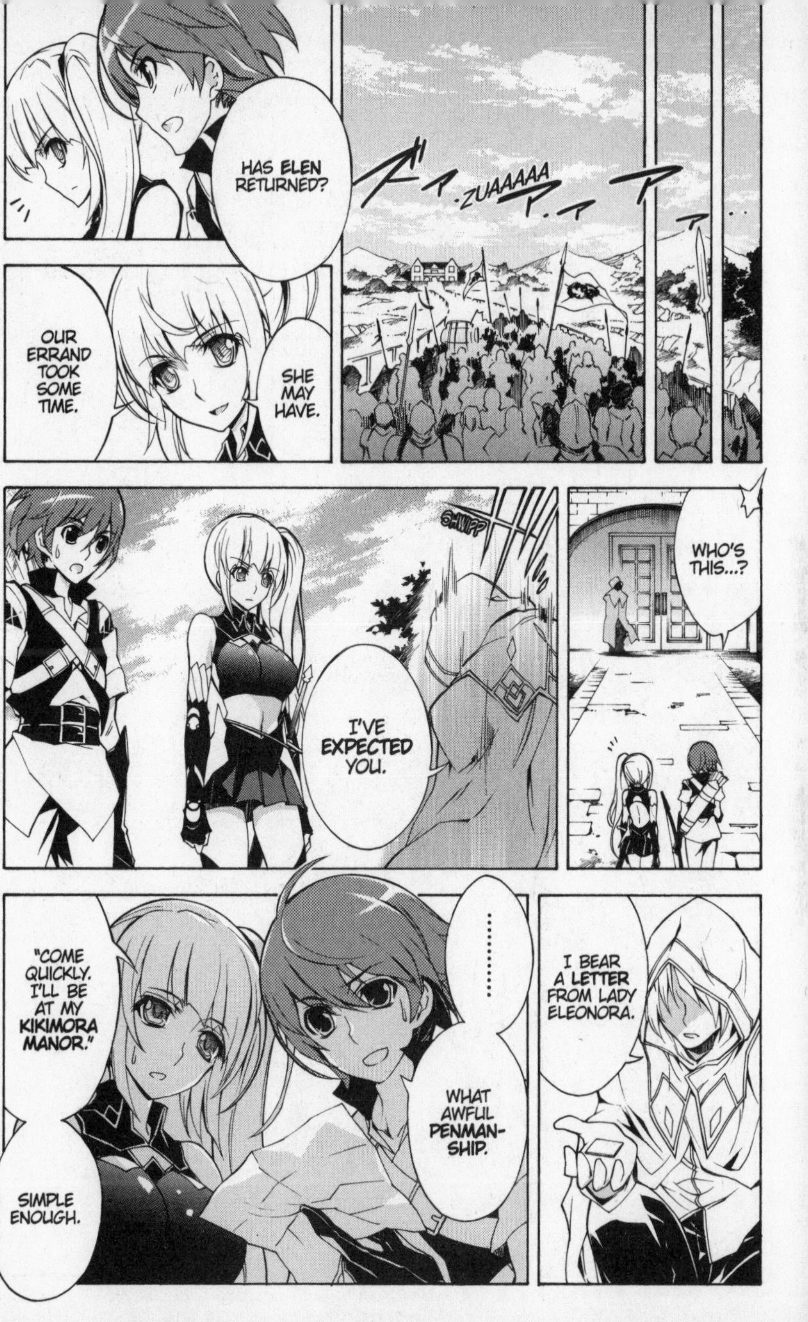
ZUAAAAA
HAS ELEN RETURNED?
SHE MAY HAVE.
OUR ERRAND TOOK SOME TIME.
WHO'S THIS...?
SHWIPP
I'VE EXPECTED YOU.
I BEAR A LETTER FROM LADY ELEONORA.
......
"COME QUICKLY. I'LL BE AT MY KIKIMORA MANOR."
WHAT AWFUL PENMAN-SHIP.
SIMPLE ENOUGH.

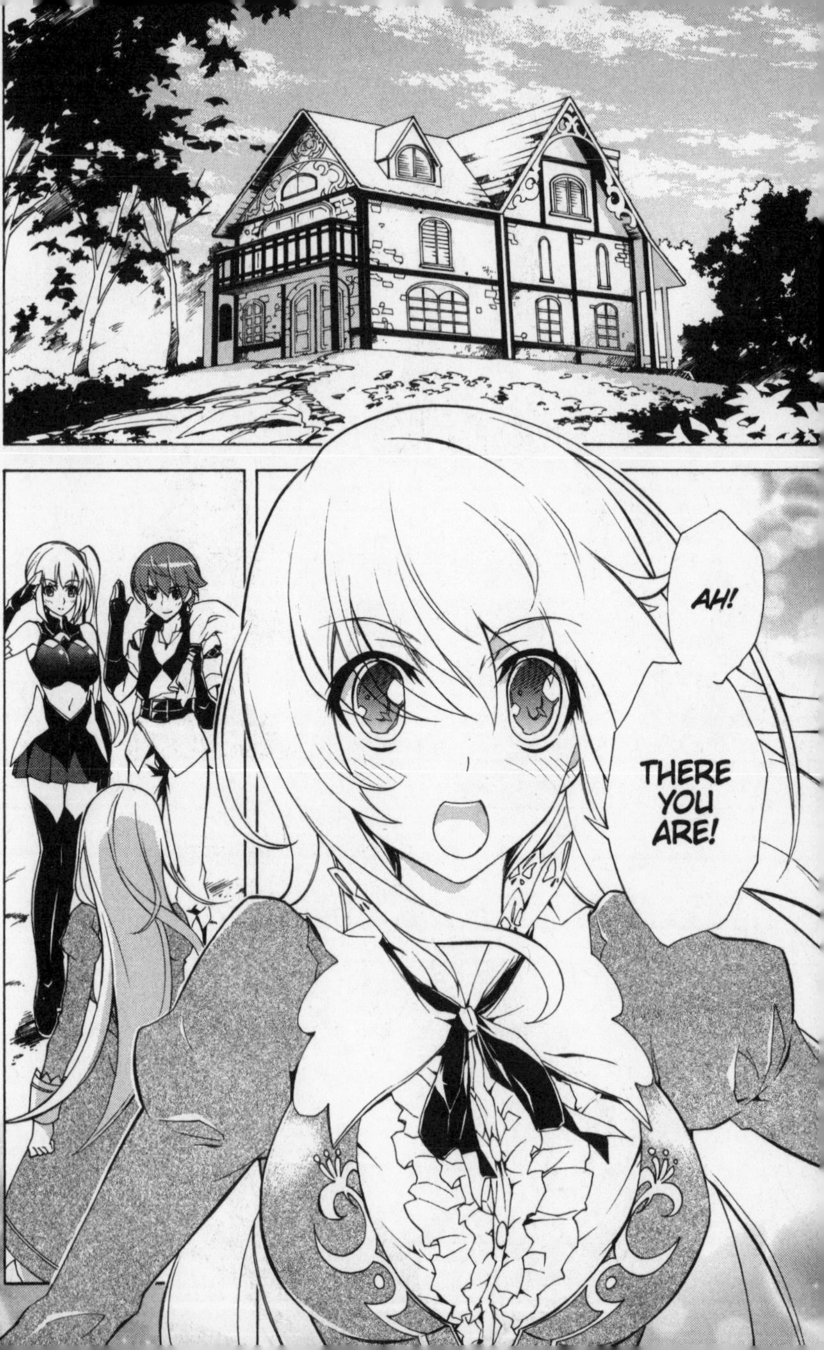
AH!
THERE YOU ARE!

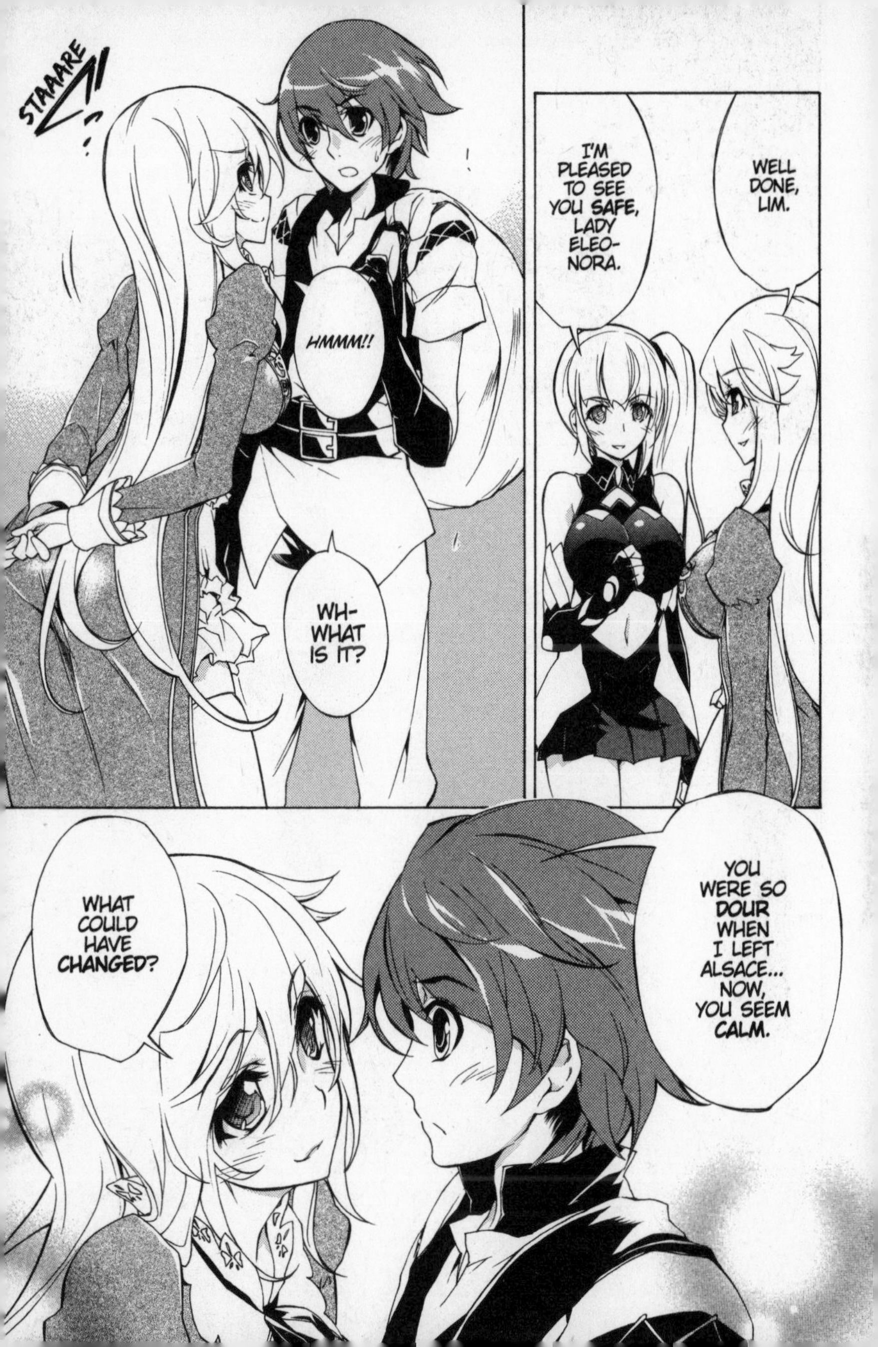
WELL DONE, LIM.
I'M PLEASED TO SEE YOU SAFE, LADY ELEO-NORA.
STAAARE
HMMM!!
WH-WHAT IS IT?
YOU WERE SO DOUR WHEN I LEFT ALSACE... NOW, YOU SEEM CALM.
WHAT COULD HAVE CHANGED?

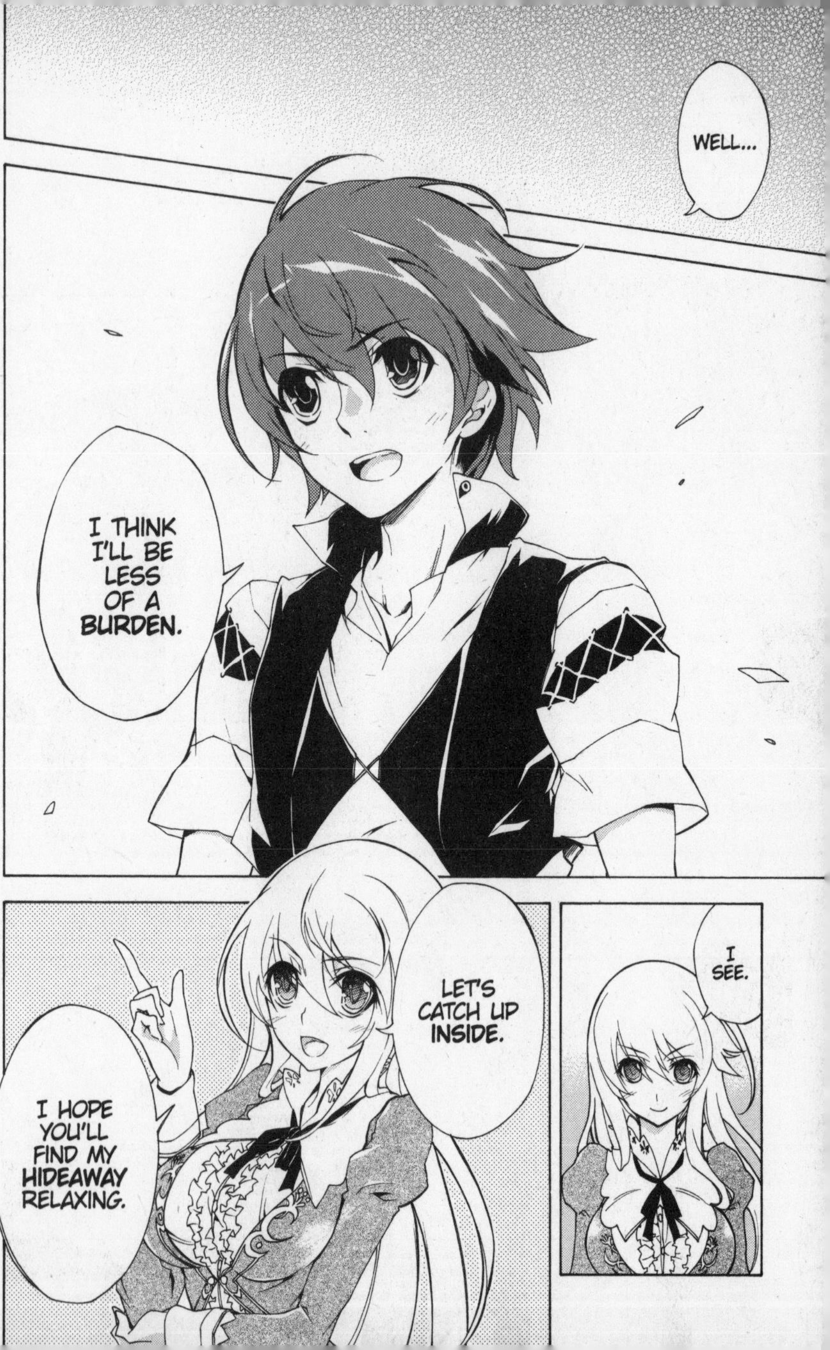
WELL...
I THINK I'LL BE LESS OF A BURDEN.
I SEE.
LET'S CATCH UP INSIDE.
I HOPE YOU'LL FIND MY HIDEAWAY RELAXING.

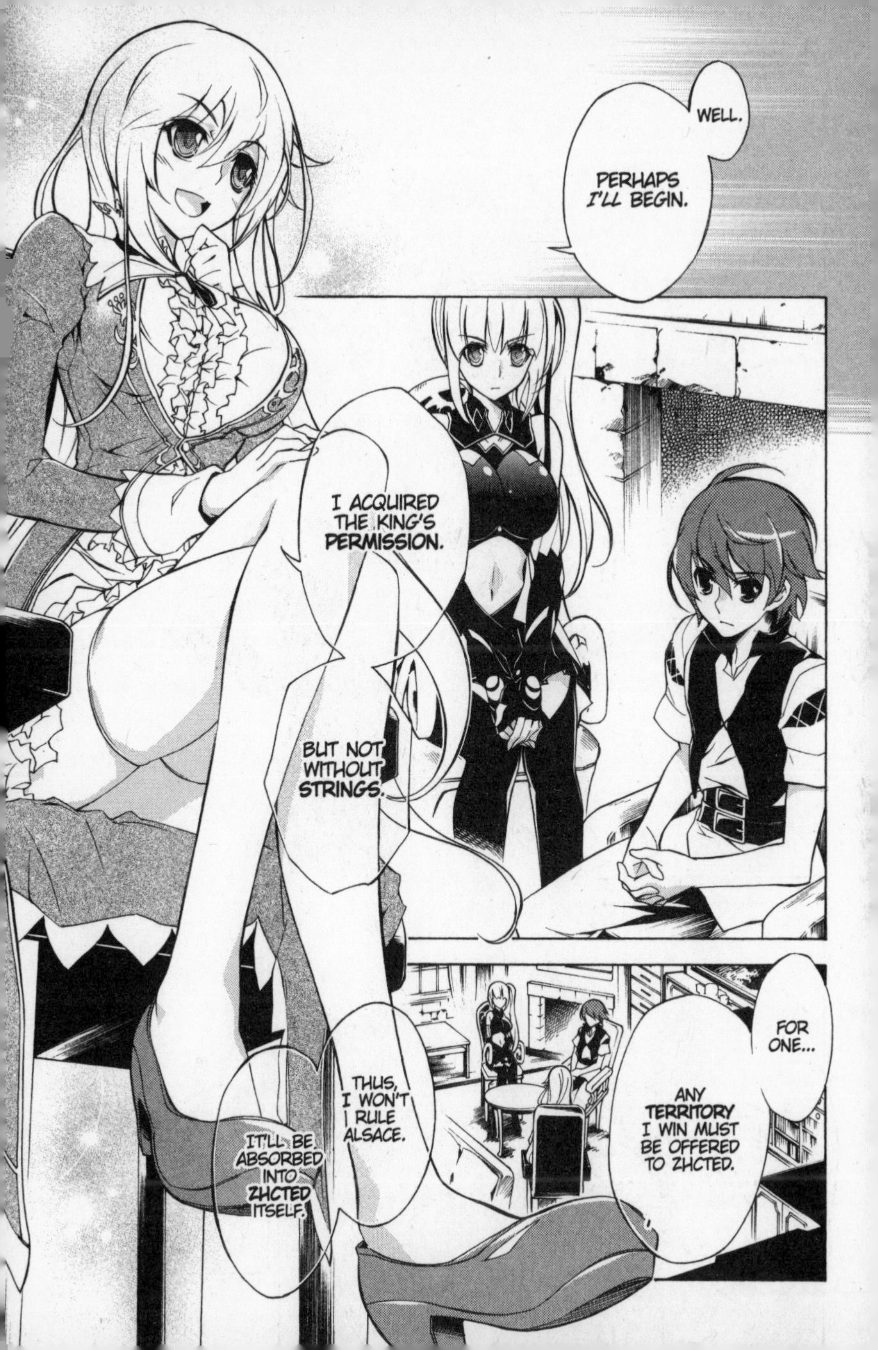
WELL.
PERHAPS I'LL BEGIN.
I ACQUIRED THE KING'S PERMISSION.
BUT NOT WITHOUT STRINGS.
FOR ONE...
ANY TERRITORY I WIN MUST BE OFFERED TO ZHCTED.
THUS, I WON'T RULE ALSACE.
IT'LL BE ABSORBED INTO ZHCTED ITSELF.

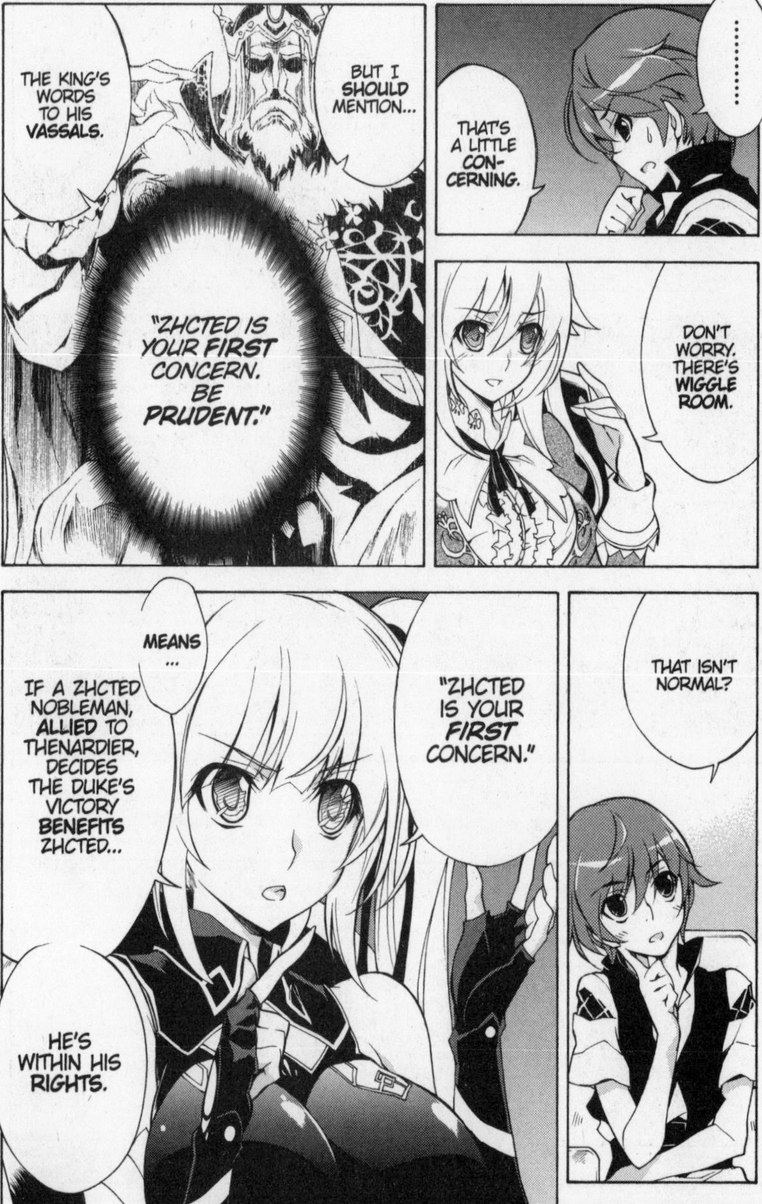
......
THAT'S A LITTLE CON-CERNING.
DON'T WORRY. THERE'S WIGGLE ROOM.
BUT I SHOULD MENTION...
THE KING'S WORDS TO HIS VASSALS.
"ZHCTED IS YOUR FIRST CONCERN. BE PRUDENT."
THAT ISN'T NORMAL?
"ZHCTED IS YOUR FIRST CONCERN."
MEANS ...
IF A ZHCTED NOBLEMAN, ALLIED TO THENARDIER, DECIDES THE DUKE'S VICTORY BENEFITS ZHCTED...
HE'S WITHIN HIS RIGHTS.

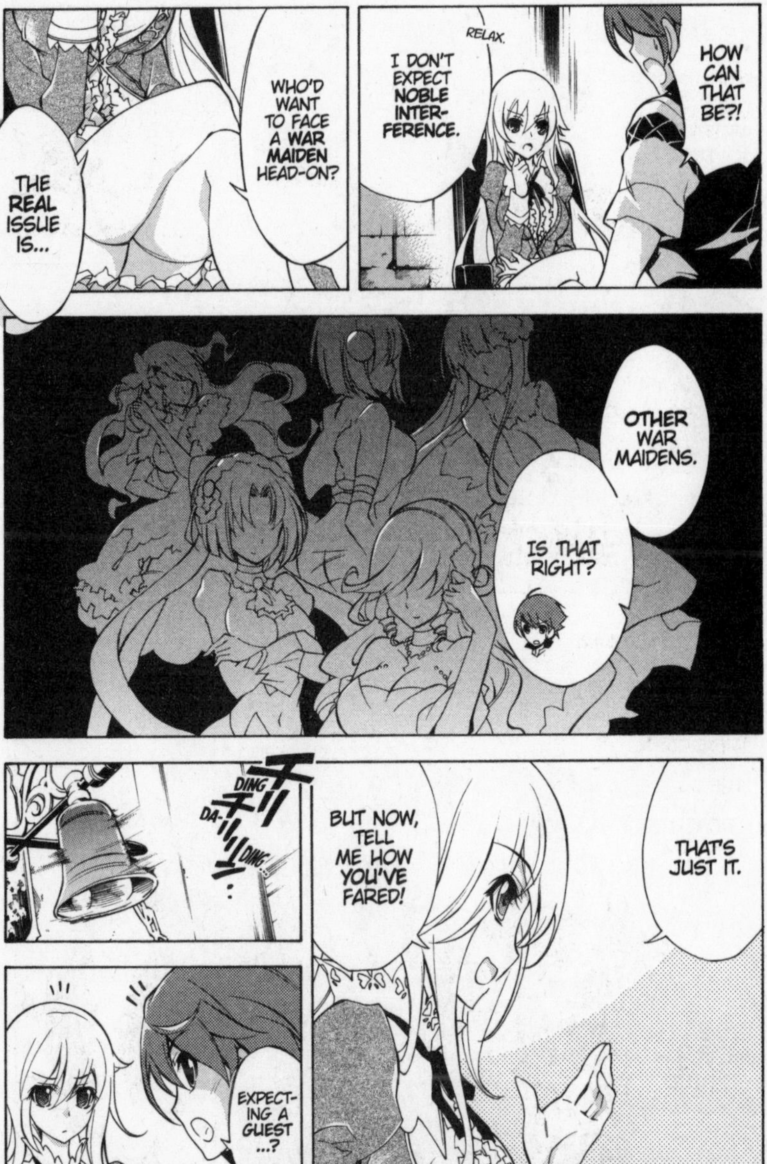
HOW CAN THAT BE?!
RELAX.
I DON'T EXPECT NOBLE INTERFERENCE.
WHO'D WANT TO FACE A WAR MAIDEN HEAD-ON?
THE REAL ISSUE IS...
OTHER WAR MAIDENS.
IS THAT RIGHT?
THAT'S JUST IT.
BUT NOW, TELL ME HOW YOU'VE FARED!
DING
DA-
DING
EXPECTING A GUEST...?

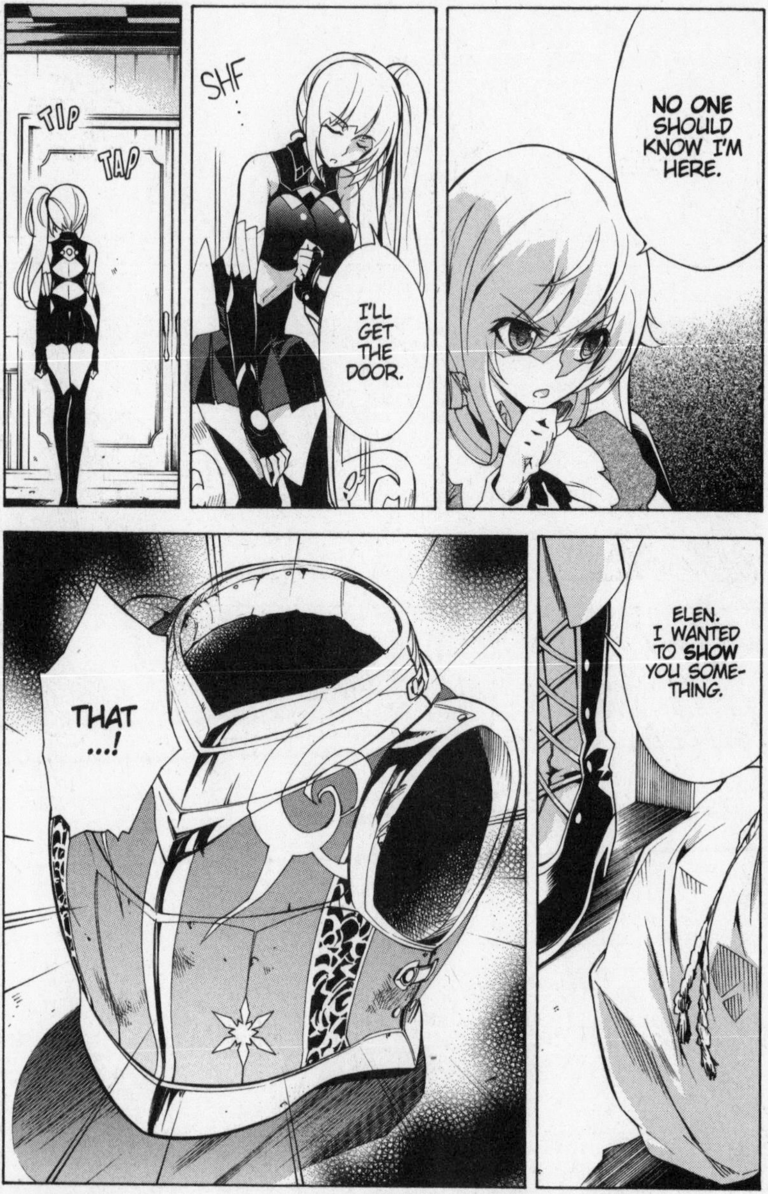
NO ONE SHOULD KNOW I'M HERE.
SHF...
I'LL GET THE DOOR.
TIP
TAP
ELEN. I WANTED TO SHOW YOU SOMETHING.
THAT ...!

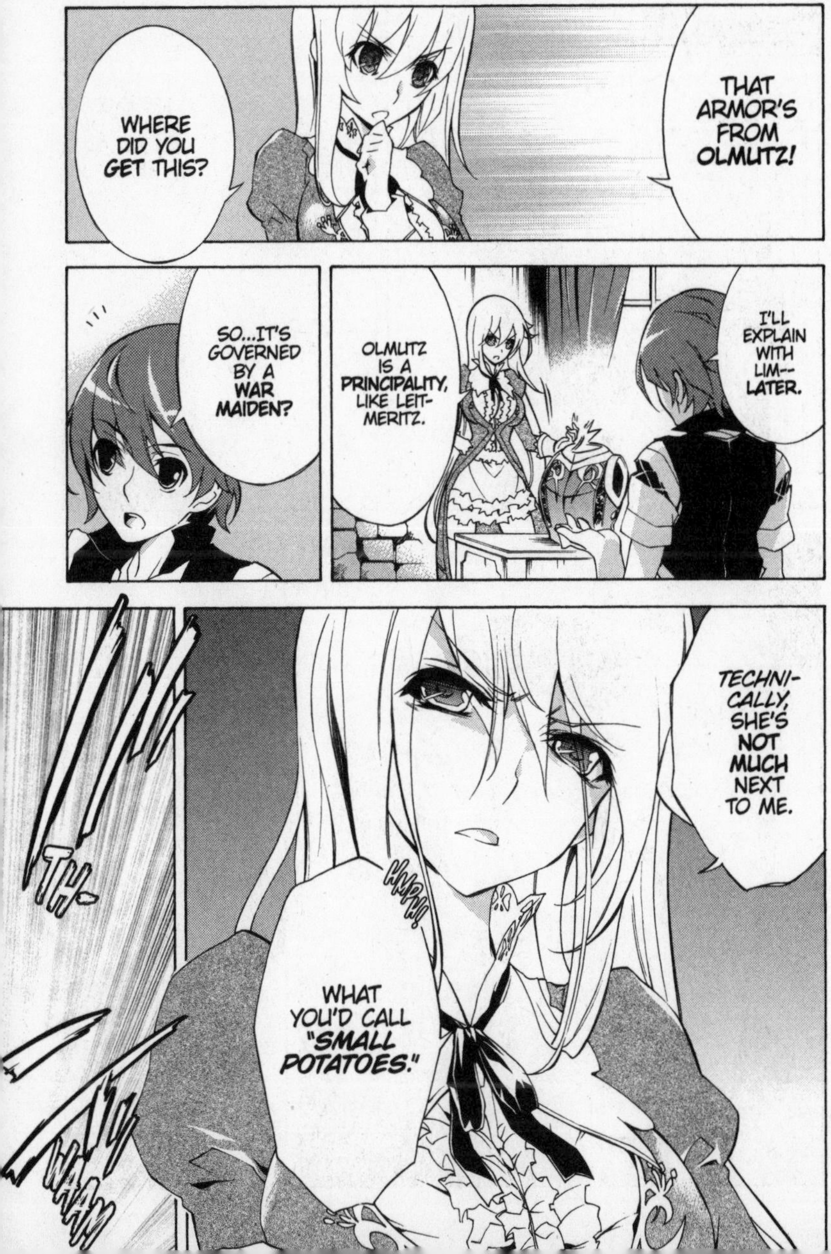
THAT ARMOR'S FROM OLMUTZ!
WHERE DID YOU GET THIS?
I'LL EXPLAIN WITH LIM-- LATER.
OLMUTZ IS A PRINCIPALITY, LIKE LEIT-MERITZ.
SO...IT'S GOVERNED BY A WAR MAIDEN?
TECHNI-CALLY, SHE'S NOT MUCH NEXT TO ME.
HMPH!!
WHAT YOU'D CALL "SMALL POTATOES."
TH-
WHAM

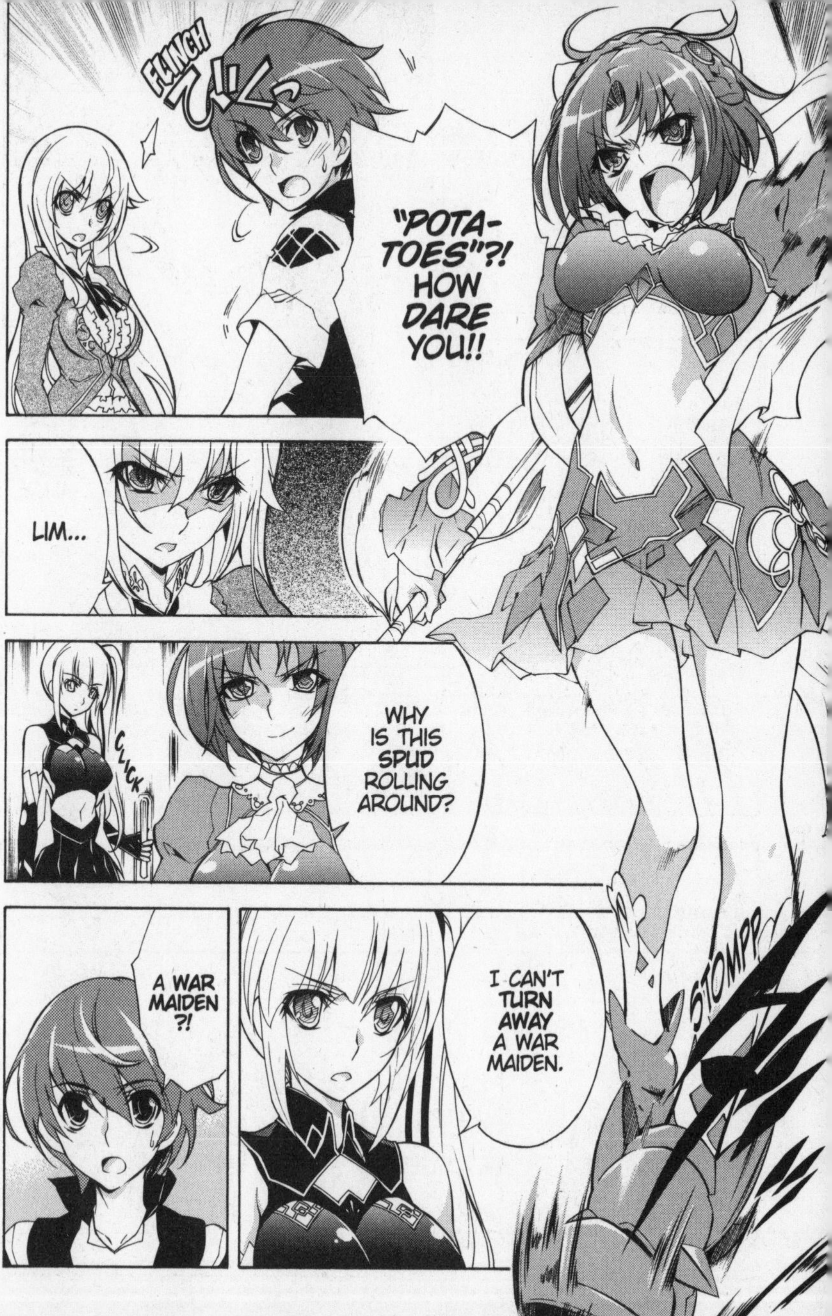
"POTATOES"?! HOW DARE YOU!!
FLINCH
LIM...
WHY IS THIS SPUD ROLLING AROUND?
CLICK
STOMPP
I CAN'T TURN AWAY A WAR MAIDEN.
A WAR MAIDEN?!

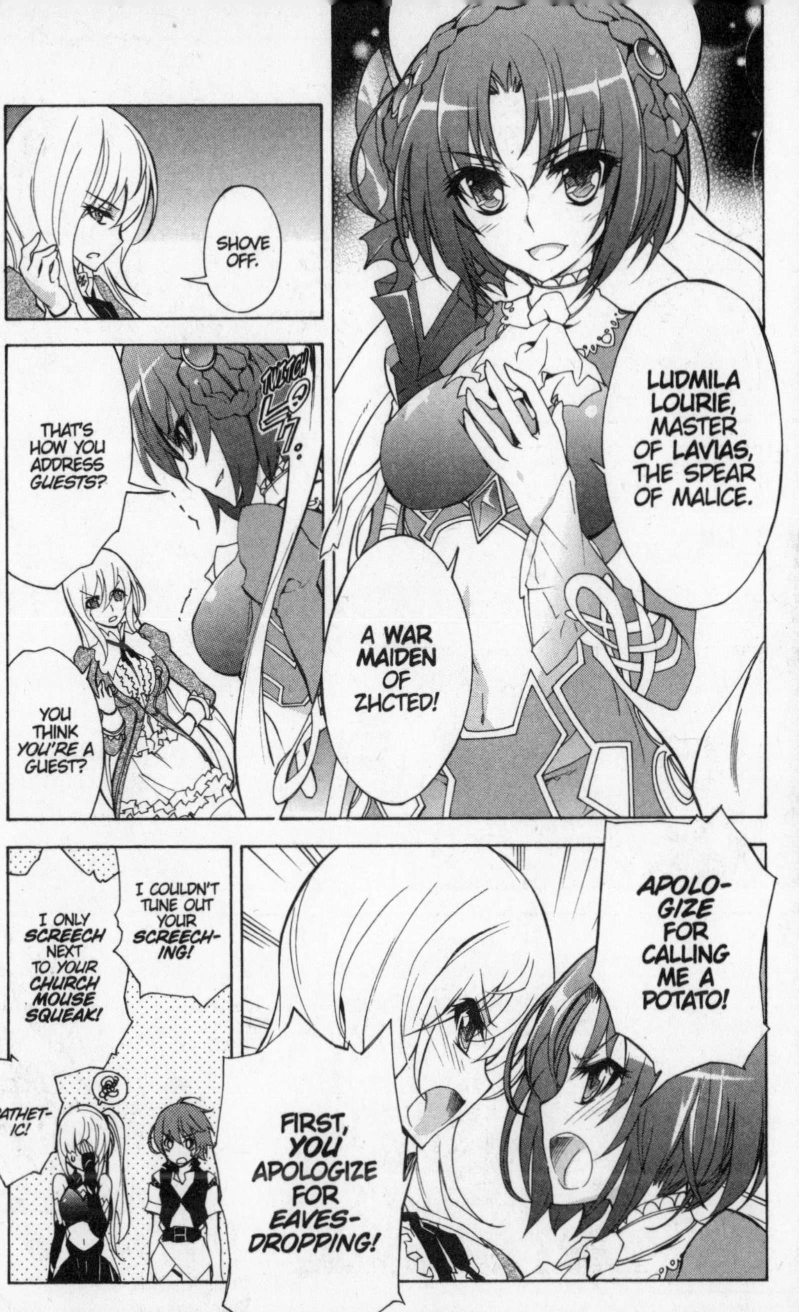
LUDMILA LOURIE, MASTER OF LAVIAS, THE SPEAR OF MALICE.
A WAR MAIDEN OF ZHCTED!
SHOVE OFF.
TWITCH
THAT'S HOW YOU ADDRESS GUESTS?
YOU THINK YOU'RE A GUEST?
APOLOGIZE FOR CALLING ME A POTATO!
FIRST, YOU APOLOGIZE FOR EAVES-DROPPING!
I COULDN'T TUNE OUT YOUR SCREECH-ING!
I ONLY SCREECH NEXT TO YOUR CHURCH MOUSE SQUEAK!
PATHET-IC!

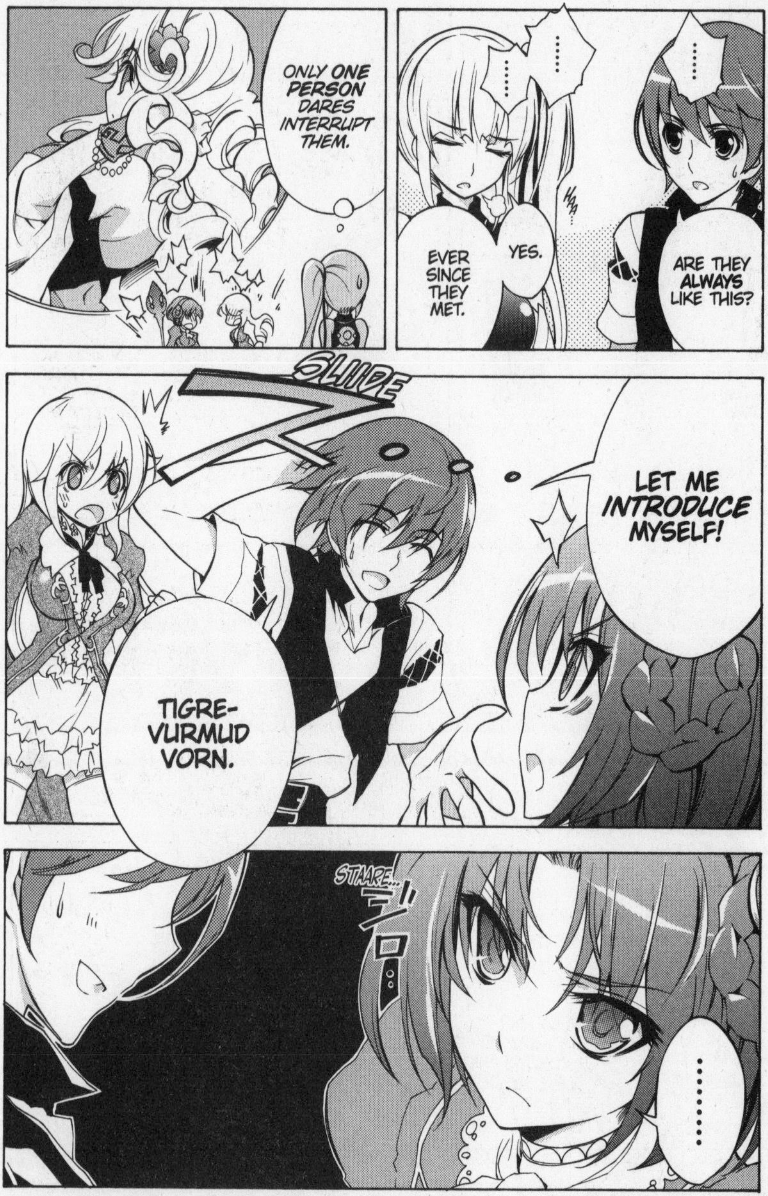
……
……
……
HAA
ARE THEY ALWAYS LIKE THIS?
YES.
EVER SINCE THEY MET.
ONLY ONE PERSON DARES INTERRUPT THEM.
SLIIDE
LET ME INTRODUCE MYSELF!
TIGRE-VURMUD VORN.
STAARE...
……

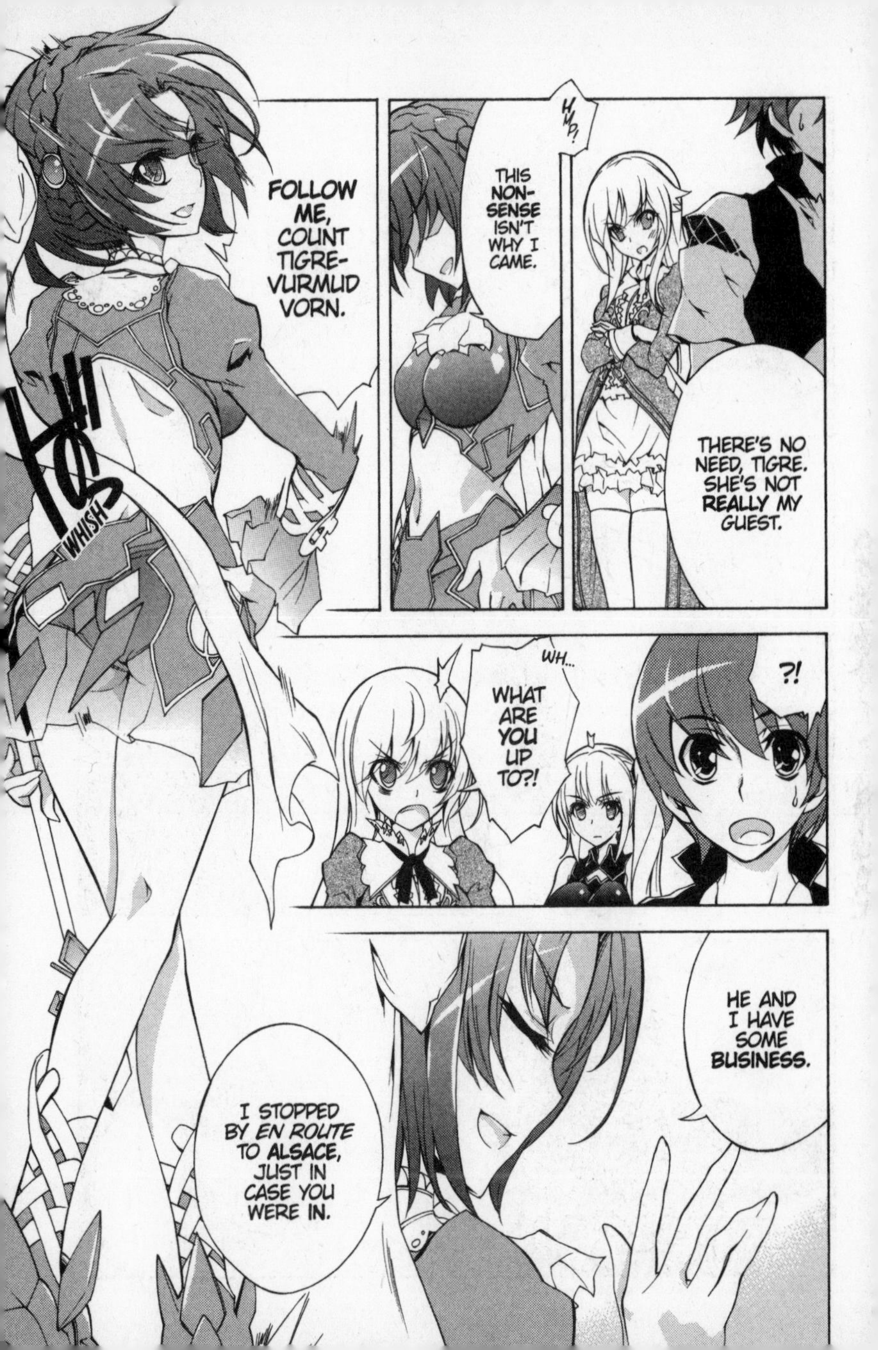
THERE'S NO NEED, TIGRE. SHE'S NOT REALLY MY GUEST.
HMP!
THIS NONSENSE ISN'T WHY I CAME.
?!
WH...
WHAT ARE YOU UP TO?!
HE AND I HAVE SOME BUSINESS.
I STOPPED BY *EN ROUTE* TO ALSACE, JUST IN CASE YOU WERE IN.
FOLLOW ME, COUNT TIGREVURMUD VORN.
WHISH

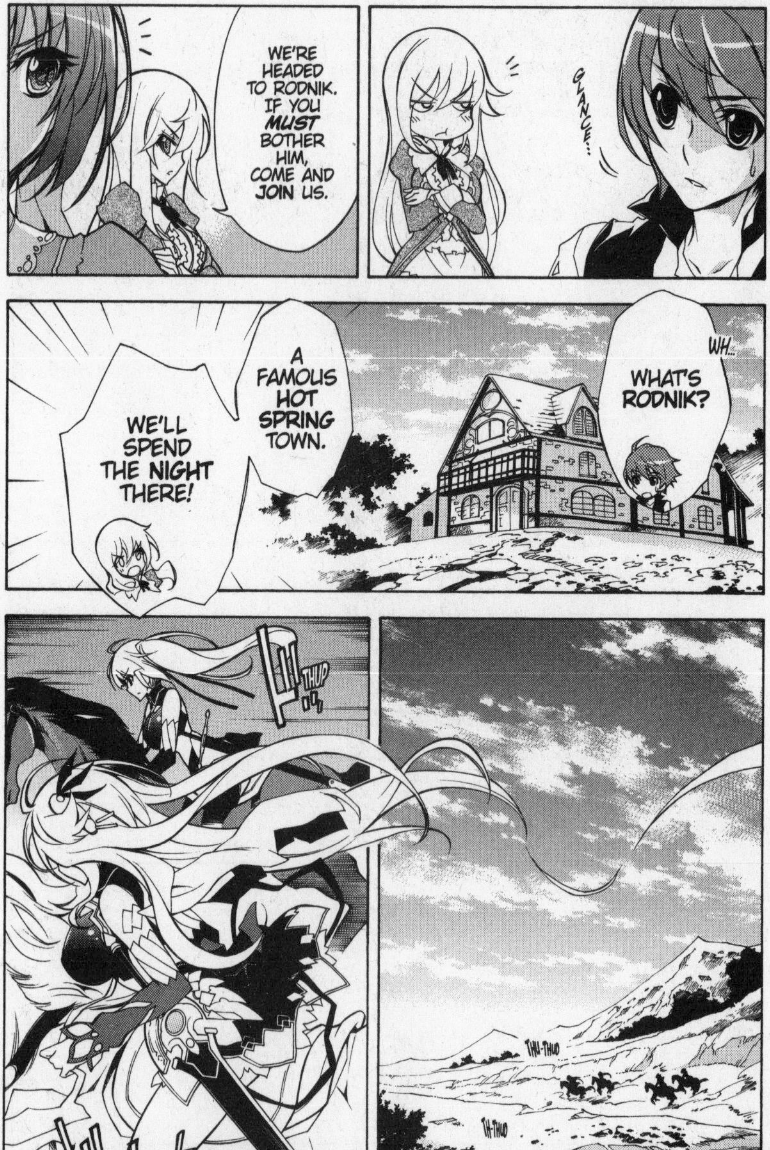
GLANCE...
WE'RE HEADED TO RODNIK. IF YOU *MUST* BOTHER HIM, COME AND JOIN US.
WH... WHAT'S RODNIK?
A FAMOUS HOT SPRING TOWN.
WE'LL SPEND THE NIGHT THERE!
THU-THUD
TH-THUD
THUP
THUP BA LUP

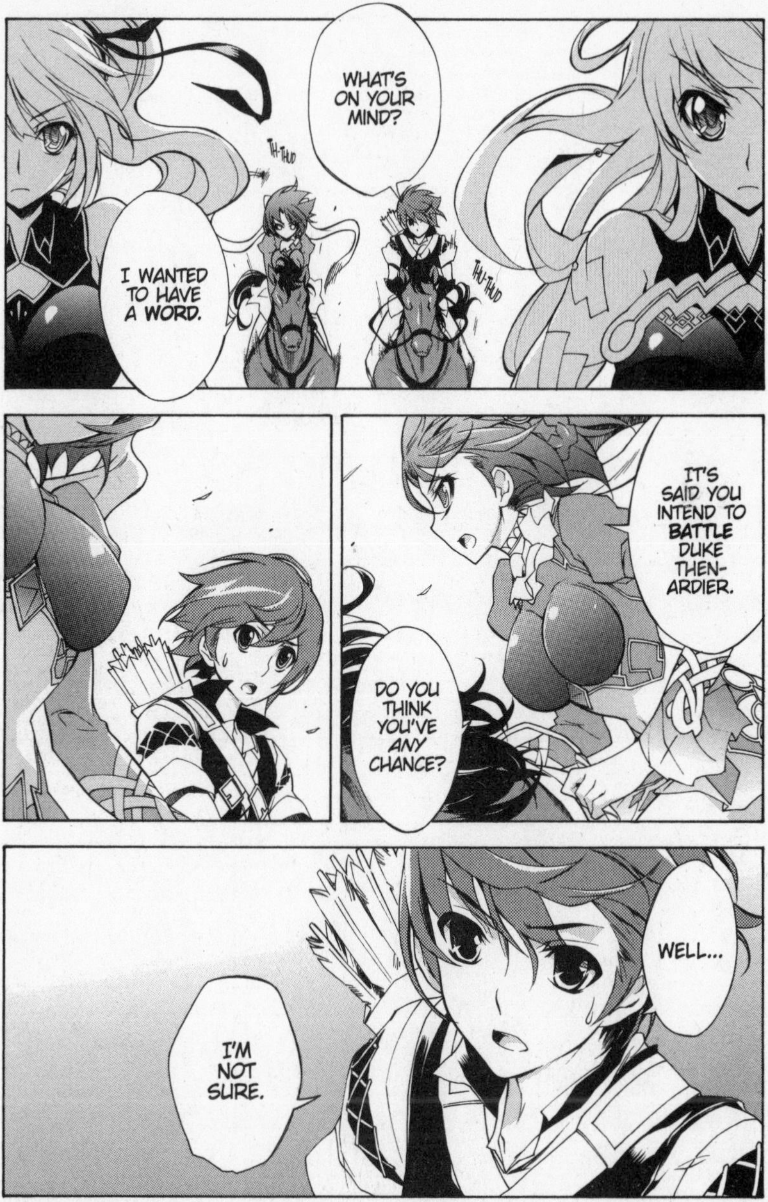
WHAT'S ON YOUR MIND?
THU-THUD
TH-THUD
I WANTED TO HAVE A WORD.
IT'S SAID YOU INTEND TO BATTLE DUKE THEN-ARDIER.
DO YOU THINK YOU'VE ANY CHANCE?
WELL...
I'M NOT SURE.

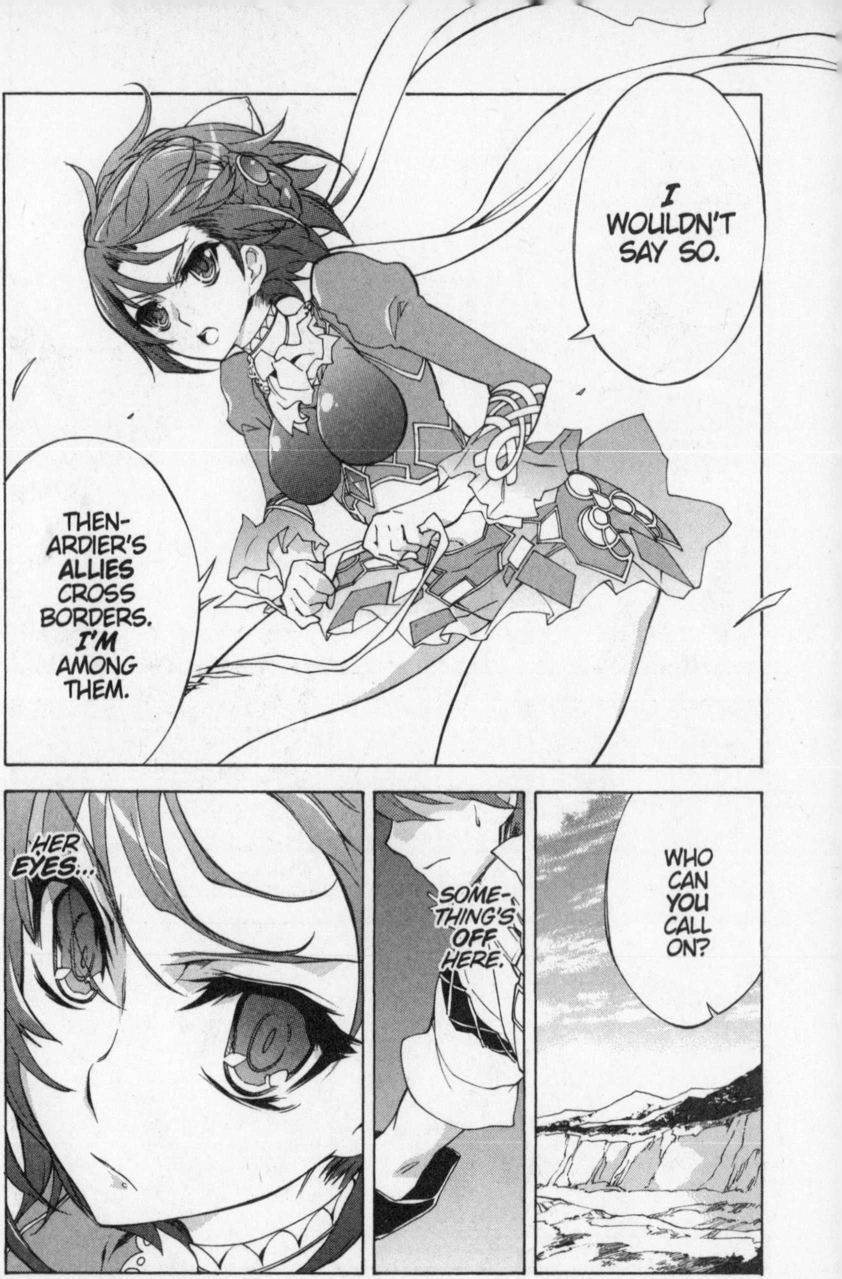
I WOULDN'T SAY SO.
THEN-ARDIER'S ALLIES CROSS BORDERS. I'M AMONG THEM.
WHO CAN YOU CALL ON?
SOME-THING'S OFF HERE.
HER EYES...

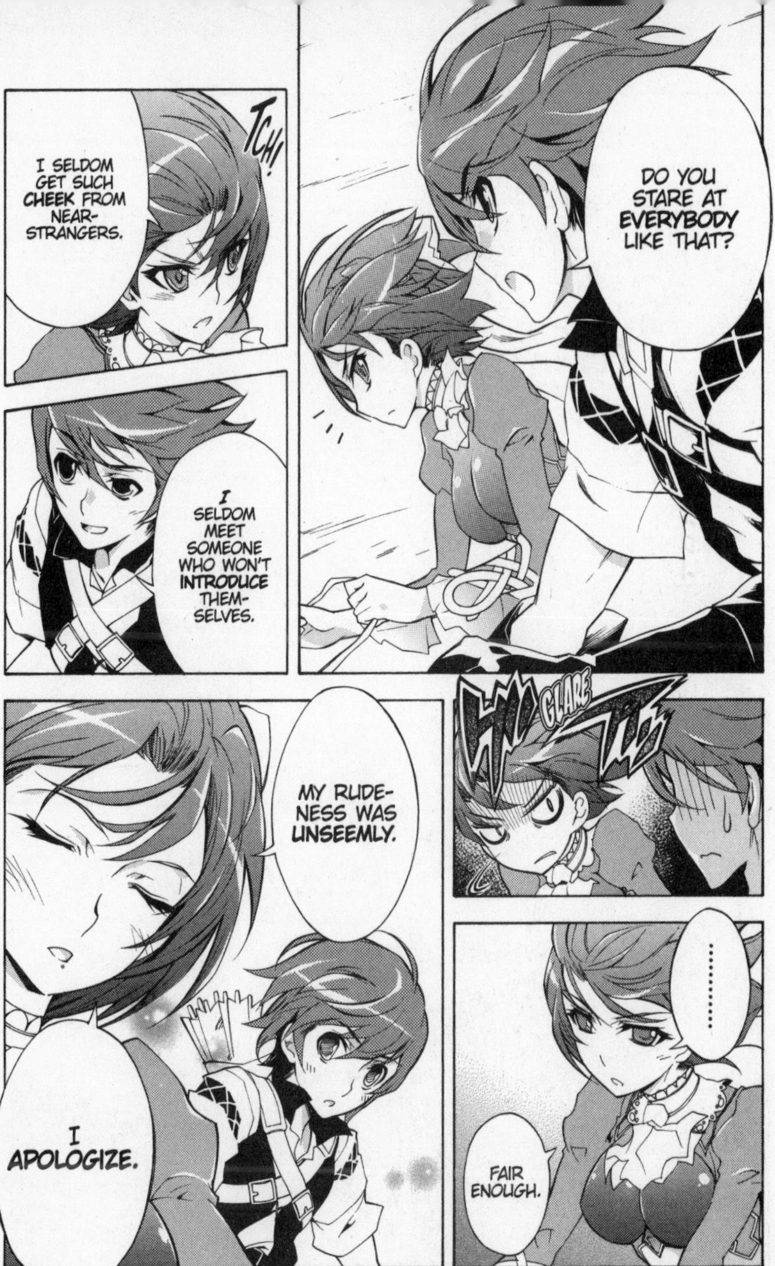
DO YOU STARE AT EVERYBODY LIKE THAT?
TCH!
I SELDOM GET SUCH CHEEK FROM NEAR-STRANGERS.
I SELDOM MEET SOMEONE WHO WON'T INTRODUCE THEM-SELVES.
GLARE
MY RUDE-NESS WAS UNSEEMLY.
I APOLOGIZE.
......
FAIR ENOUGH.

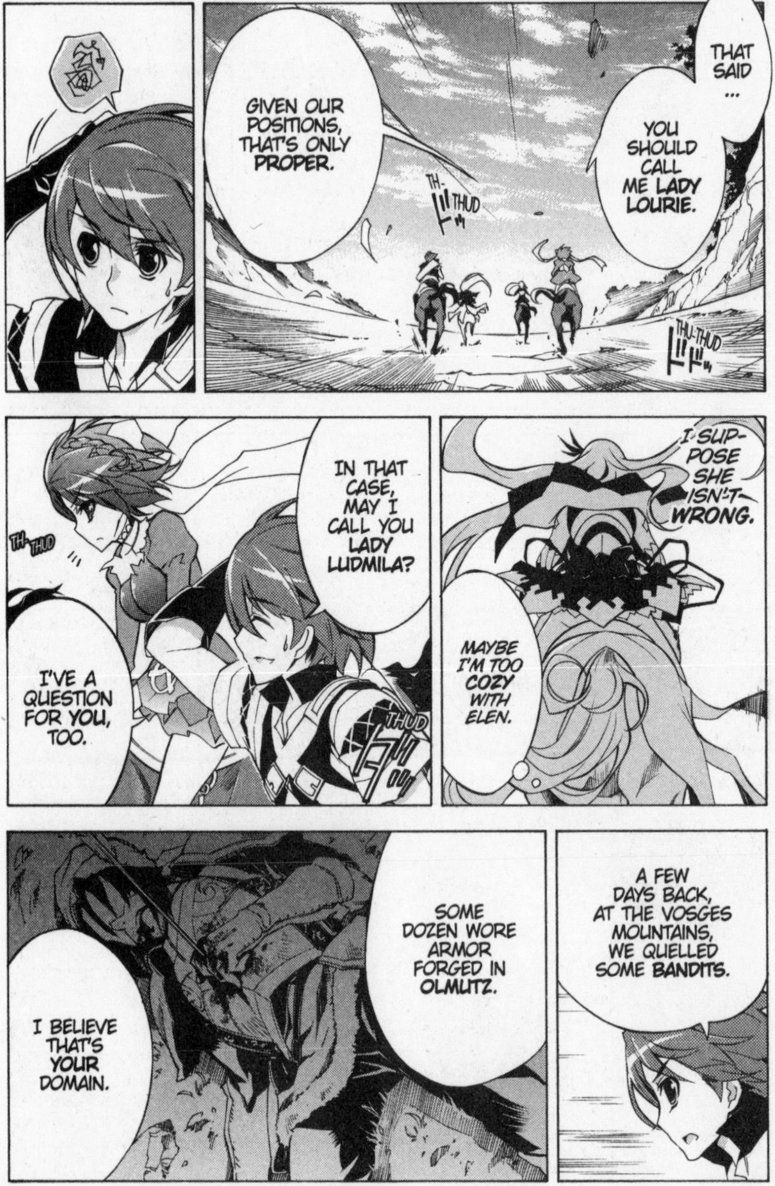
THAT SAID...
YOU SHOULD CALL ME LADY LOURIE.
GIVEN OUR POSITIONS, THAT'S ONLY PROPER.
TH-THUD
THU-THUD
I SUP-POSE SHE ISN'T WRONG.
MAYBE I'M TOO COZY WITH ELEN.
IN THAT CASE, MAY I CALL YOU LADY LUDMILA?
TH-THUD
I'VE A QUESTION FOR YOU, TOO.
THUD
A FEW DAYS BACK, AT THE VOSGES MOUNTAINS, WE QUELLED SOME BANDITS.
SOME DOZEN WORE ARMOR FORGED IN OLMUTZ.
I BELIEVE THAT'S YOUR DOMAIN.

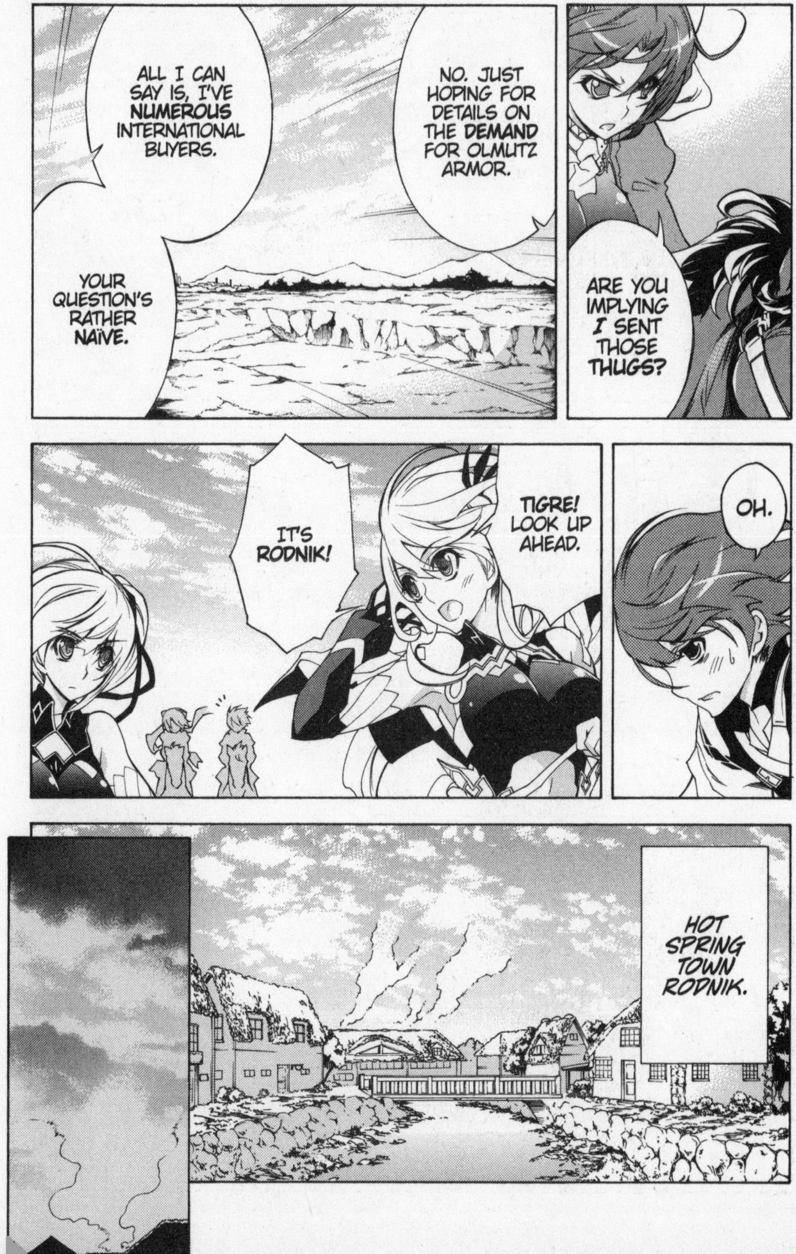
ARE YOU IMPLYING I SENT THOSE THUGS?
NO. JUST HOPING FOR DETAILS ON THE DEMAND FOR OLMUTZ ARMOR.
ALL I CAN SAY IS, I'VE NUMEROUS INTERNATIONAL BUYERS.
YOUR QUESTION'S RATHER NAÏVE.
OH.
TIGRE! LOOK UP AHEAD.
IT'S RODNIK!
HOT SPRING TOWN RODNIK.

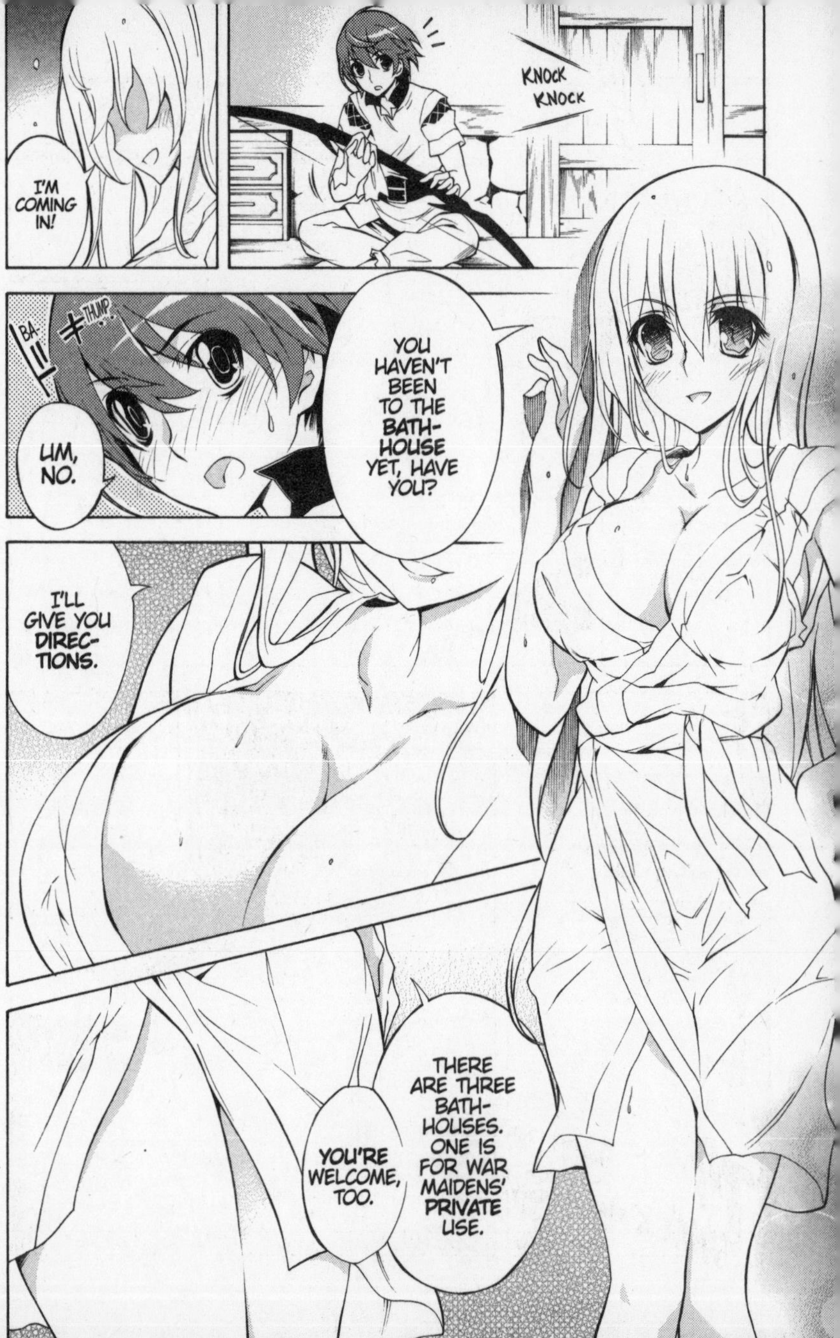
KNOCK KNOCK
I'M COMING IN!
YOU HAVEN'T BEEN TO THE BATH-HOUSE YET, HAVE YOU?
BA-THUMP
UM, NO.
I'LL GIVE YOU DIREC-TIONS.
THERE ARE THREE BATH-HOUSES. ONE IS FOR WAR MAIDENS' PRIVATE USE.
YOU'RE WELCOME, TOO.

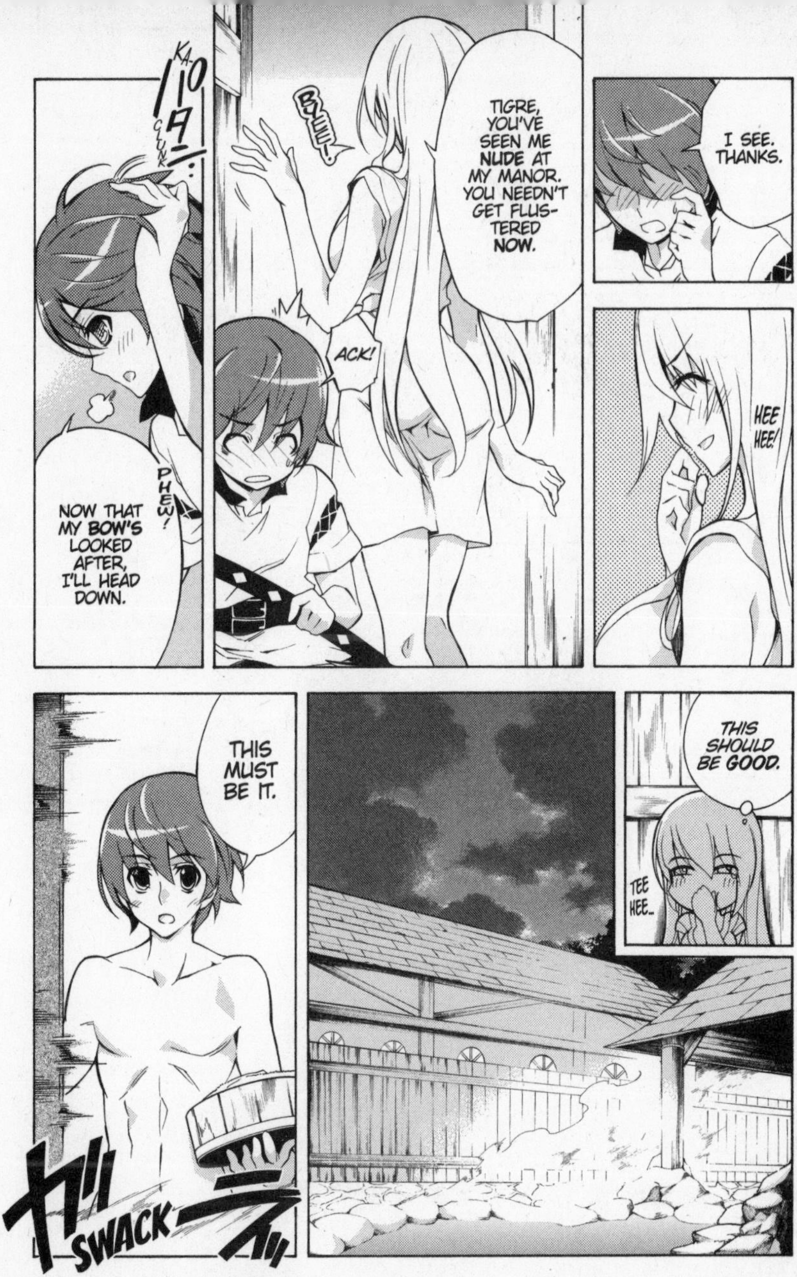
I SEE. THANKS.
HEE HEE!
TIGRE, YOU'VE SEEN ME NUDE AT MY MANOR. YOU NEEDN'T GET FLUSTERED NOW.
BYEEE!
ACK!
KA-CLUNK
PHEW!
NOW THAT MY BOW'S LOOKED AFTER, I'LL HEAD DOWN.
THIS SHOULD BE GOOD.
TEE HEE..
THIS MUST BE IT.
SWACK

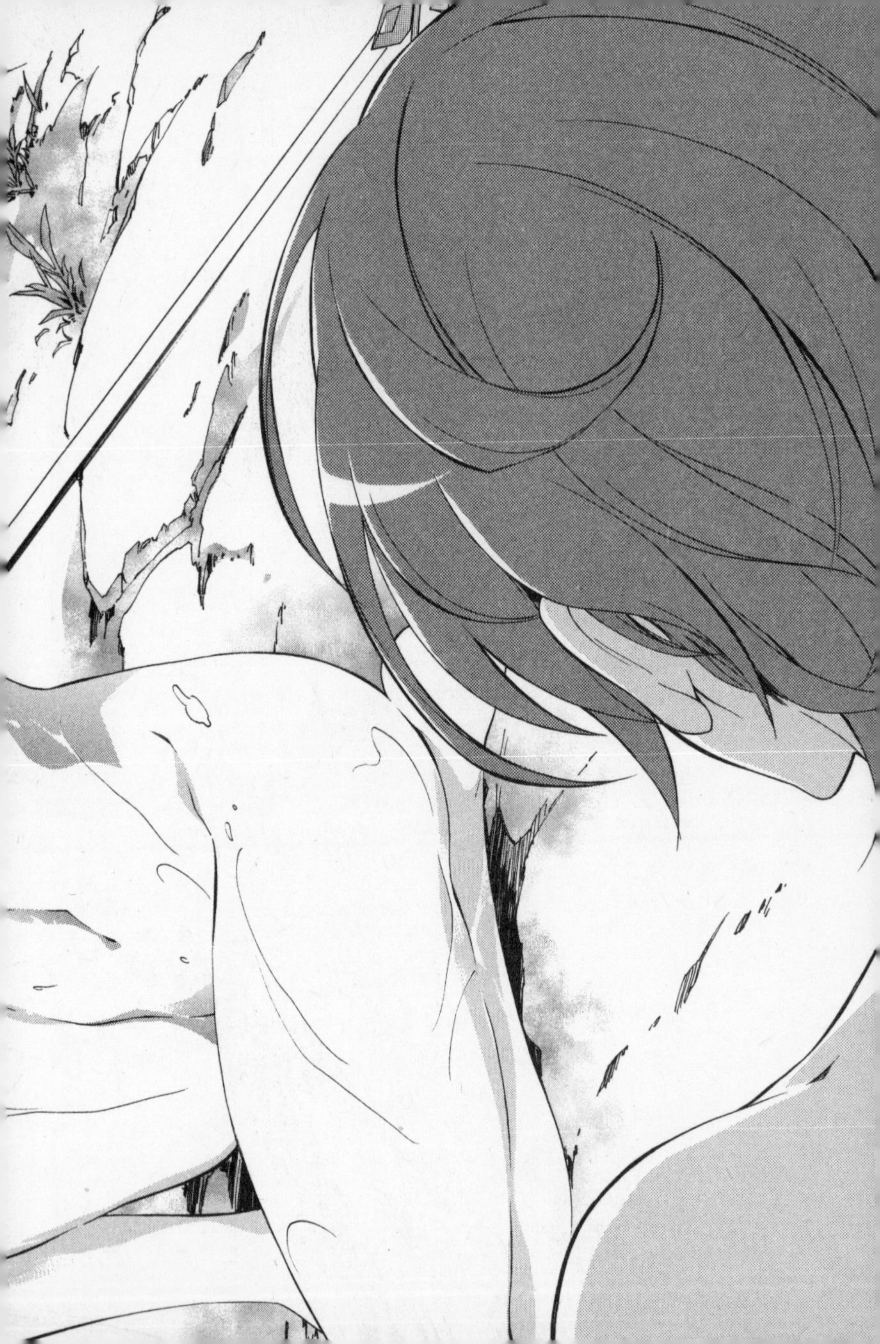

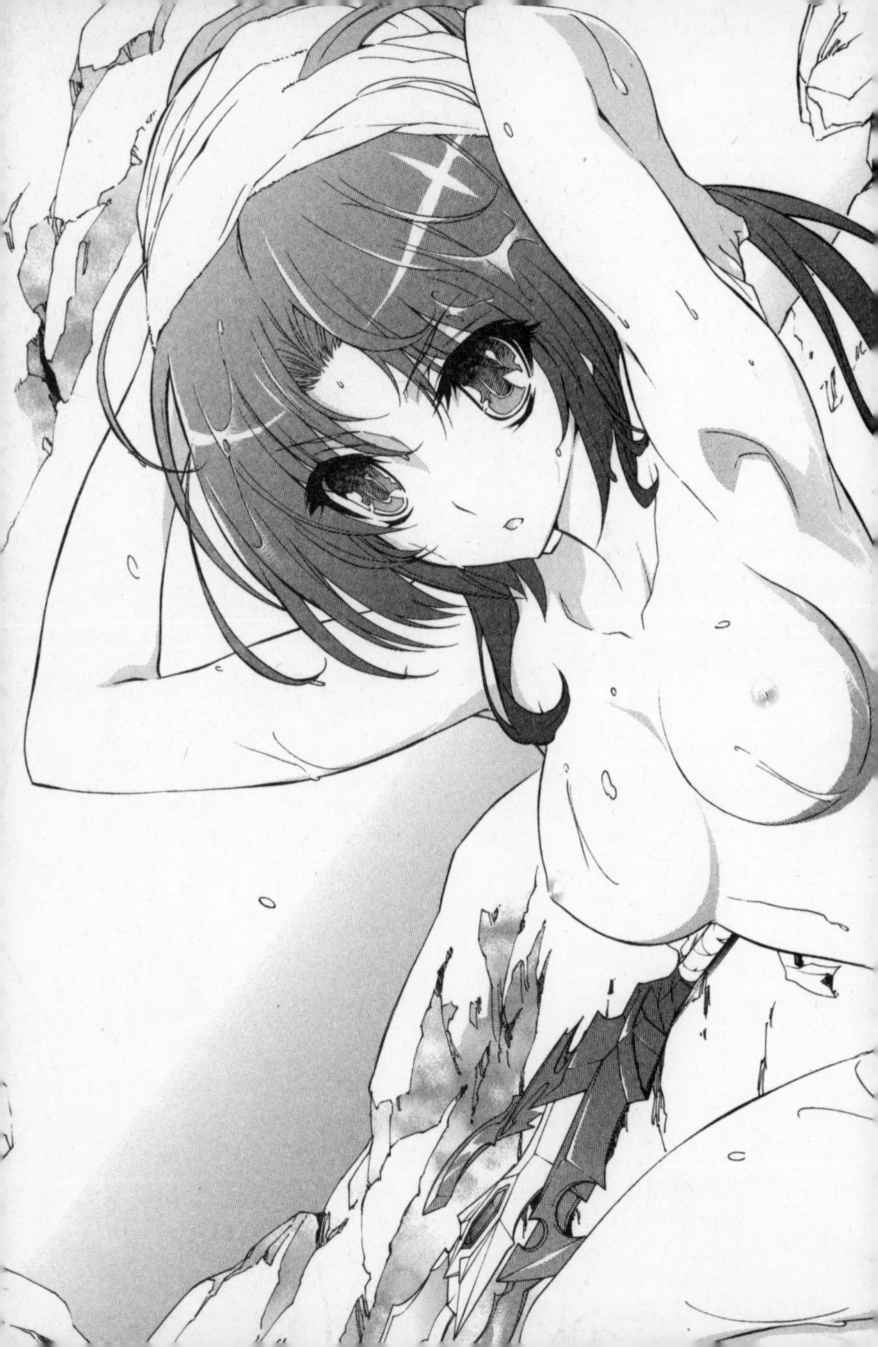

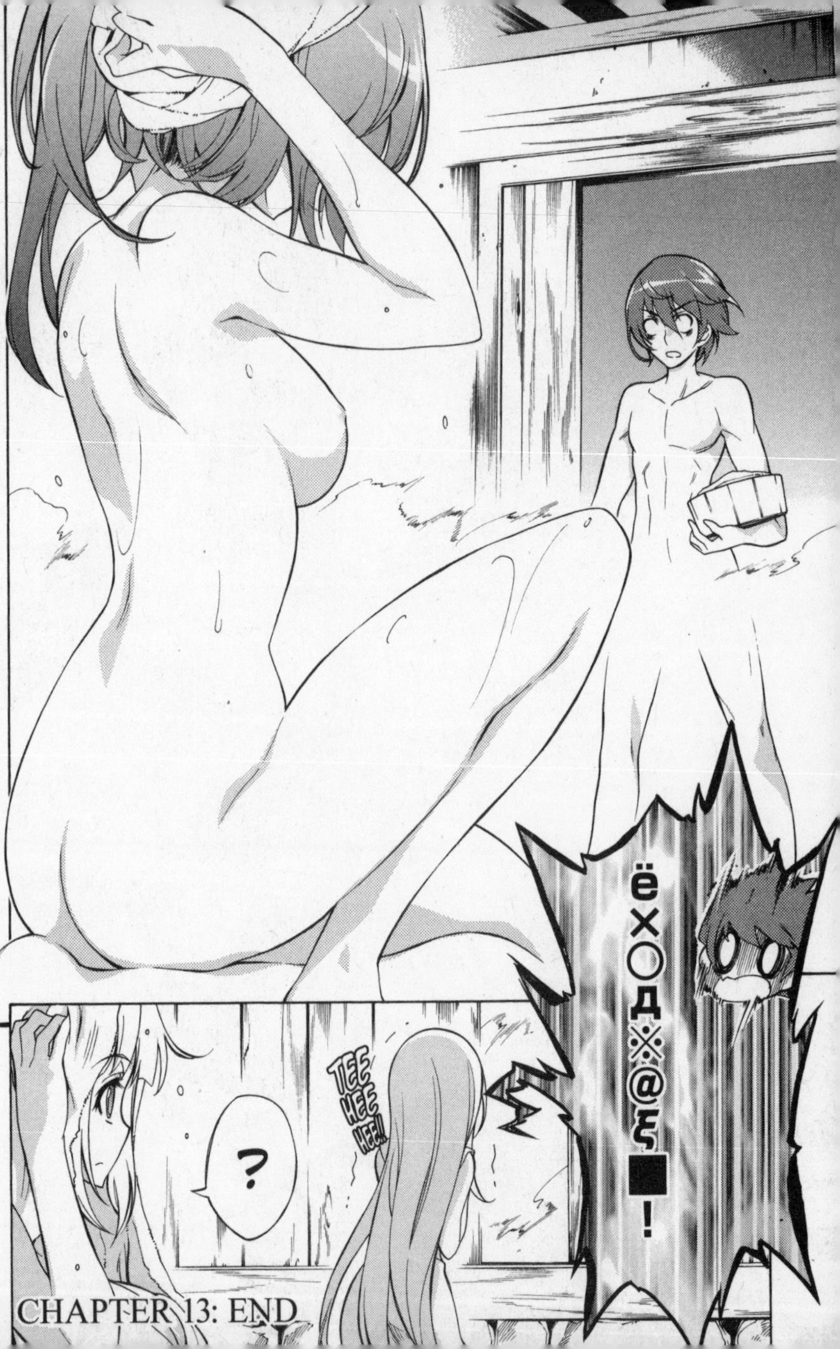
ёx○д※@ξ■!
TEE HEE HEE!!
?

CHAPTER 13: END

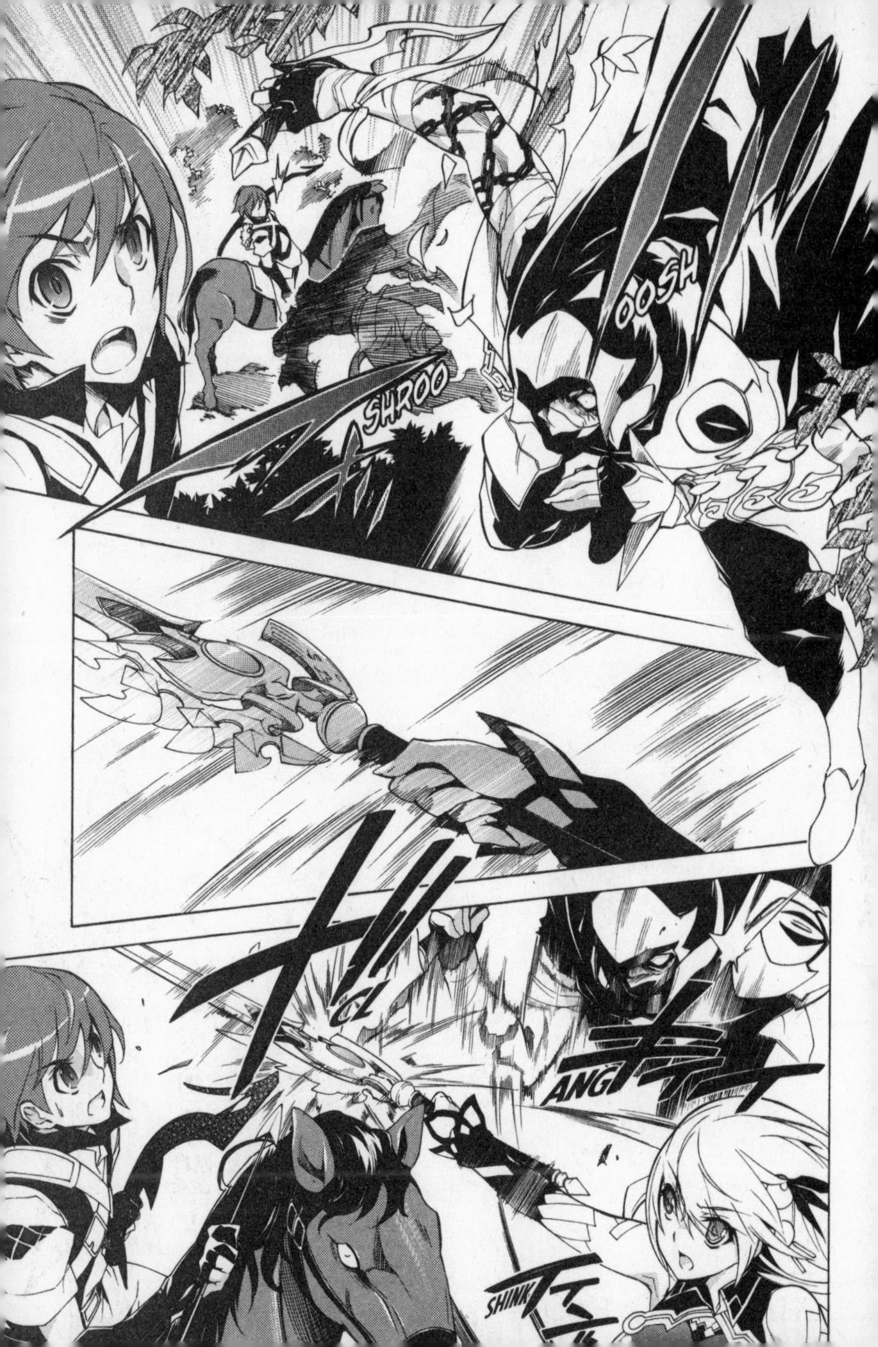
OOSH
SHROO
ANG
SHINK

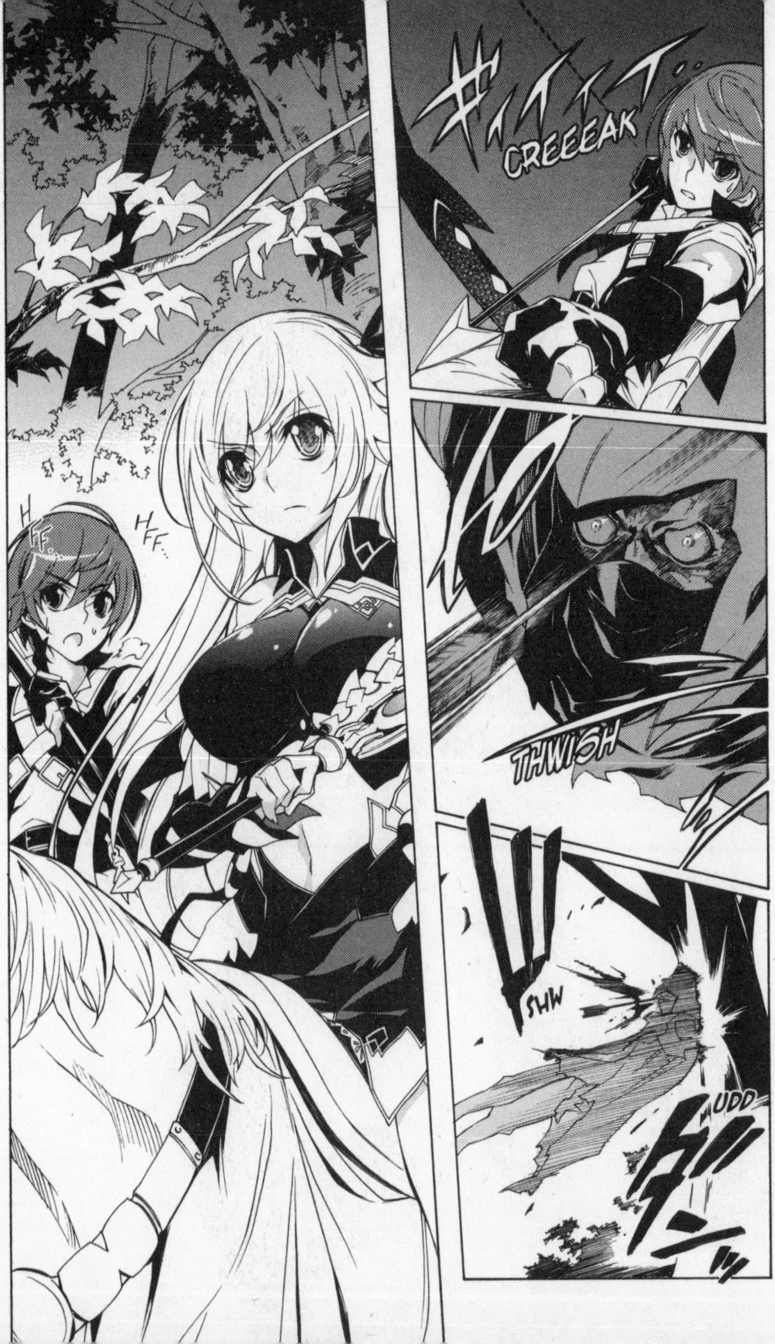
CREEEAK
THWISH
SHW
UDD
HFF
HFF...

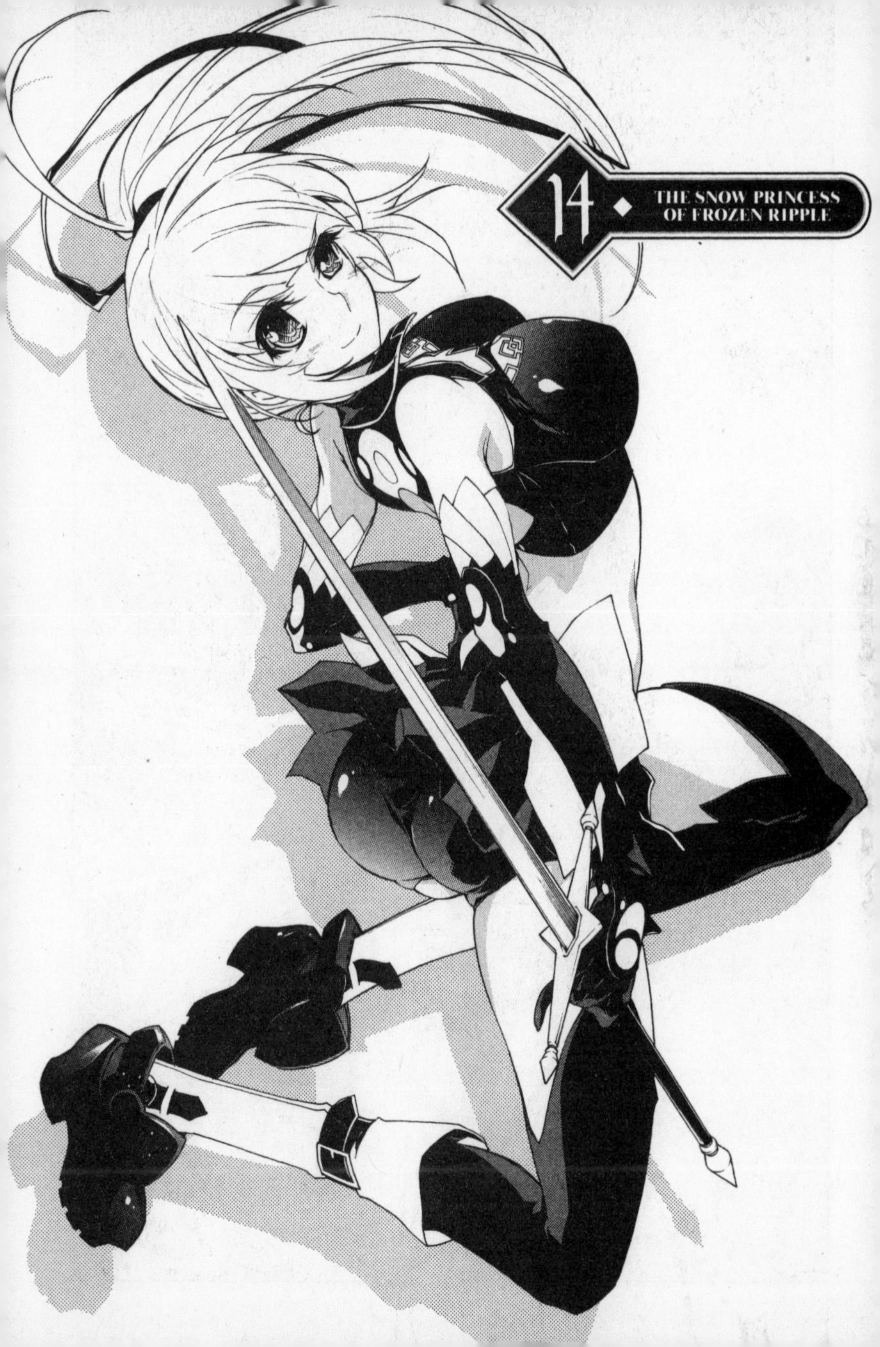
14
THE SNOW PRINCESS
OF FROZEN RIPPLE

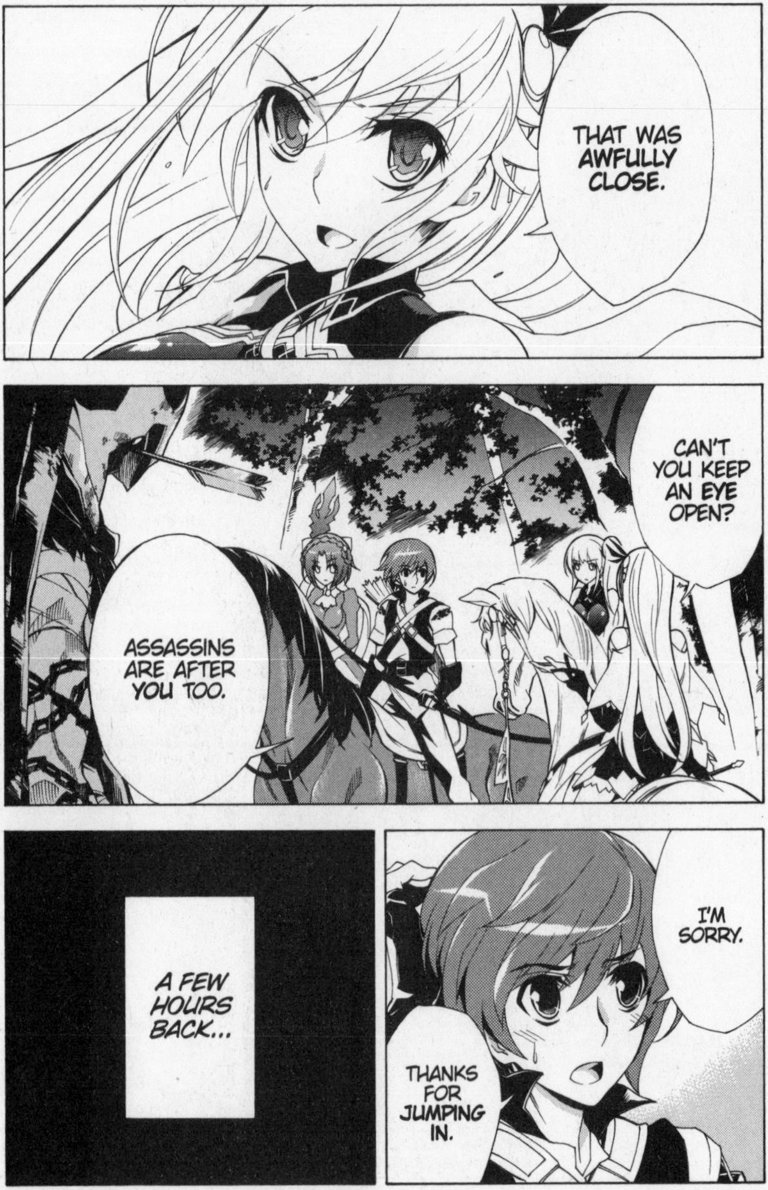
THAT WAS AWFULLY CLOSE.
CAN'T YOU KEEP AN EYE OPEN?
ASSASSINS ARE AFTER YOU TOO.
I'M SORRY.
THANKS FOR JUMPING IN.
A FEW HOURS BACK...

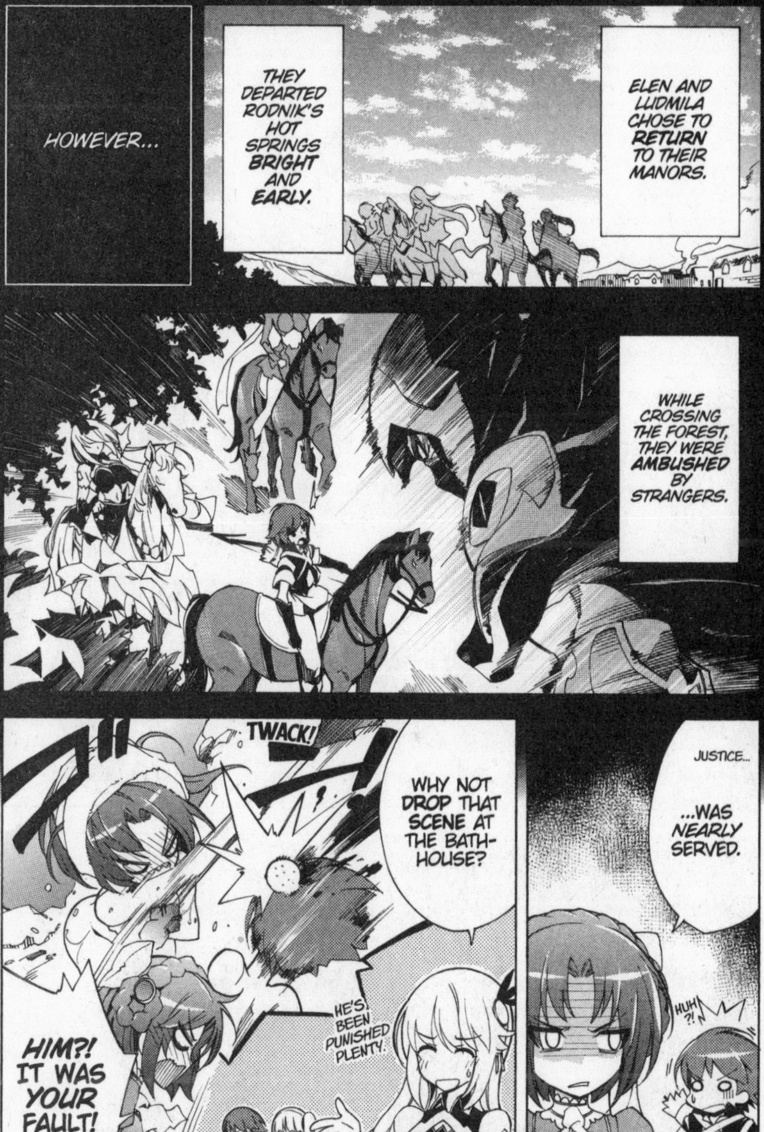
ELEN AND LUDMILA CHOSE TO RETURN TO THEIR MANORS.
THEY DEPARTED RODNIK'S HOT SPRINGS BRIGHT AND EARLY.
HOWEVER...
WHILE CROSSING THE FOREST, THEY WERE AMBUSHED BY STRANGERS.
JUSTICE...
...WAS NEARLY SERVED.
HUH ?!
TWACK!
WHY NOT DROP THAT SCENE AT THE BATH-HOUSE?
HE'S BEEN PUNISHED PLENTY.
HIM?! IT WAS YOUR FAULT!

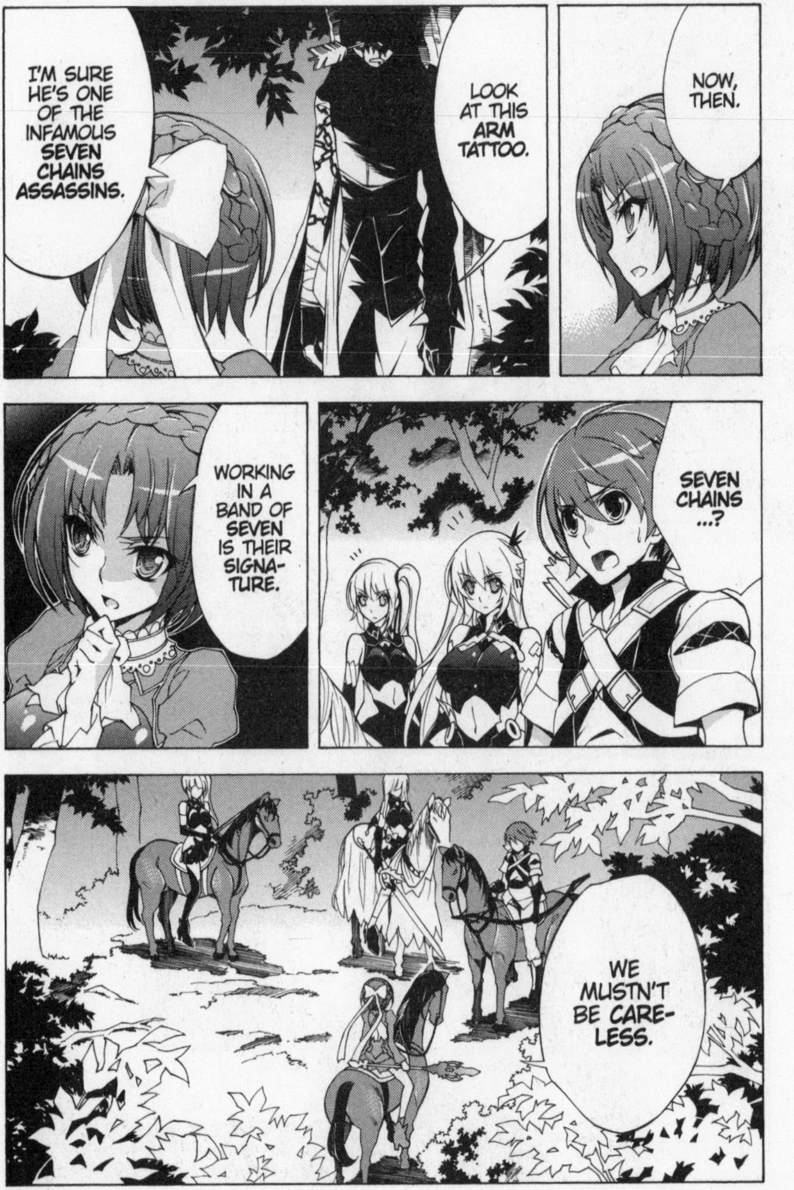
NOW, THEN.
LOOK AT THIS ARM TATTOO.
I'M SURE HE'S ONE OF THE INFAMOUS SEVEN CHAINS ASSASSINS.
SEVEN CHAINS ...?
WORKING IN A BAND OF SEVEN IS THEIR SIGNATURE.
WE MUSTN'T BE CARELESS.

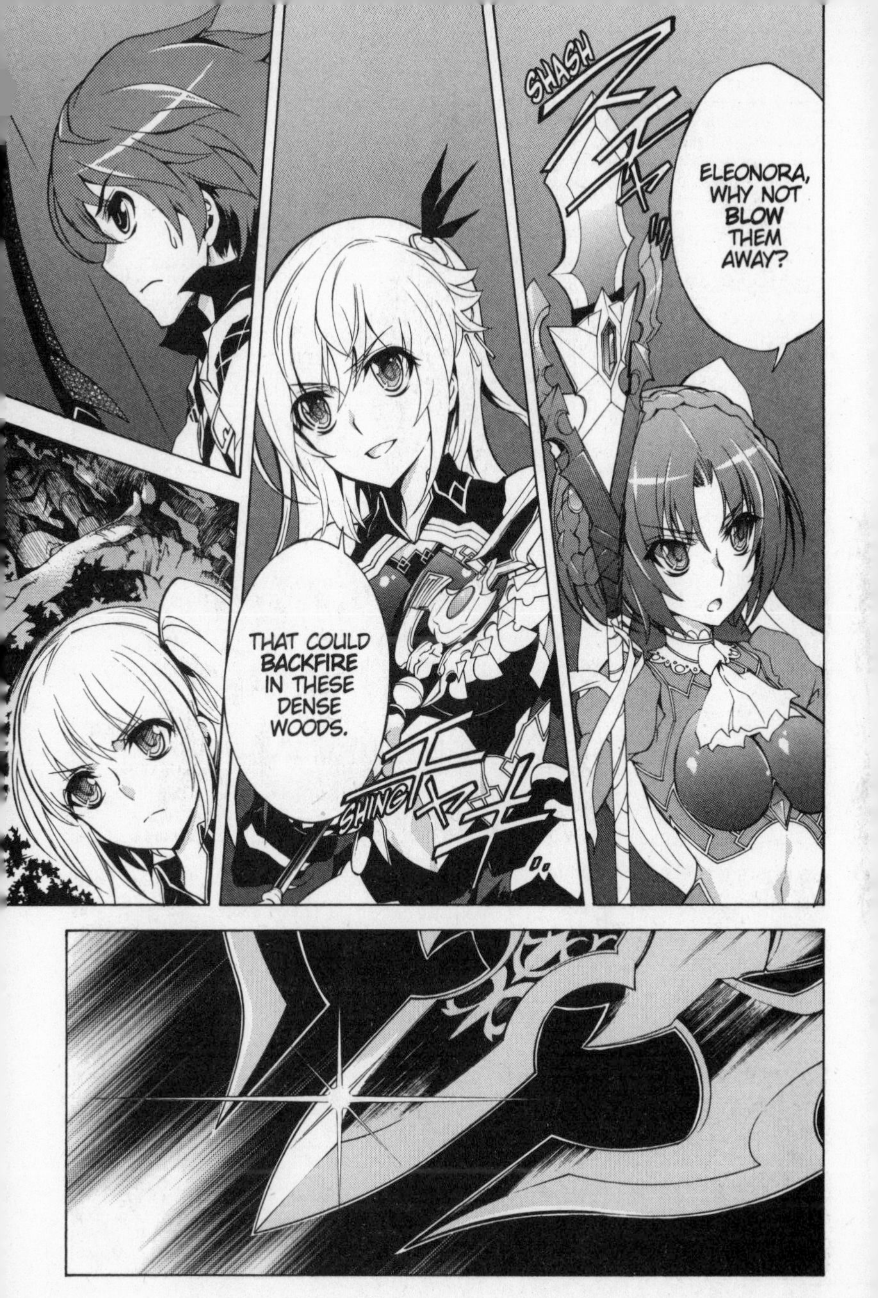
SHASH
ELEONORA, WHY NOT BLOW THEM AWAY?
THAT COULD BACKFIRE IN THESE DENSE WOODS.
SHING

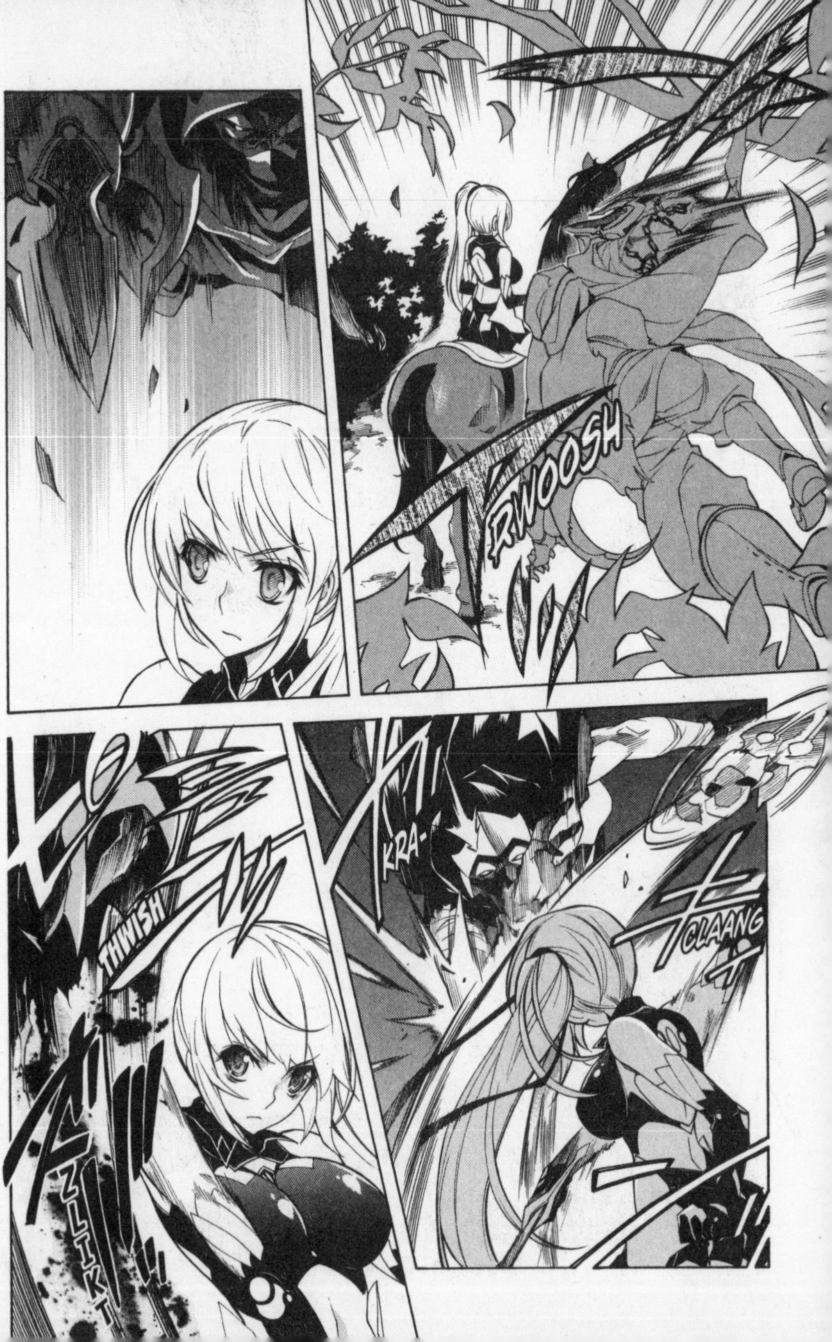

RWOOSH
CLAANG
KRA-
THWISH
ZLIKT

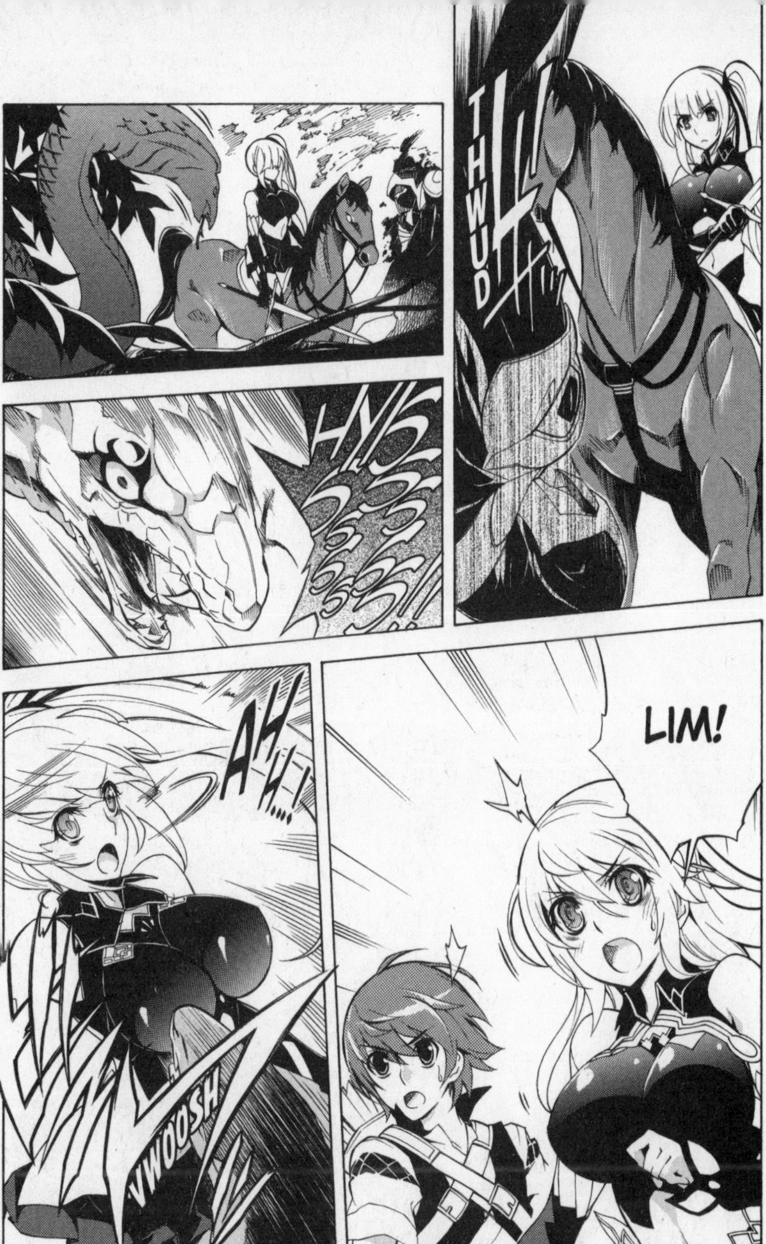
THWUD
HYISSSSSSSS...!!
LIM!
AH...!
VWOOSH

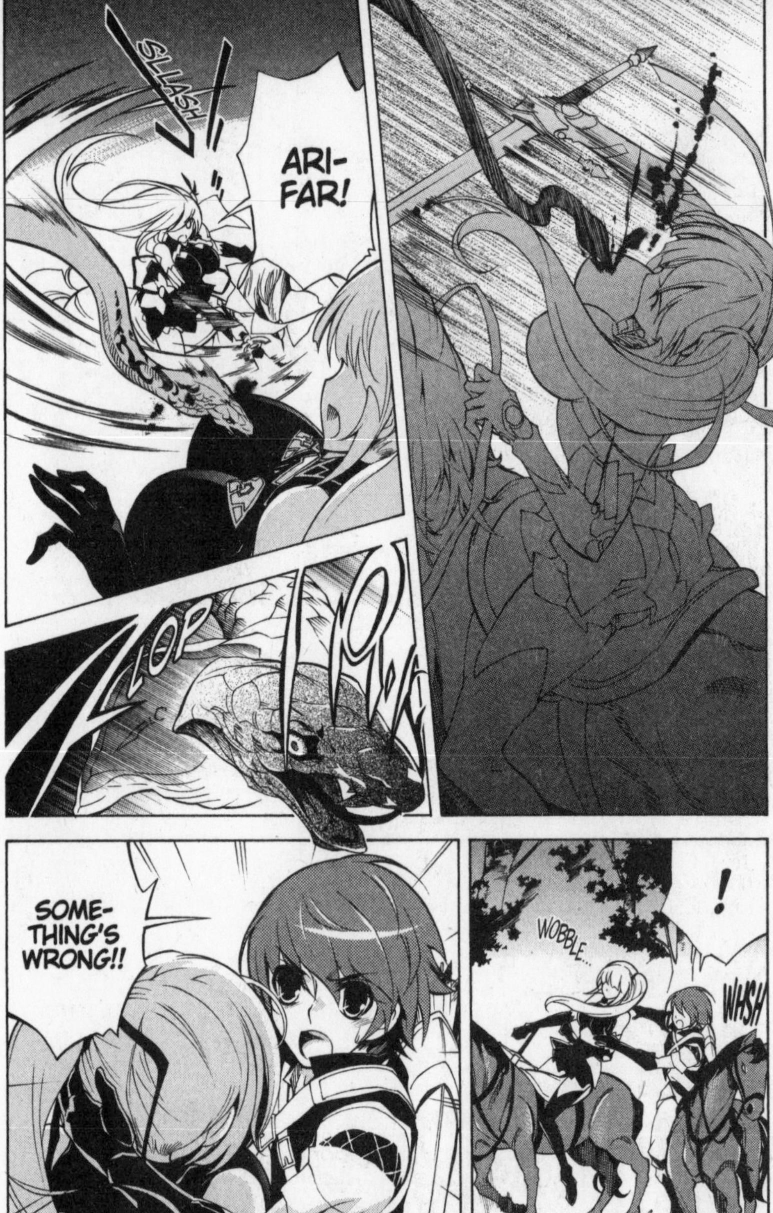
!!
SLASH
ARI-FAR!
ZLOP
POW
!
WOBBLE...
WHSH
SOME-THING'S WRONG!!

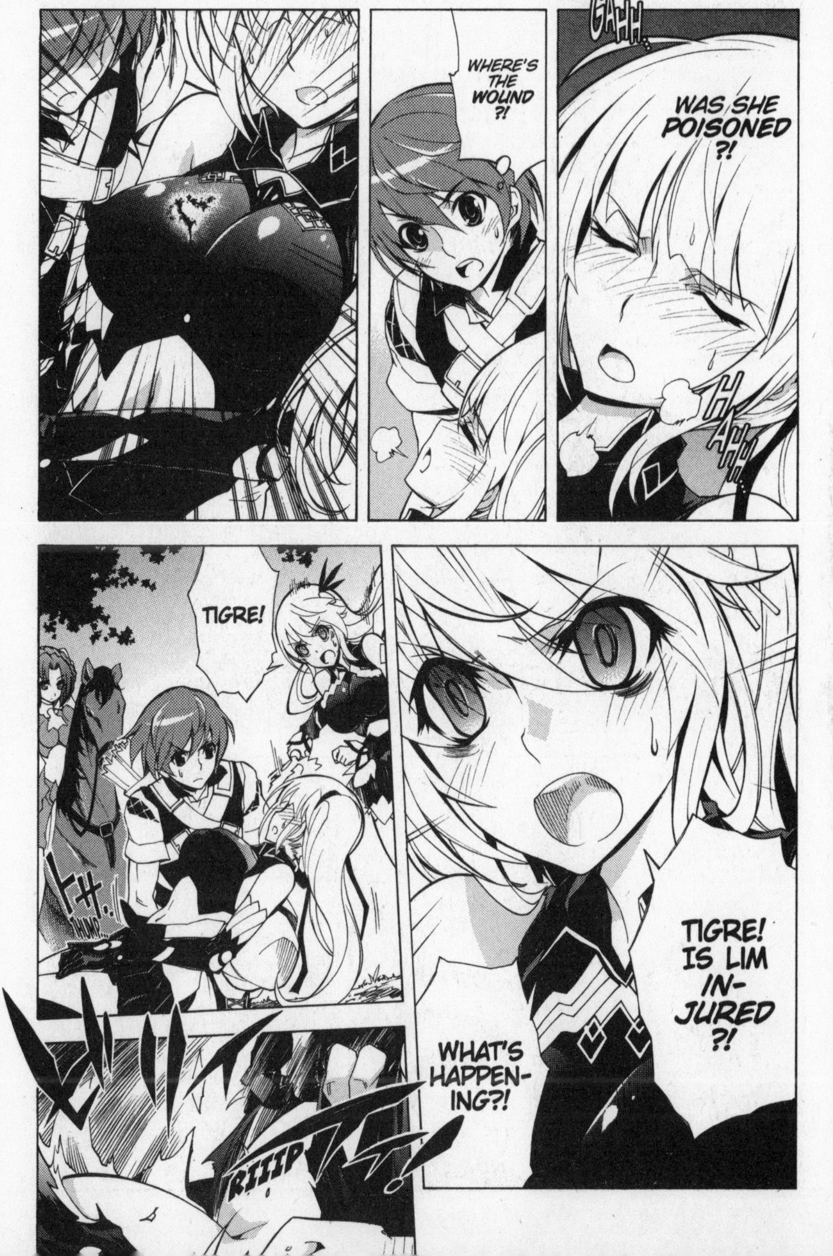
GAHH
WAS SHE POISONED?!
HAH HAH
WHERE'S THE WOUND?!
TIGRE! IS LIM IN-JURED?!
WHAT'S HAPPEN-ING?!
TIGRE!
THUMP
RIIIP

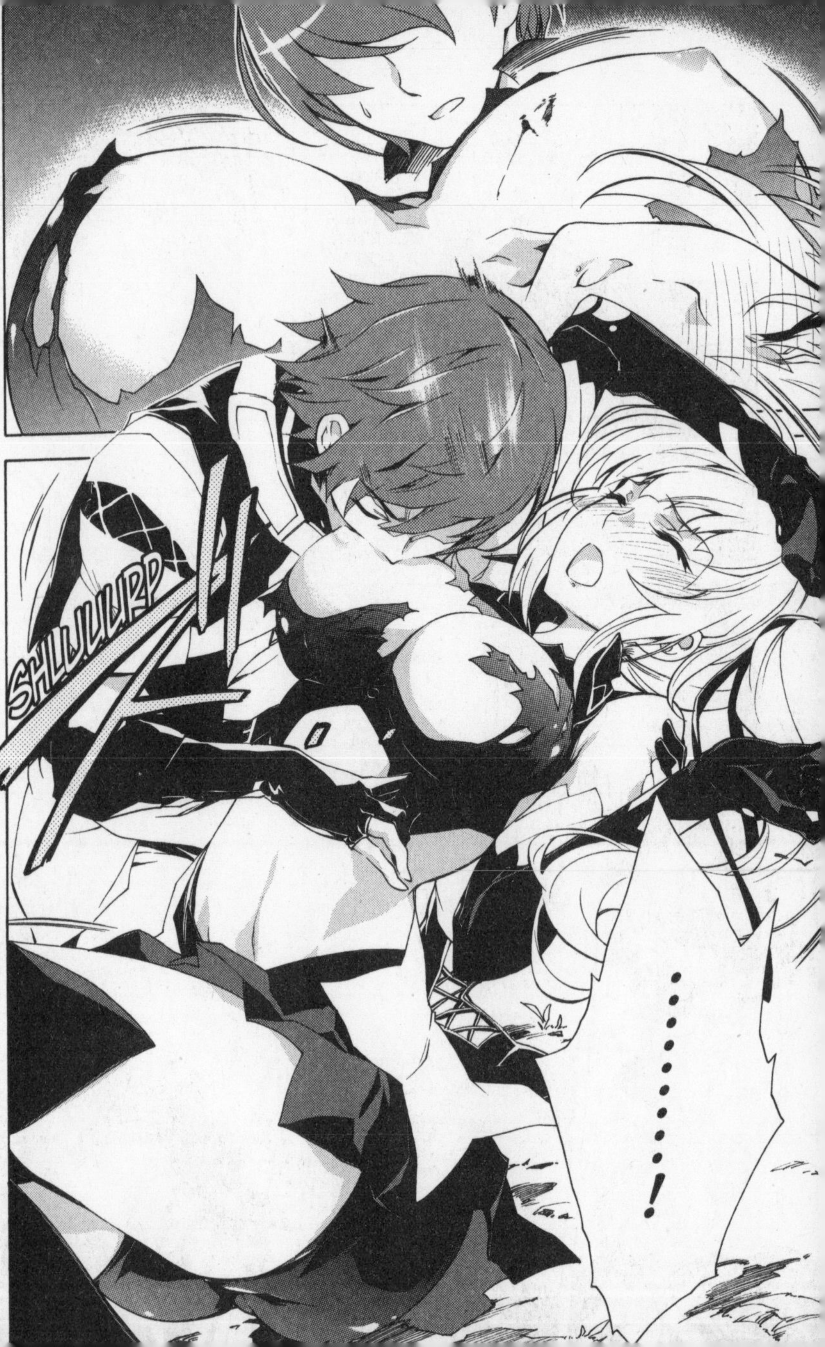
SHLUULURP
.........!

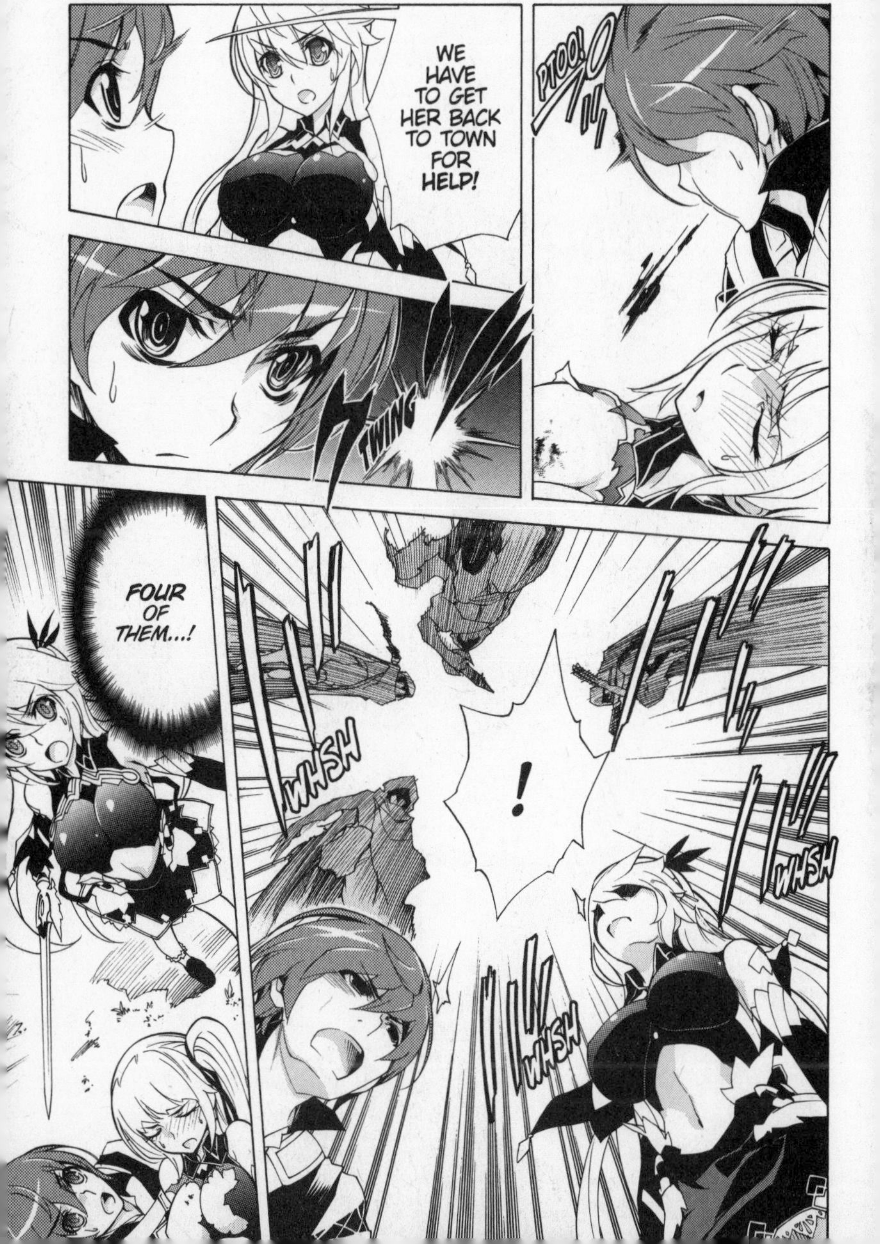
PTOO!
WE HAVE TO GET HER BACK TO TOWN FOR HELP!
TWING
WHSH
!
WHSH
WHSH
FOUR OF THEM...!

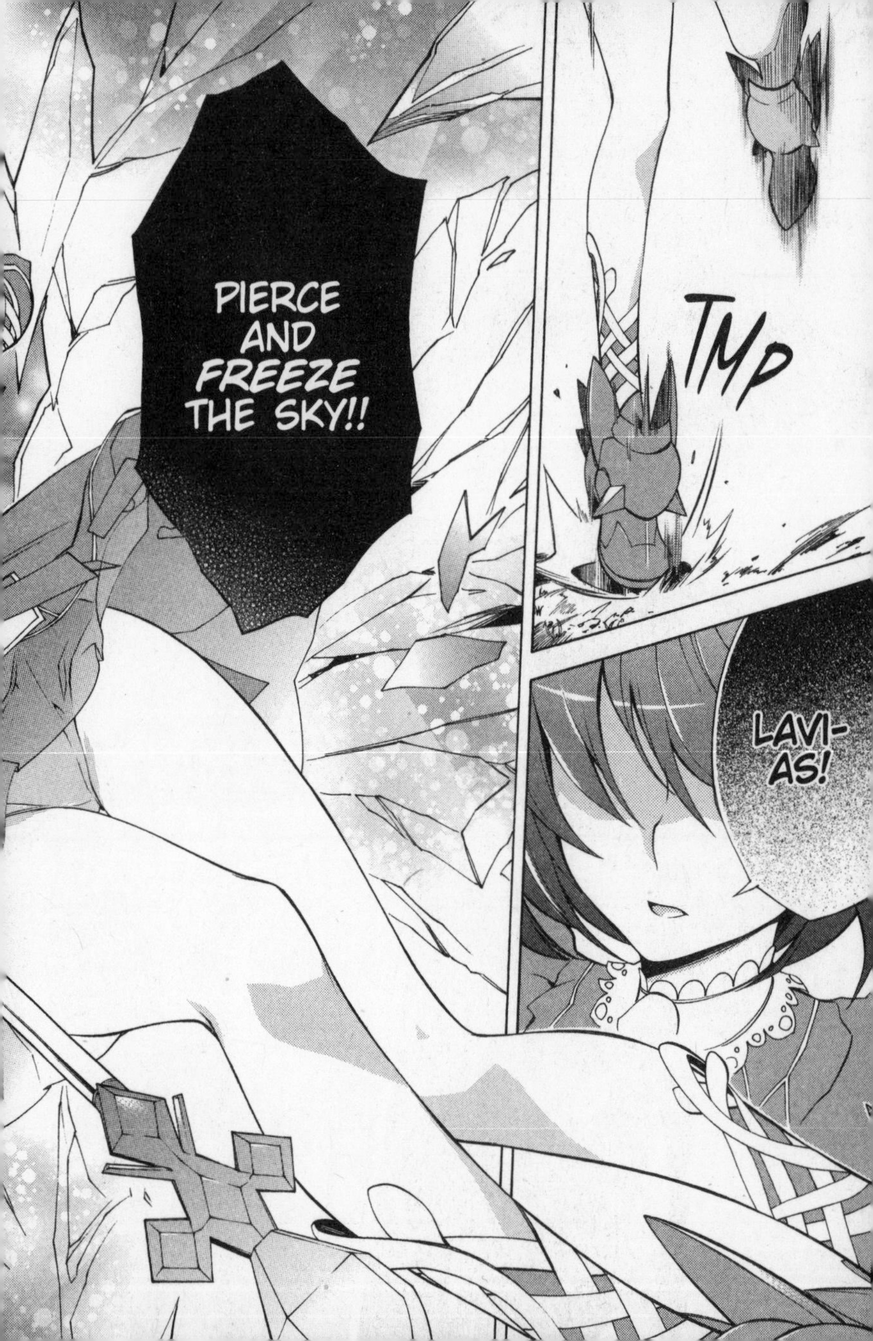
TMP
LAVI-AS!
PIERCE AND FREEZE THE SKY!!

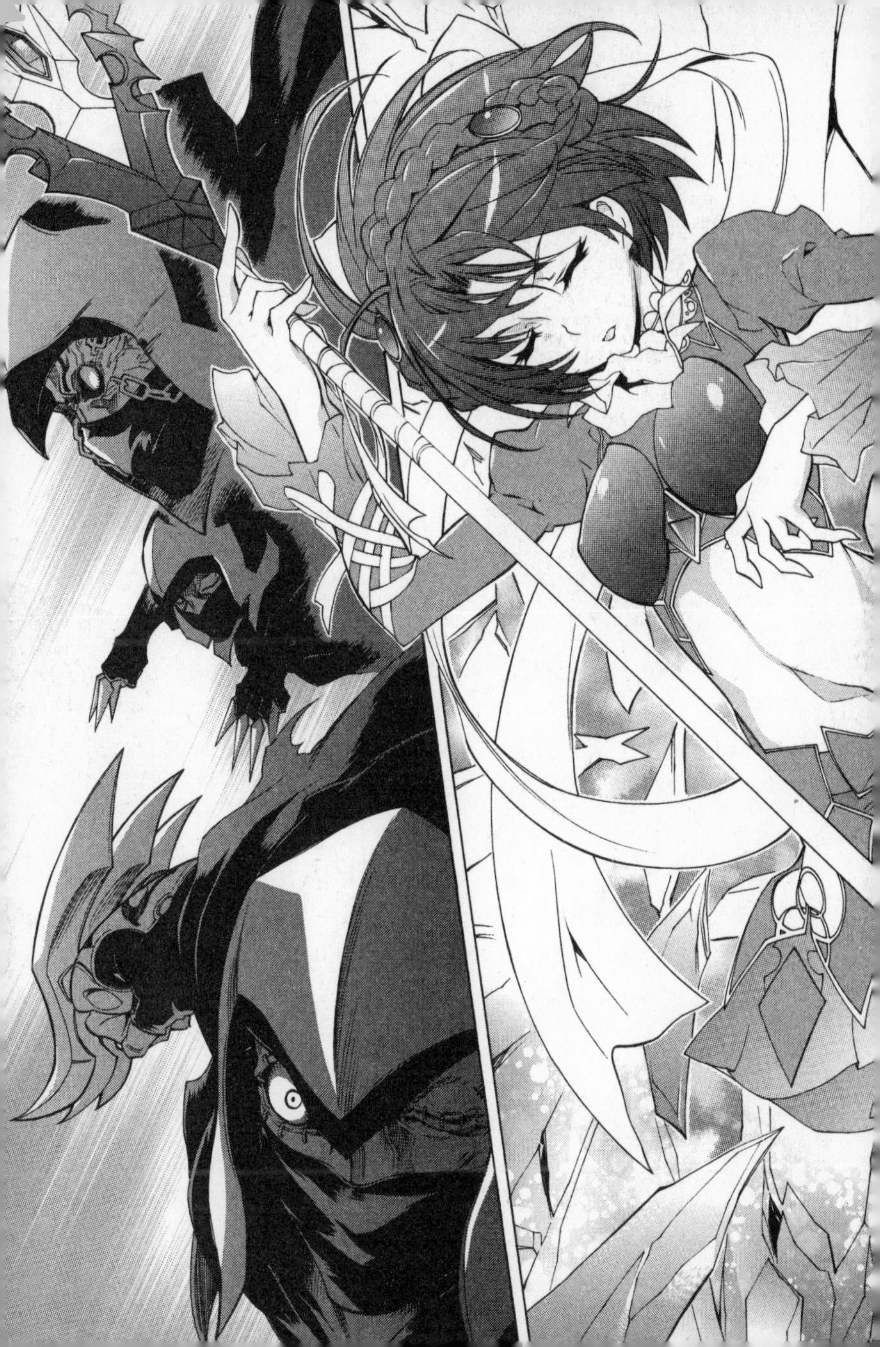

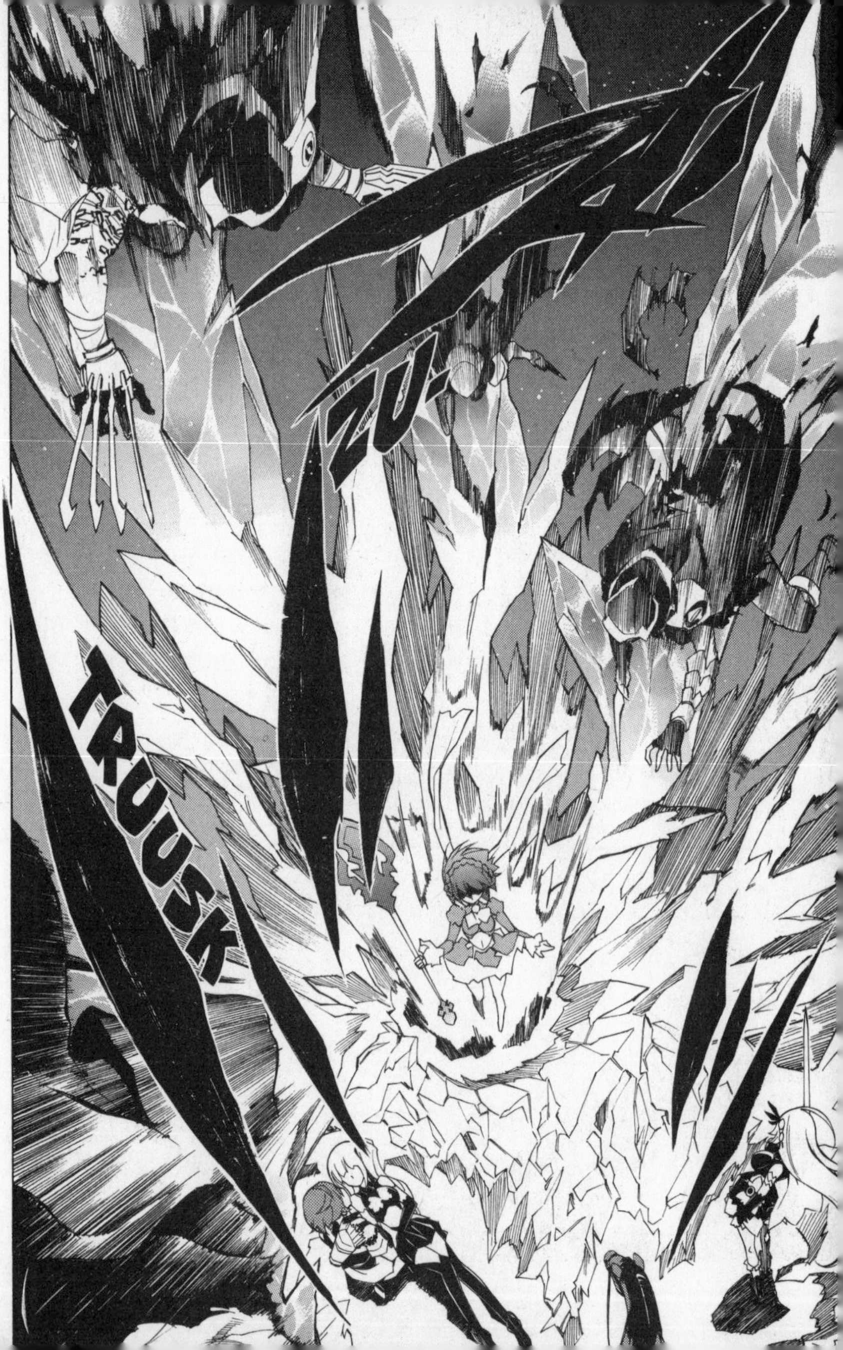
ZU-
TRUUSK

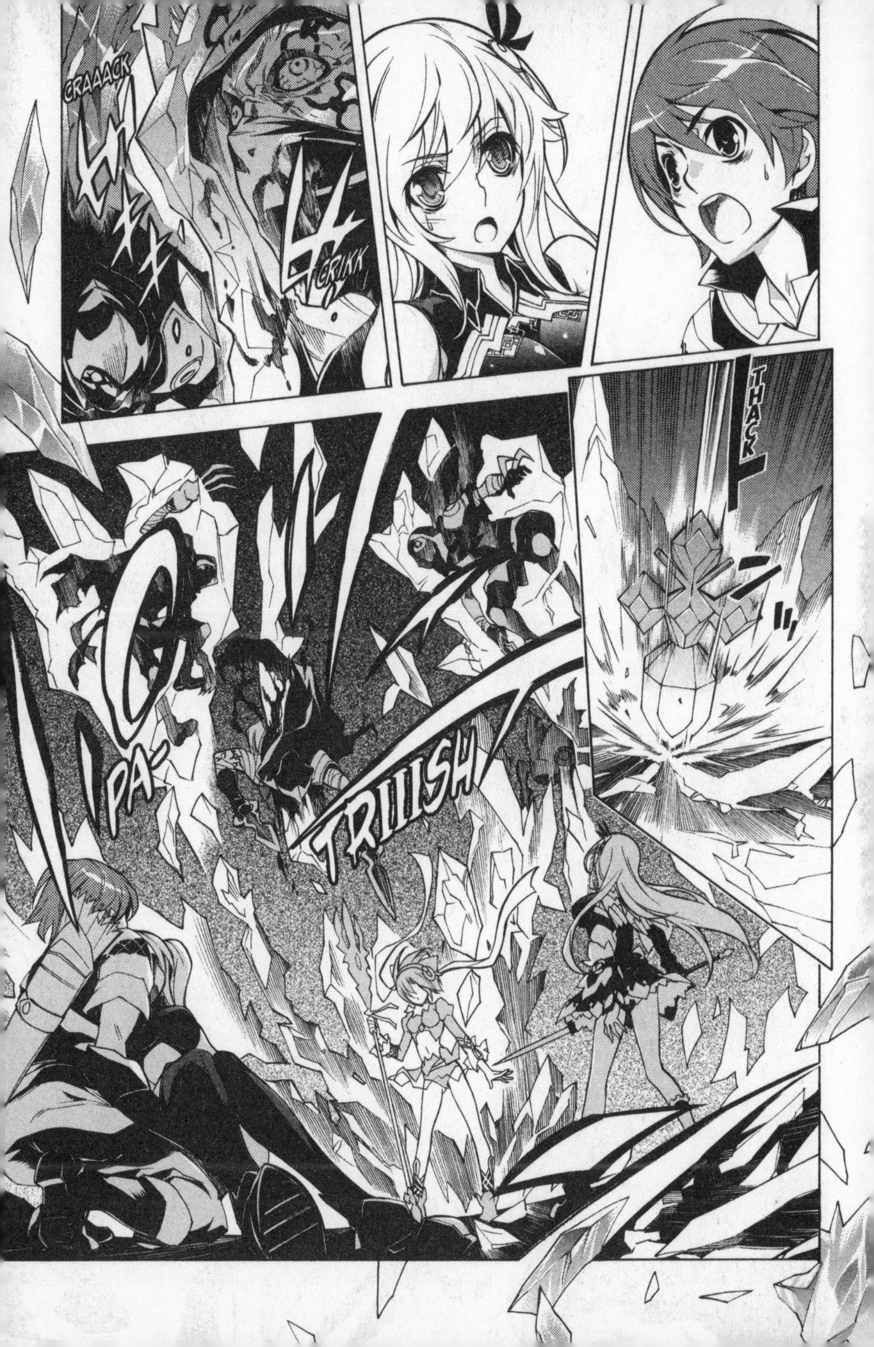
CRIKK
CRAAACK
THACK
TRIIISH
PA

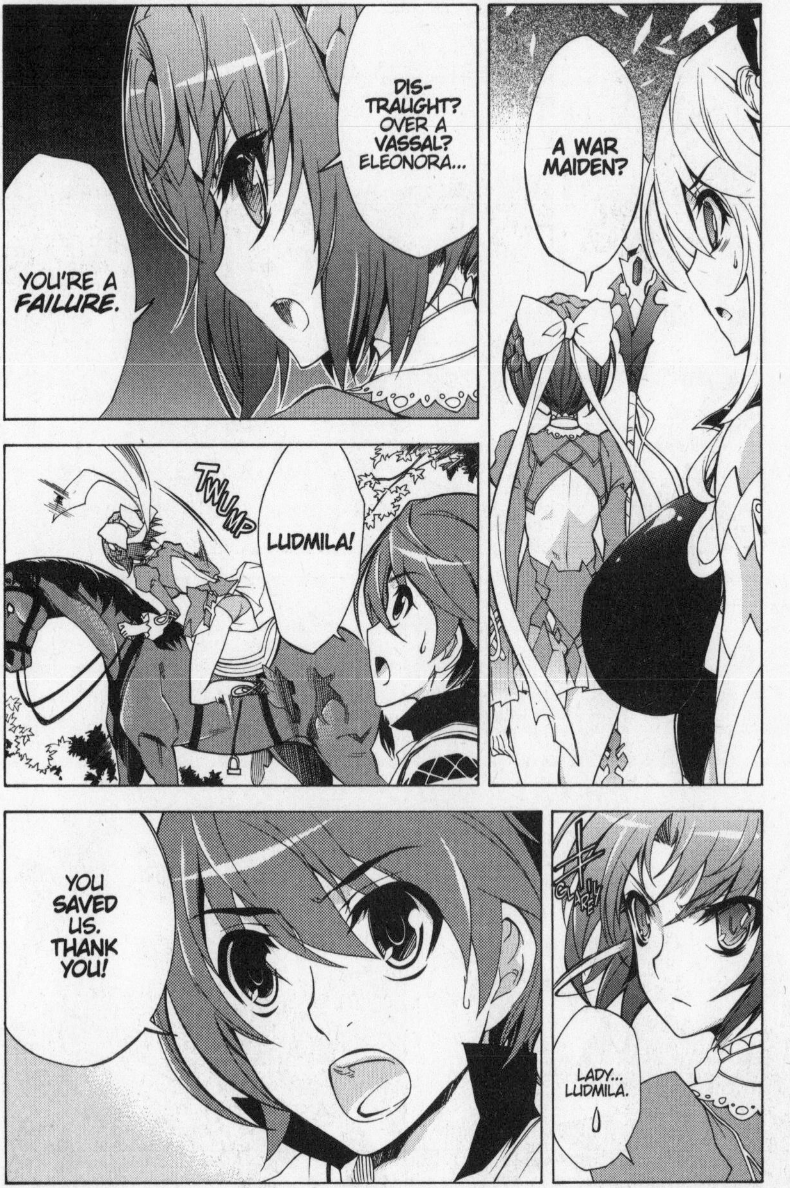
A WAR MAIDEN?
DIS-TRAUGHT? OVER A VASSAL? ELEONORA...
YOU'RE A *FAILURE.*
TWUMP
LUDMILA!
LADY... LUDMILA.
YOU SAVED US. THANK YOU!

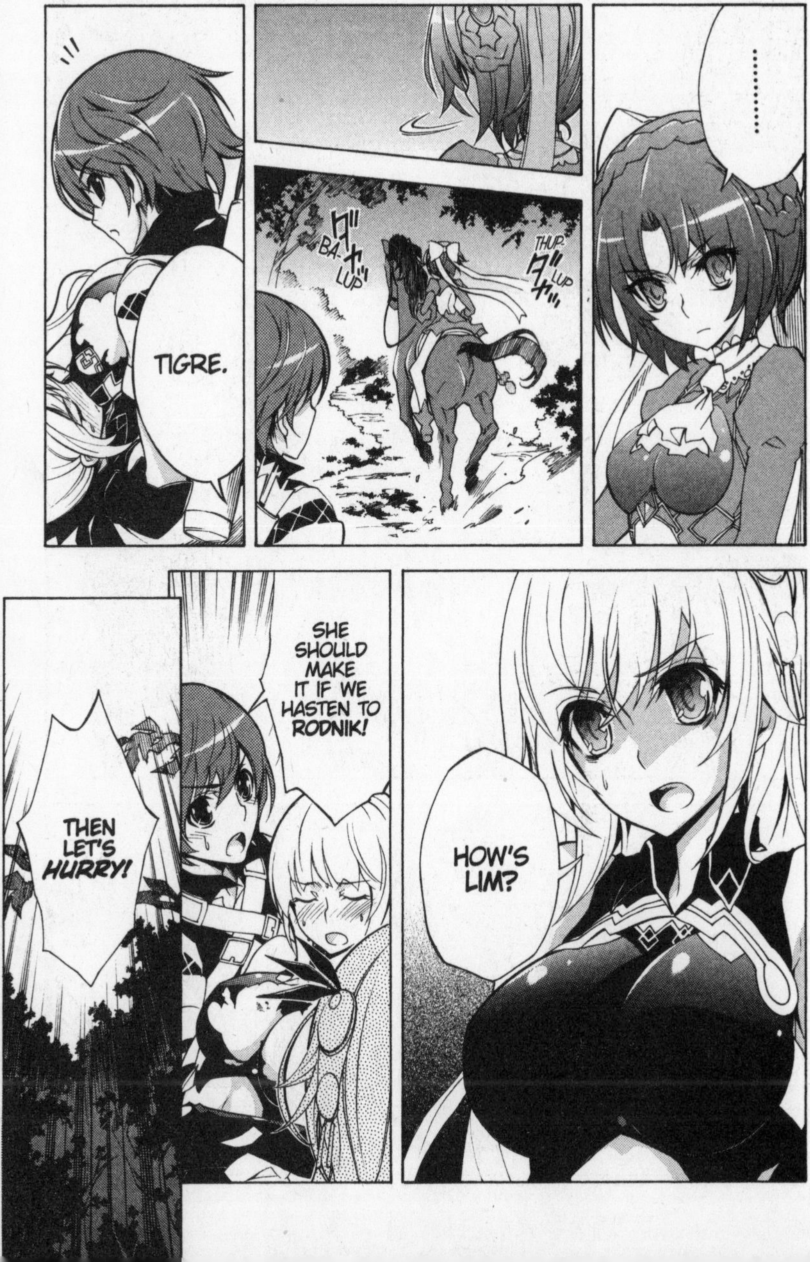
……
THUP-LUP
BA-LUP
TIGRE.
HOW'S LIM?
SHE SHOULD MAKE IT IF WE HASTEN TO RODNIK!
THEN LET'S *HURRY!*

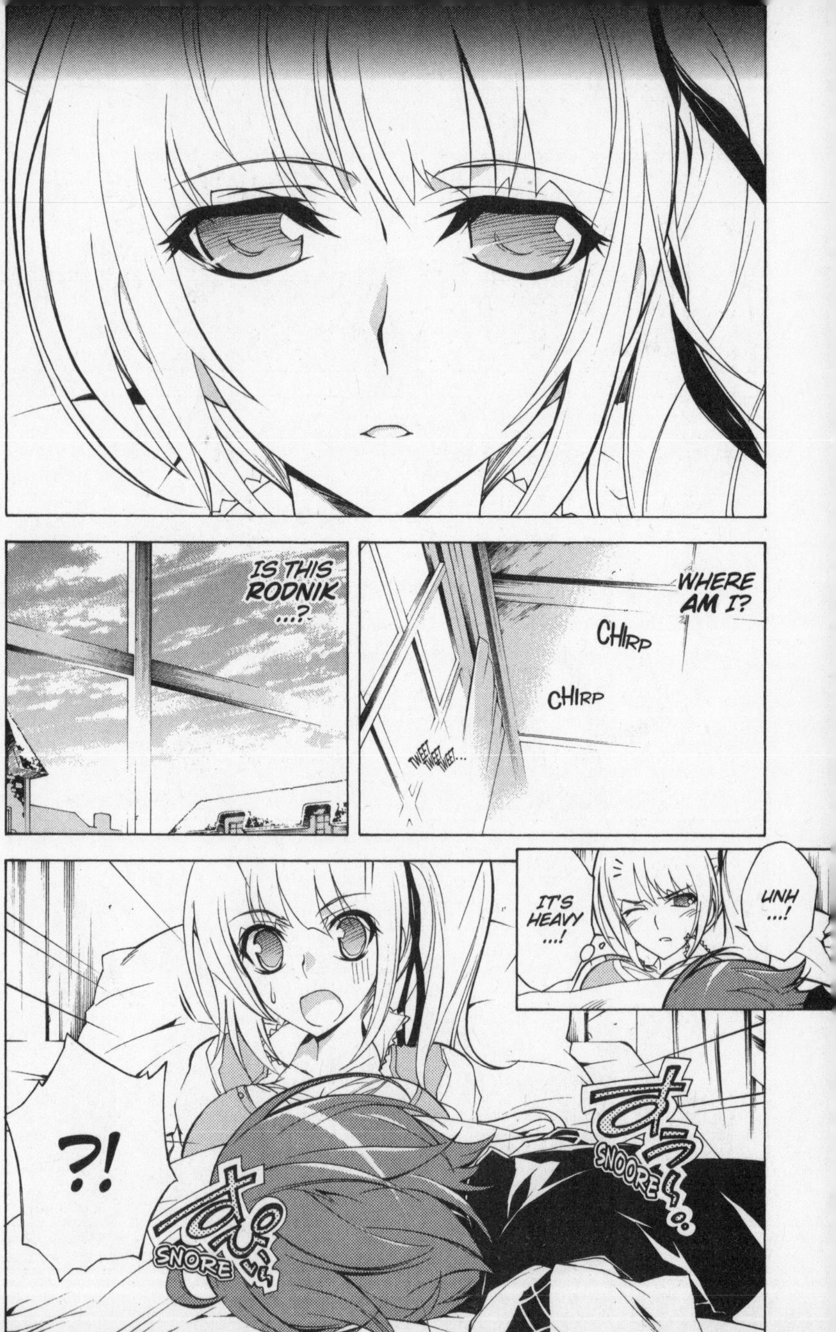
WHERE AM I?
CHIRP
CHIRP
TWEET TWEET TWEET...
IS THIS RODNIK ...?
UNH ...!
IT'S HEAVY ...!
?!
SNOORE
SNORE

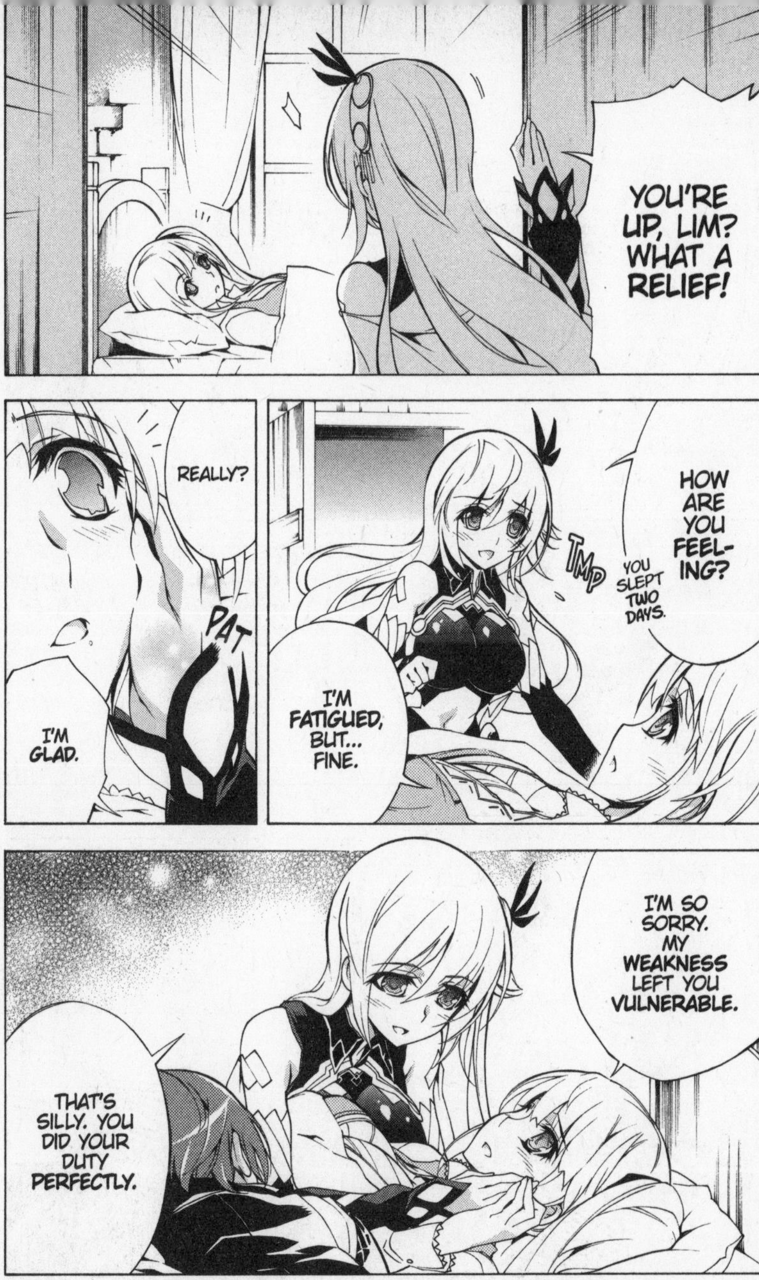
YOU'RE UP, LIM? WHAT A RELIEF!
HOW ARE YOU FEELING?
YOU SLEPT TWO DAYS.
TMP
I'M FATIGUED, BUT... FINE.
REALLY?
PAT
I'M GLAD.
I'M SO SORRY. MY WEAKNESS LEFT YOU VULNERABLE.
THAT'S SILLY. YOU DID YOUR DUTY PERFECTLY.

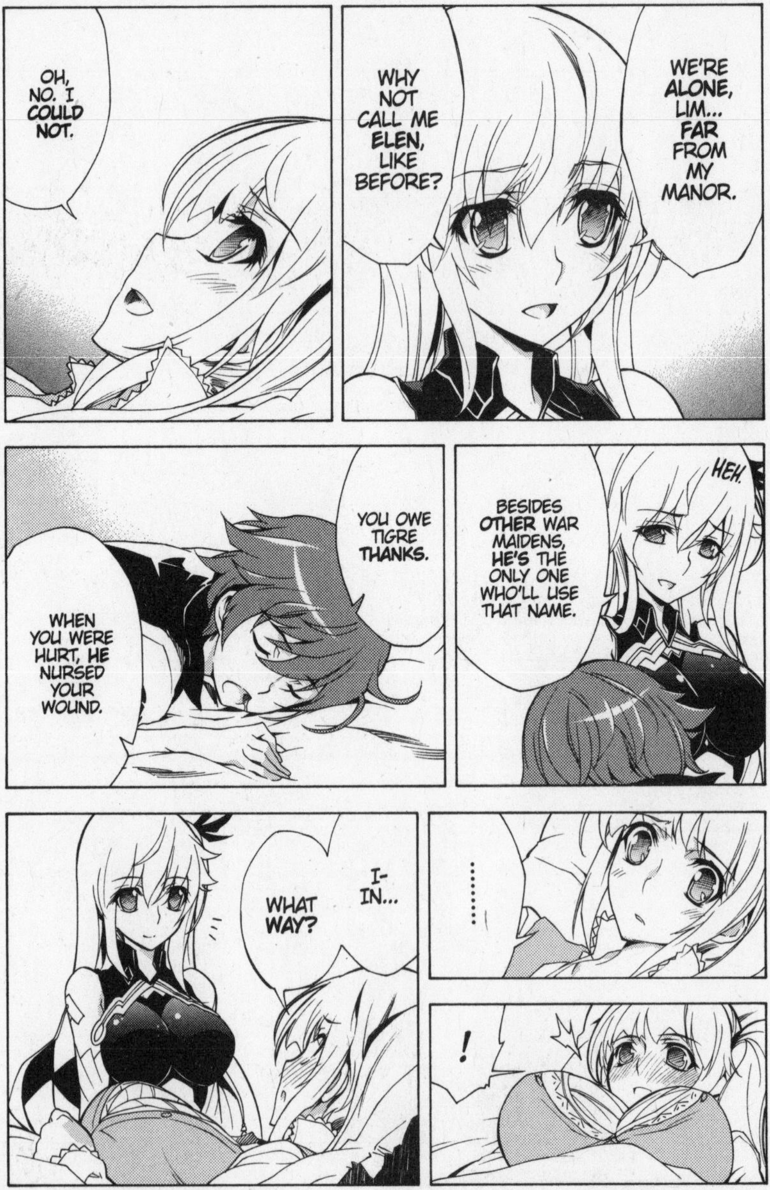
WE'RE ALONE, LIM... FAR FROM MY MANOR.
WHY NOT CALL ME ELEN, LIKE BEFORE?
OH, NO. I COULD NOT.
HEH.
BESIDES OTHER WAR MAIDENS, HE'S THE ONLY ONE WHO'LL USE THAT NAME.
YOU OWE TIGRE THANKS.
WHEN YOU WERE HURT, HE NURSED YOUR WOUND.
......
!
I- IN...
WHAT WAY?

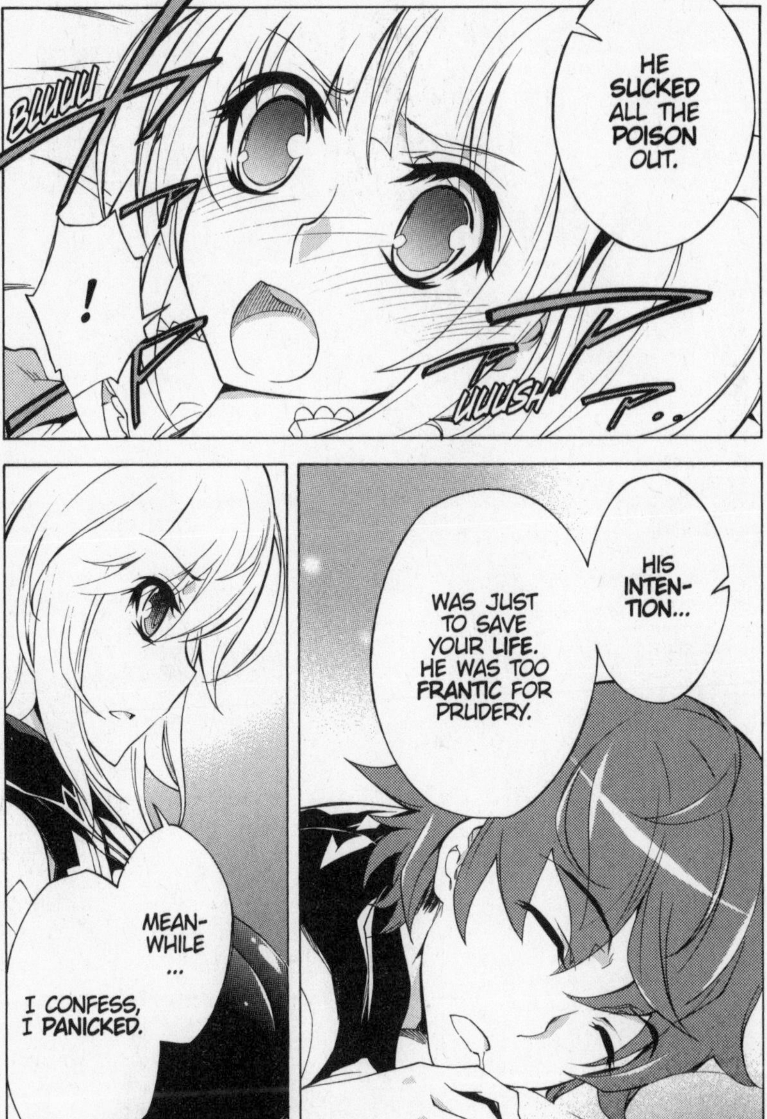
HE SUCKED ALL THE POISON OUT.
BLUUU
!
UUUSH
HIS INTEN-TION...
WAS JUST TO SAVE YOUR LIFE. HE WAS TOO FRANTIC FOR PRUDERY.
MEAN-WHILE ...
I CONFESS, I PANICKED.

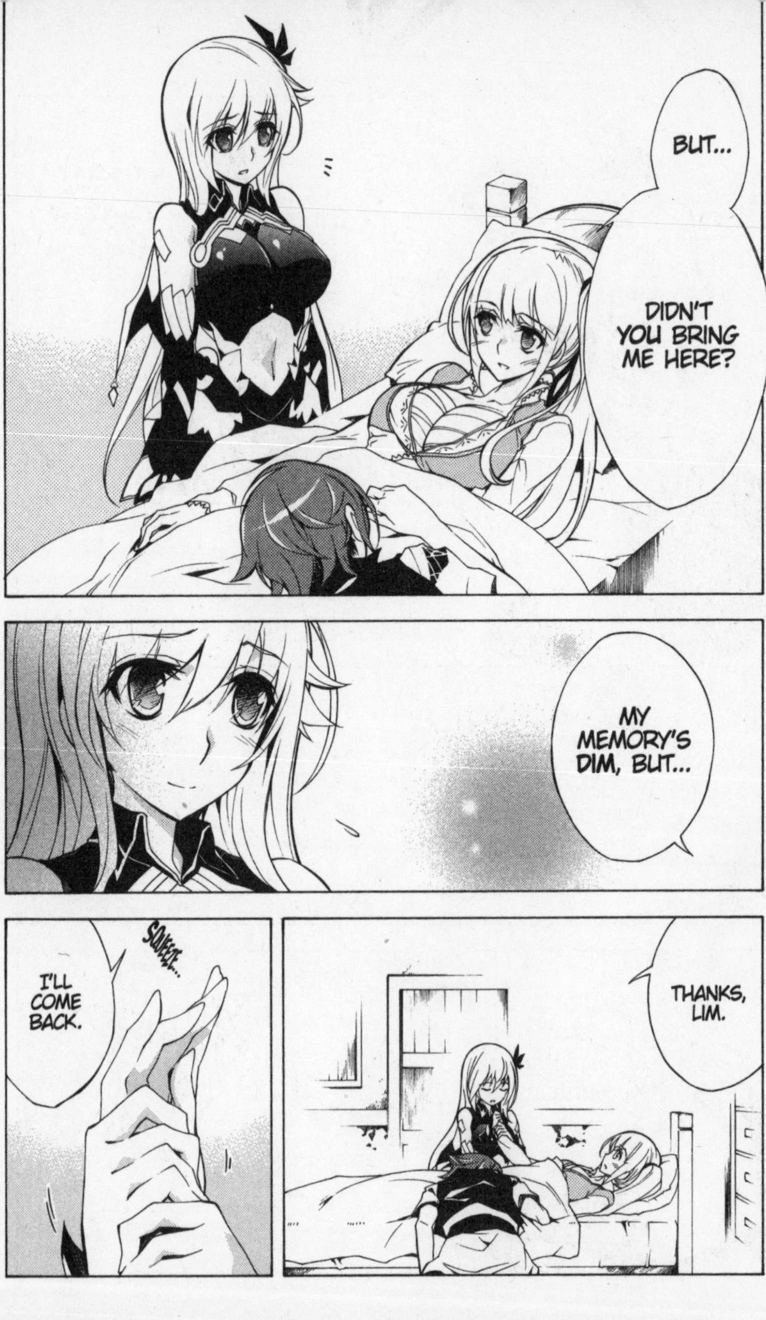
BUT...
DIDN'T YOU BRING ME HERE?
MY MEMORY'S DIM, BUT...
THANKS, LIM.
SQUEEZE...
I'LL COME BACK.

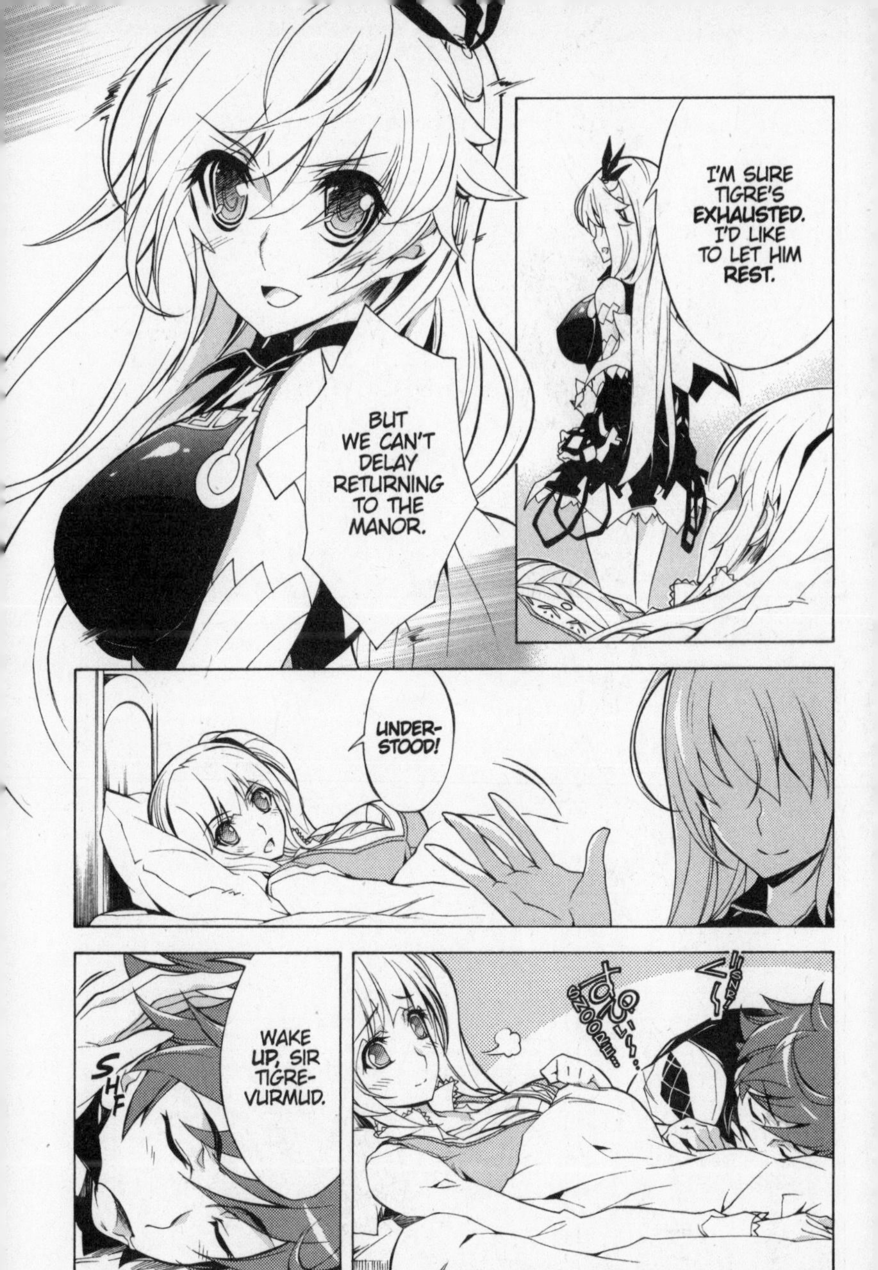
I'M SURE TIGRE'S EXHAUSTED. I'D LIKE TO LET HIM REST.
BUT WE CAN'T DELAY RETURNING TO THE MANOR.
UNDER-STOOD!
SNR...
WAKE UP, SIR TIGRE-VURMUD.
SHF

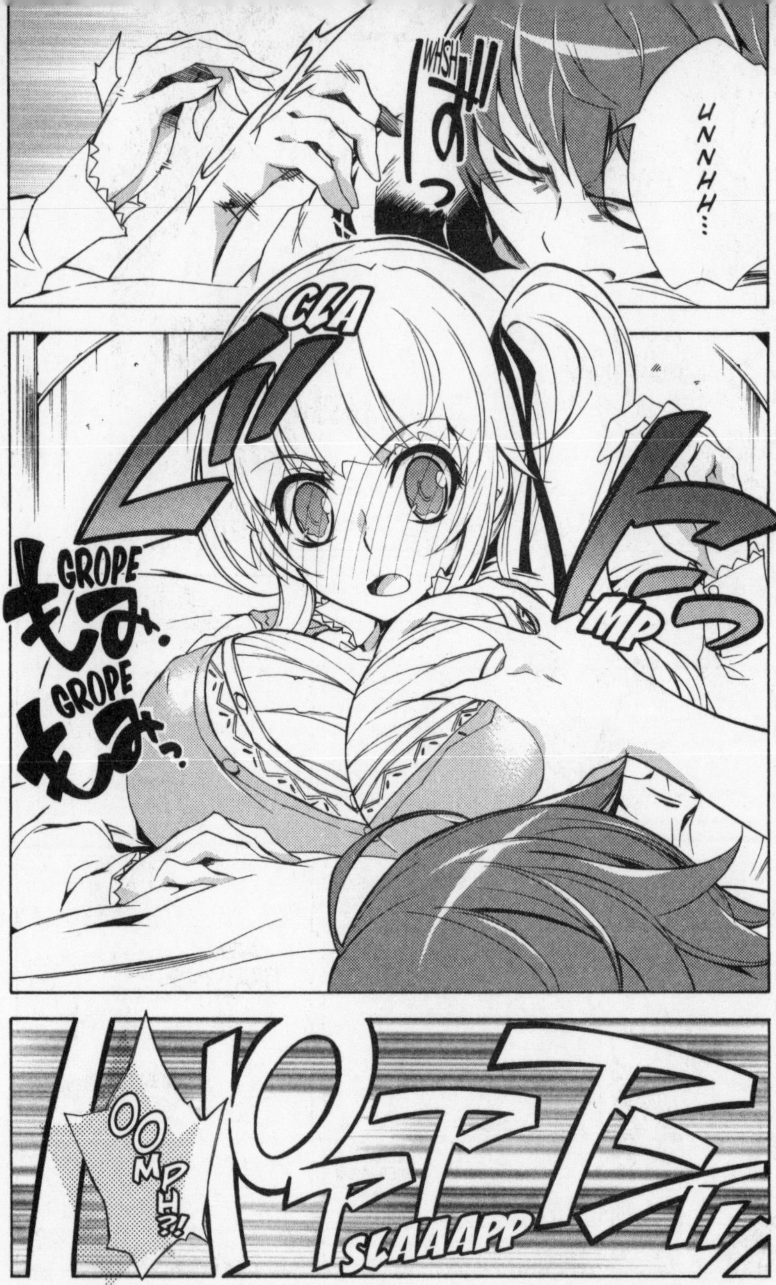
UNNHH...
WHSH
CLA
MP
GROPE
GROPE
OOMPH?!
SLAAAPP

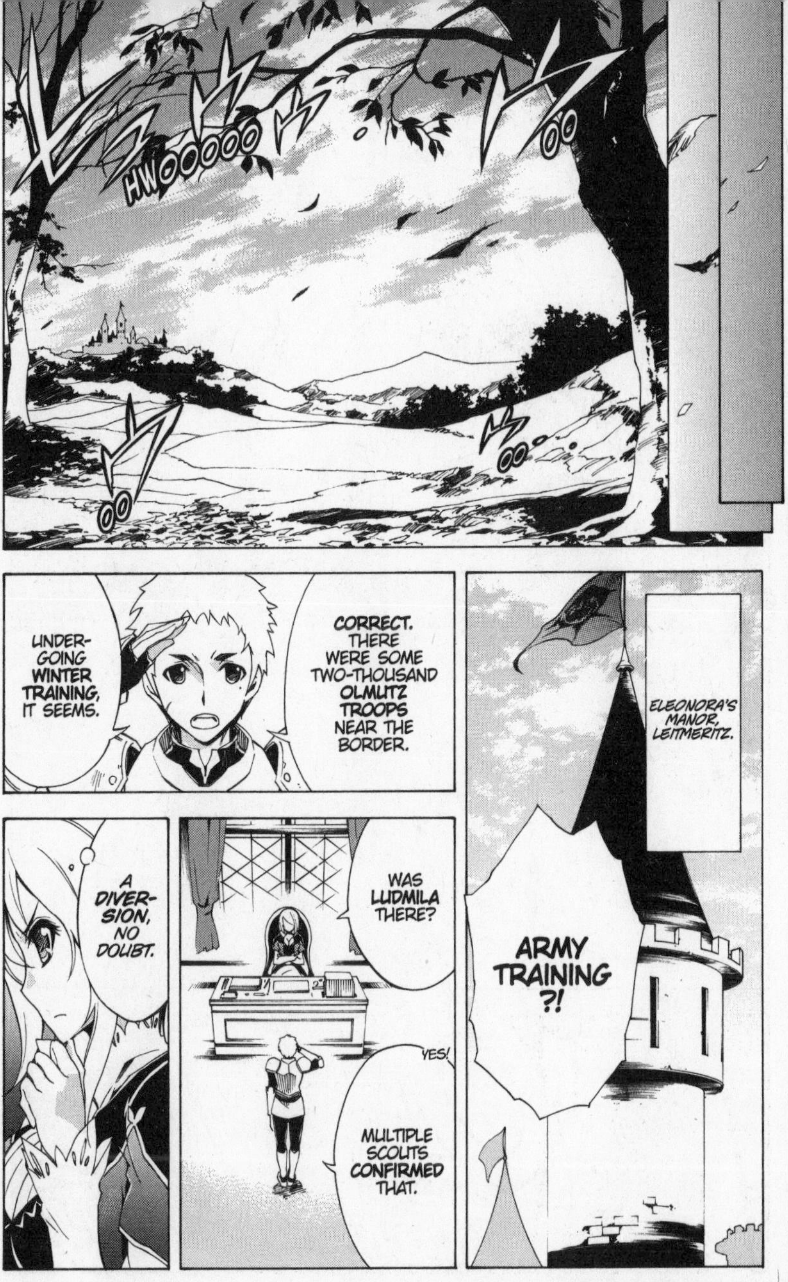
HWOOOOO
ELEONORA'S MANOR, LEITMERITZ.
ARMY TRAINING?!
CORRECT. THERE WERE SOME TWO-THOUSAND OLMUTZ TROOPS NEAR THE BORDER.
UNDER-GOING WINTER TRAINING, IT SEEMS.
WAS LUDMILA THERE?
YES!
MULTIPLE SCOUTS CONFIRMED THAT.
A DIVER-SION, NO DOUBT.

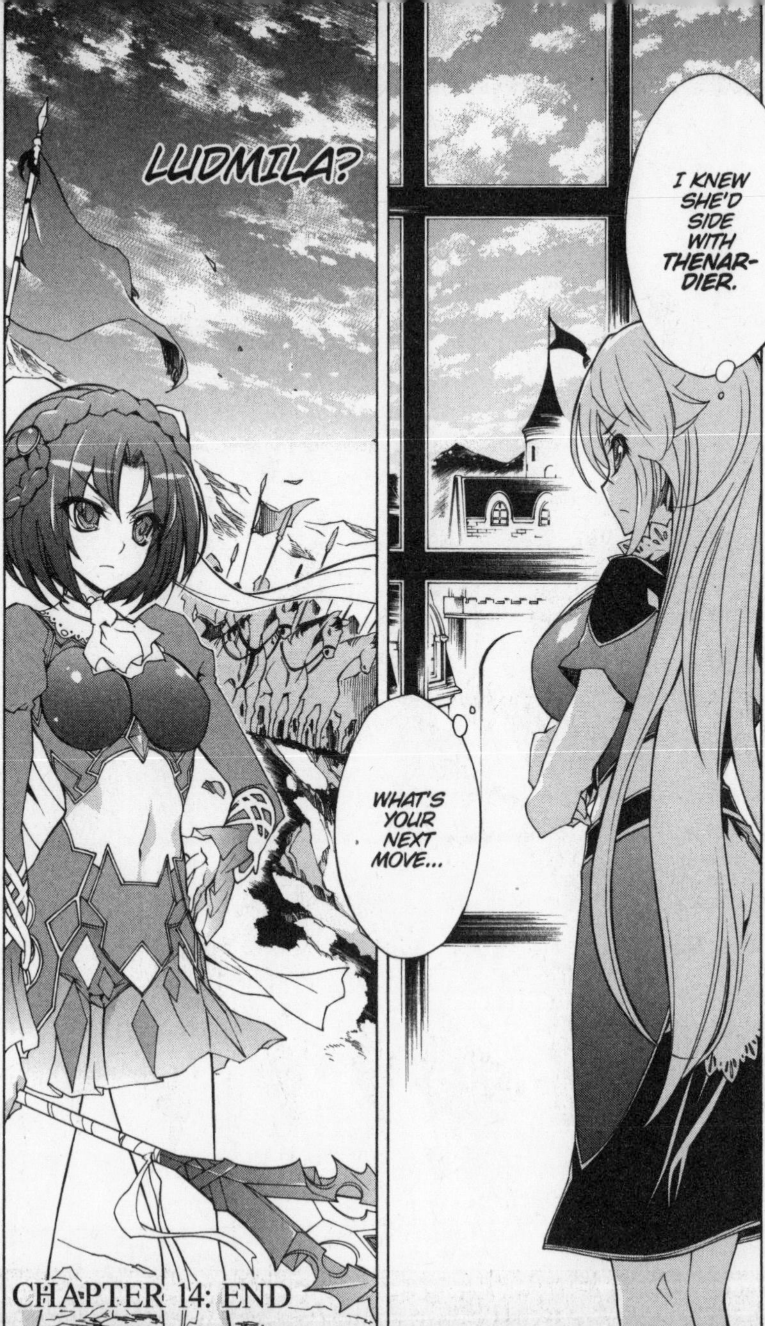
I KNEW SHE'D SIDE WITH THENARDIER.
WHAT'S YOUR NEXT MOVE...
LUDMILA?

CHAPTER 14: END

15 · THE BARRICADE

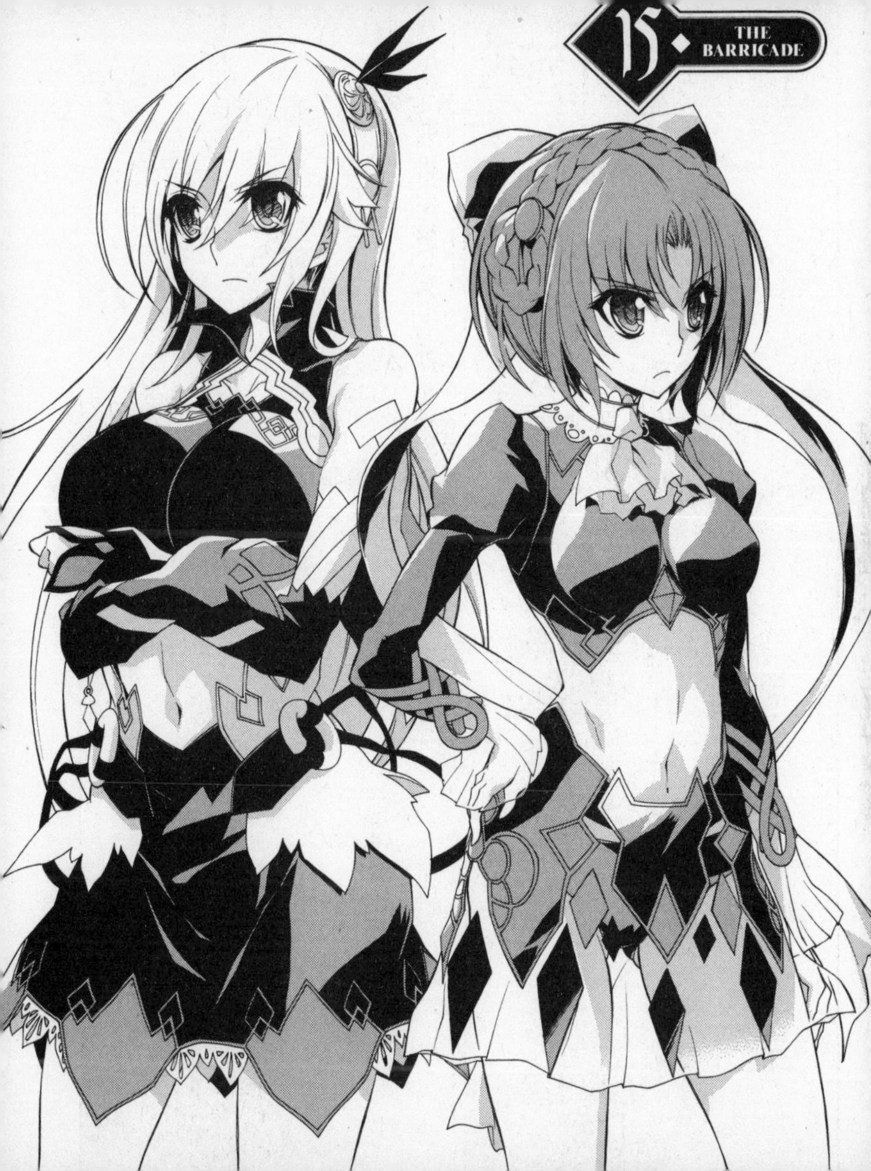

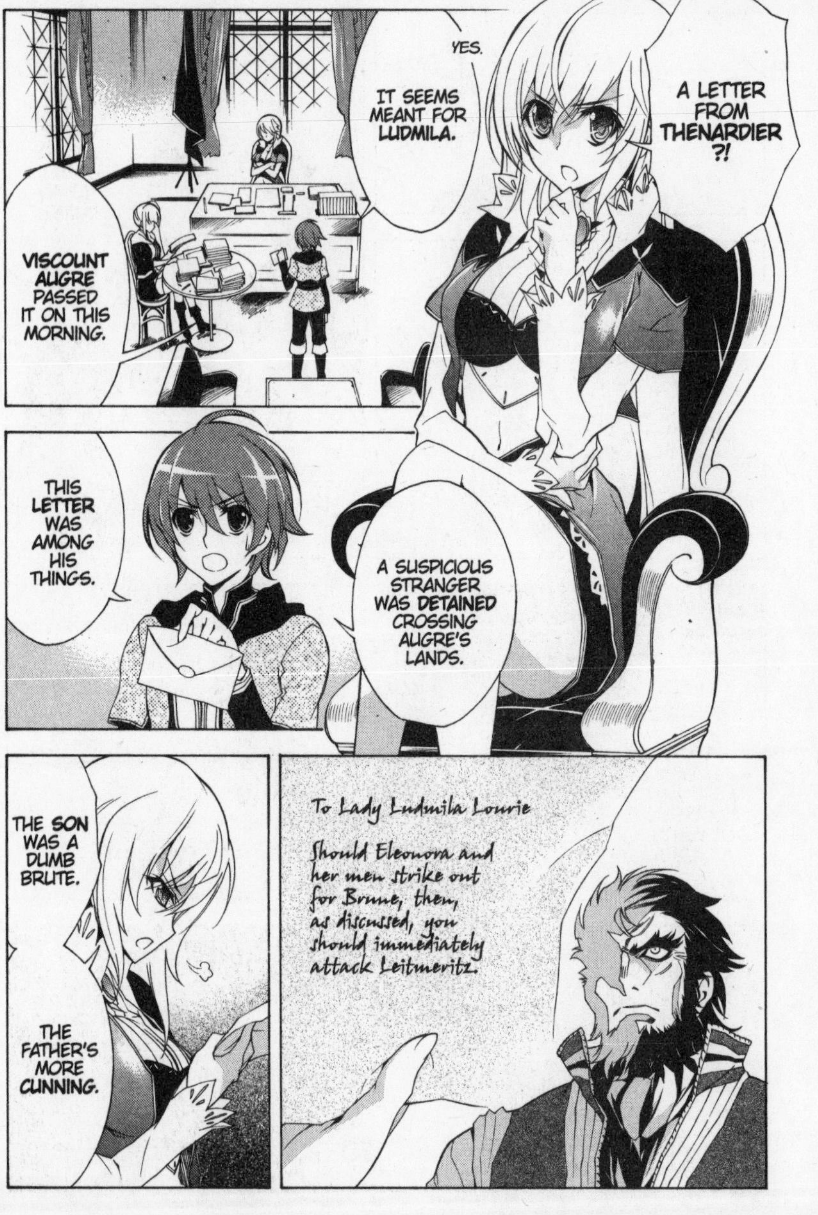
A LETTER FROM THENARDIER ?!
YES.
IT SEEMS MEANT FOR LUDMILA.
VISCOUNT AUGRE PASSED IT ON THIS MORNING.
A SUSPICIOUS STRANGER WAS DETAINED CROSSING AUGRE'S LANDS.
THIS LETTER WAS AMONG HIS THINGS.
To Lady Ludmila Lourie
Should Eleonora and her men strike out for Brune, then, as discussed, you should immediately attack Leitmeritz.
THE SON WAS A DUMB BRUTE.
THE FATHER'S MORE CUNNING.

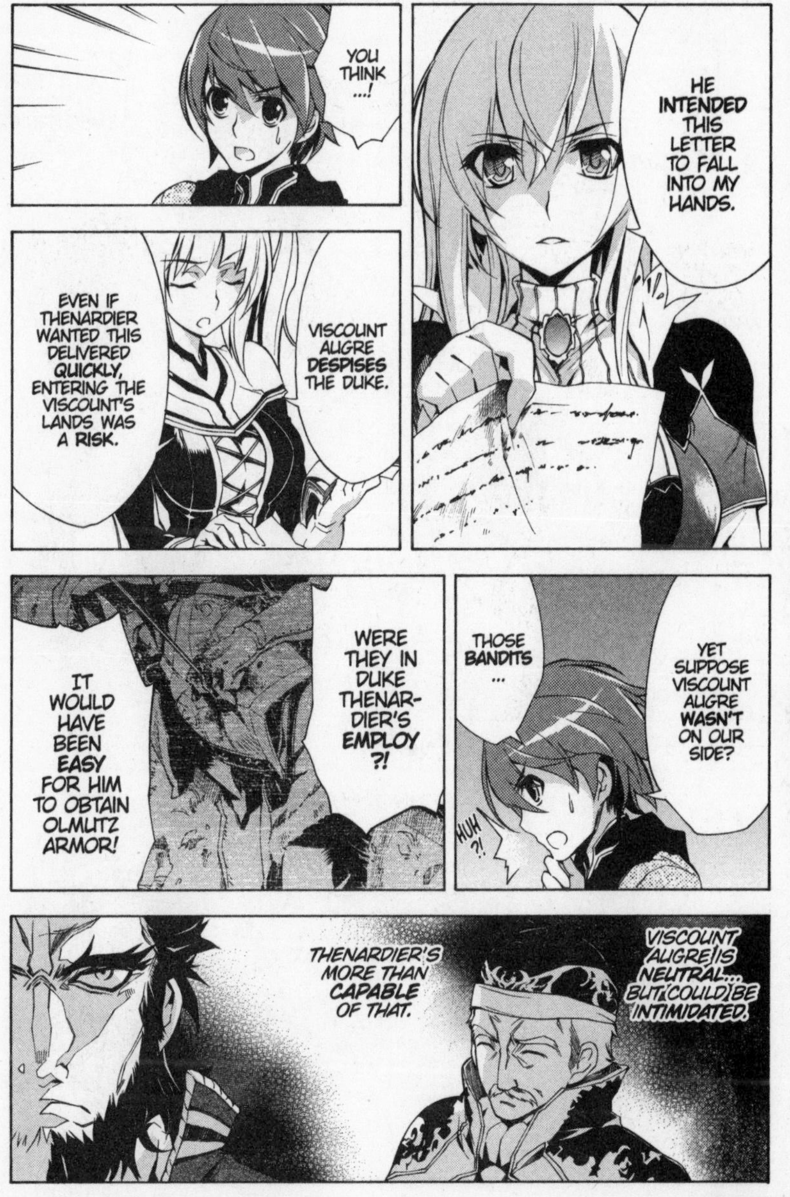
HE INTENDED THIS LETTER TO FALL INTO MY HANDS.
YOU THINK ...!
VISCOUNT AUGRE DESPISES THE DUKE.
EVEN IF THENARDIER WANTED THIS DELIVERED QUICKLY, ENTERING THE VISCOUNT'S LANDS WAS A RISK.
YET SUPPOSE VISCOUNT AUGRE WASN'T ON OUR SIDE?
HUH ?!
THOSE BANDITS ...
WERE THEY IN DUKE THENARDIER'S EMPLOY ?!
IT WOULD HAVE BEEN EASY FOR HIM TO OBTAIN OLMUTZ ARMOR!
VISCOUNT AUGRE IS NEUTRAL... BUT COULD BE INTIMIDATED.
THENARDIER'S MORE THAN CAPABLE OF THAT.

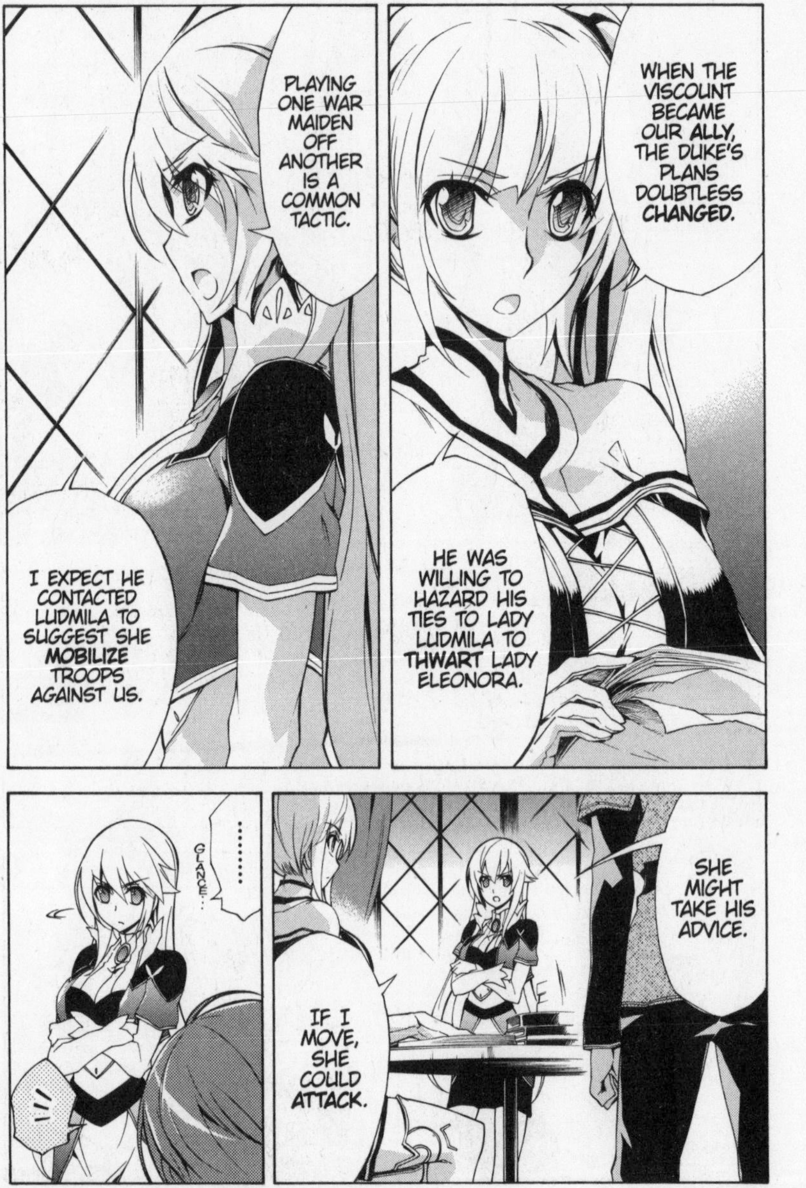
WHEN THE VISCOUNT BECAME OUR ALLY, THE DUKE'S PLANS DOUBTLESS CHANGED.
HE WAS WILLING TO HAZARD HIS TIES TO LADY LUDMILA TO THWART LADY ELEONORA.
PLAYING ONE WAR MAIDEN OFF ANOTHER IS A COMMON TACTIC.
I EXPECT HE CONTACTED LUDMILA TO SUGGEST SHE MOBILIZE TROOPS AGAINST US.
SHE MIGHT TAKE HIS ADVICE.
IF I MOVE, SHE COULD ATTACK.
....
GLANCE...

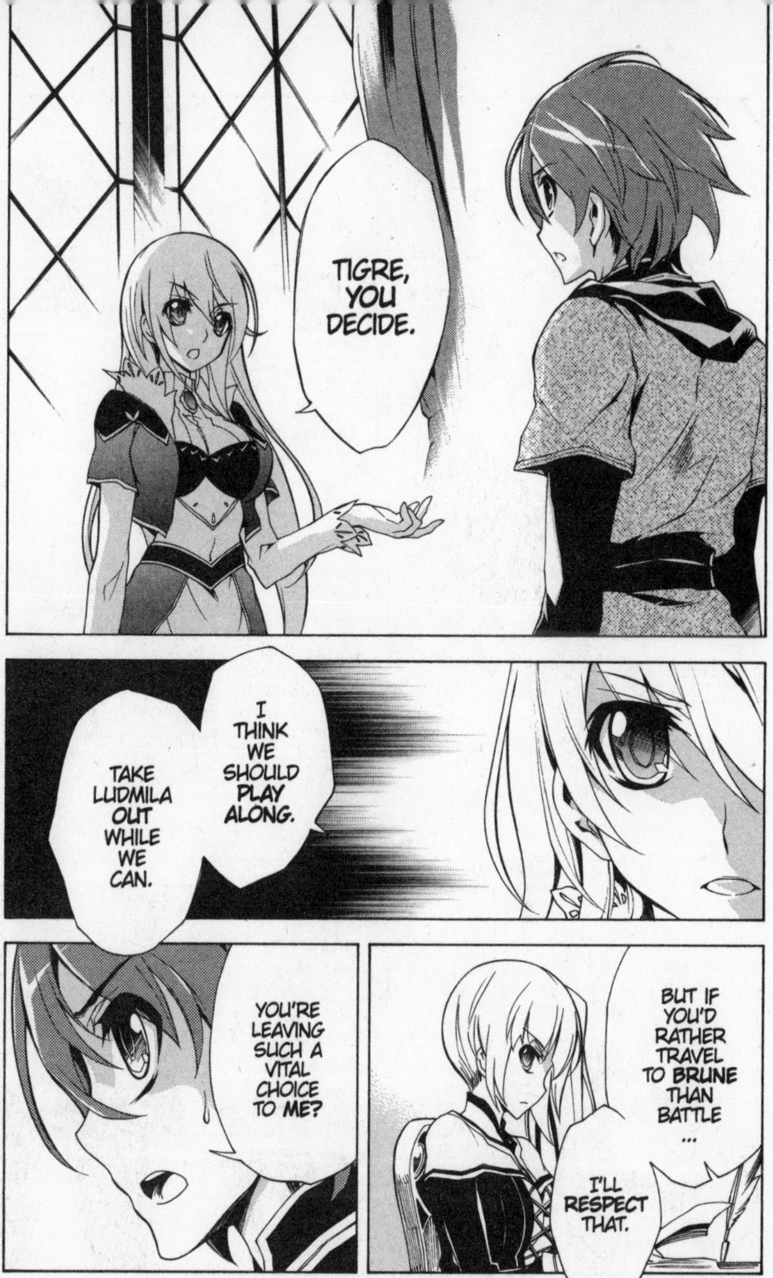
TIGRE, YOU DECIDE.
I THINK WE SHOULD PLAY ALONG.
TAKE LUDMILA OUT WHILE WE CAN.
BUT IF YOU'D RATHER TRAVEL TO BRUNE THAN BATTLE ...
I'LL RESPECT THAT.
YOU'RE LEAVING SUCH A VITAL CHOICE TO ME?

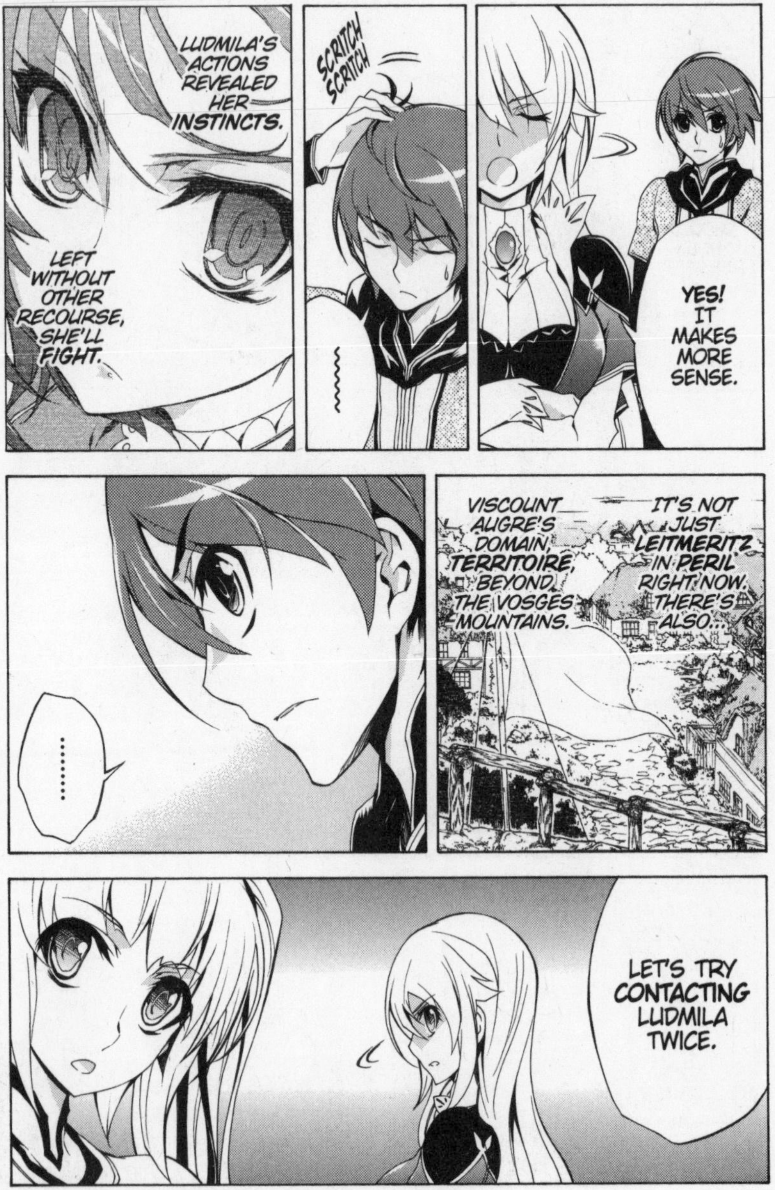
YES! IT MAKES MORE SENSE.
SCRITCH SCRITCH
LUDMILA'S ACTIONS REVEALED HER INSTINCTS.
LEFT WITHOUT OTHER RECOURSE, SHE'LL FIGHT.
IT'S NOT JUST LEITMERITZ IN PERIL RIGHT NOW. THERE'S ALSO...
VISCOUNT AUGRE'S DOMAIN, TERRITOIRE, BEYOND THE VOSGES MOUNTAINS.
....
LET'S TRY CONTACTING LUDMILA TWICE.

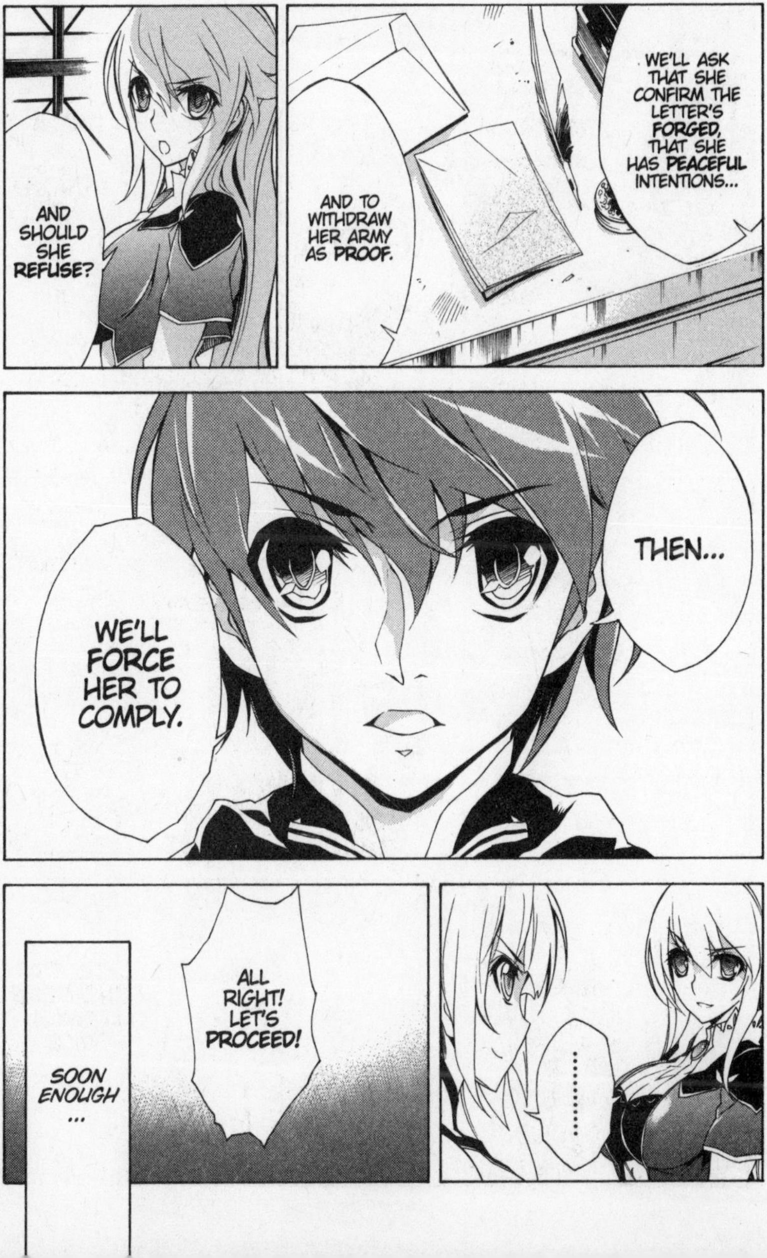
WE'LL ASK THAT SHE CONFIRM THE LETTER'S FORGED, THAT SHE HAS PEACEFUL INTENTIONS...
AND TO WITHDRAW HER ARMY AS PROOF.
AND SHOULD SHE REFUSE?
THEN...
WE'LL FORCE HER TO COMPLY.
......
ALL RIGHT! LET'S PROCEED!
SOON ENOUGH ...

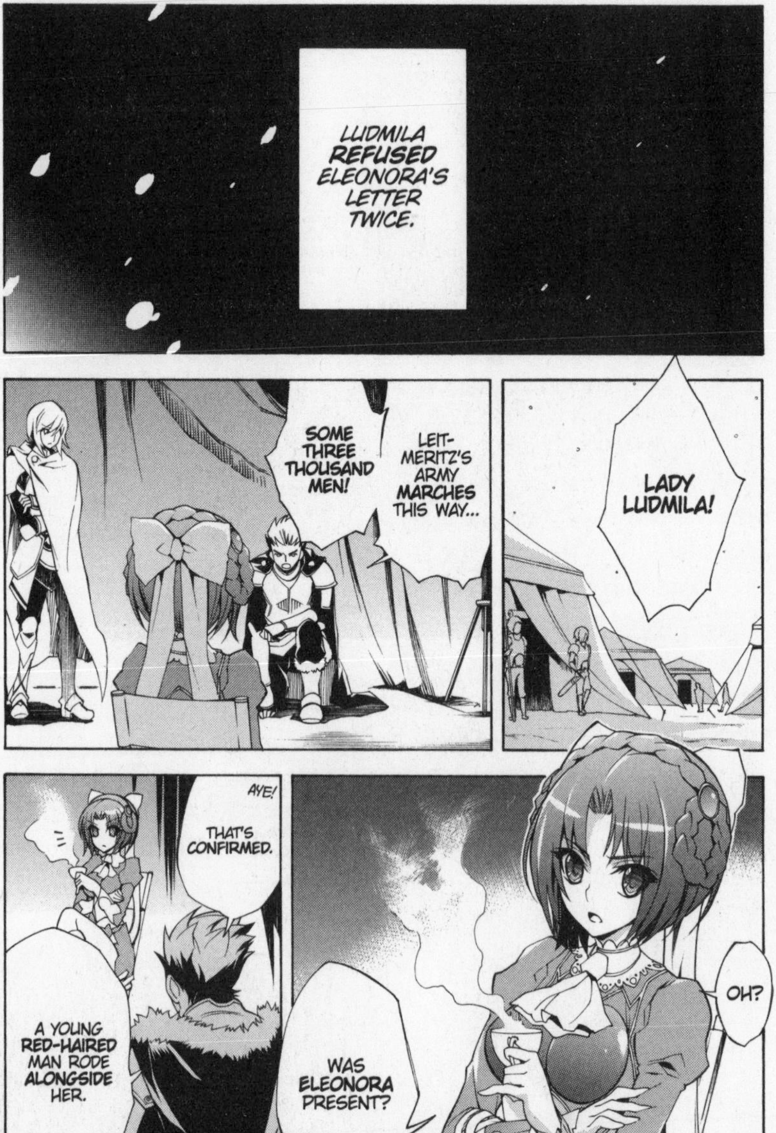

LUDMILA REFUSED ELEONORA'S LETTER TWICE.
LADY LUDMILA!
LEIT-MERITZ'S ARMY MARCHES THIS WAY...
SOME THREE THOUSAND MEN!
OH?
WAS ELEONORA PRESENT?
AYE!
THAT'S CONFIRMED.
A YOUNG RED-HAIRED MAN RODE ALONGSIDE HER.

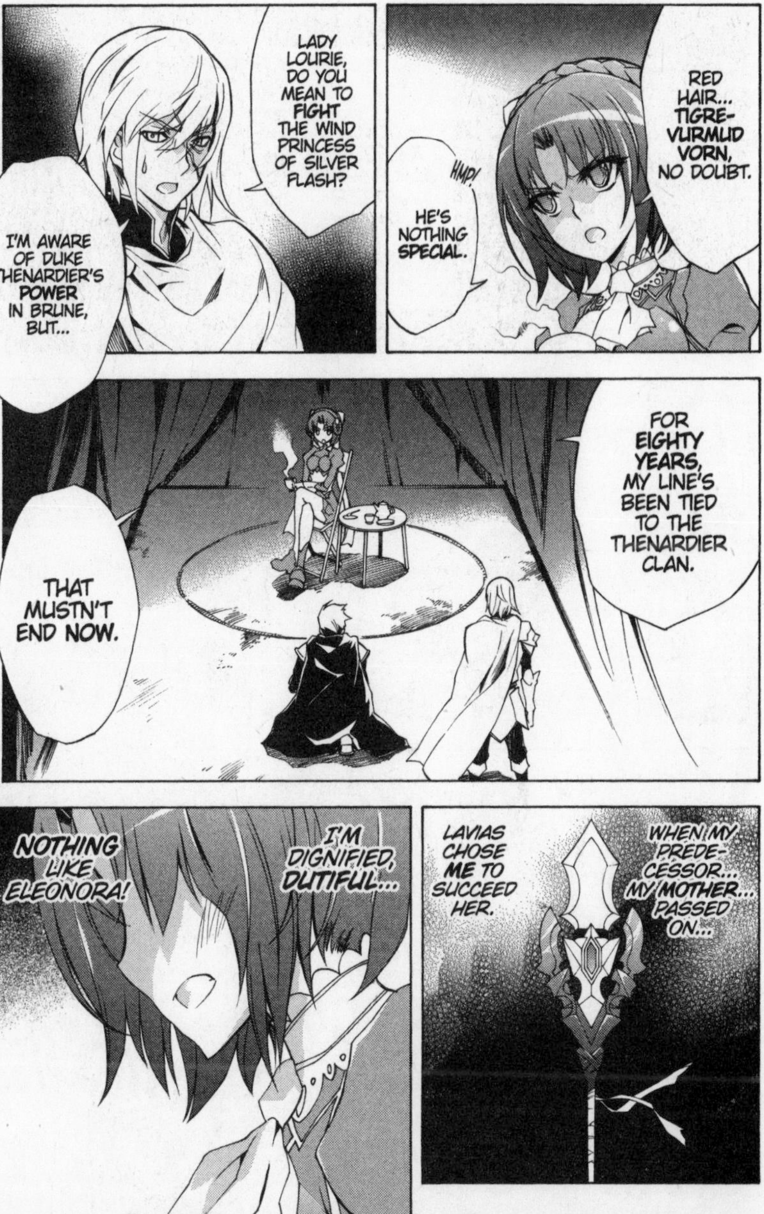
RED HAIR... TIGRE-VURMUD VORN, NO DOUBT.
HMP!
HE'S NOTHING SPECIAL.
LADY LOURIE, DO YOU MEAN TO FIGHT THE WIND PRINCESS OF SILVER FLASH?
I'M AWARE OF DUKE THENARDIER'S POWER IN BRUNE, BUT...
FOR EIGHTY YEARS, MY LINE'S BEEN TIED TO THE THENARDIER CLAN.
THAT MUSTN'T END NOW.
WHEN MY PREDE-CESSOR... MY MOTHER... PASSED ON...
LAVIAS CHOSE ME TO SUCCEED HER.
I'M DIGNIFIED, DUTIFUL...
NOTHING LIKE ELEONORA!

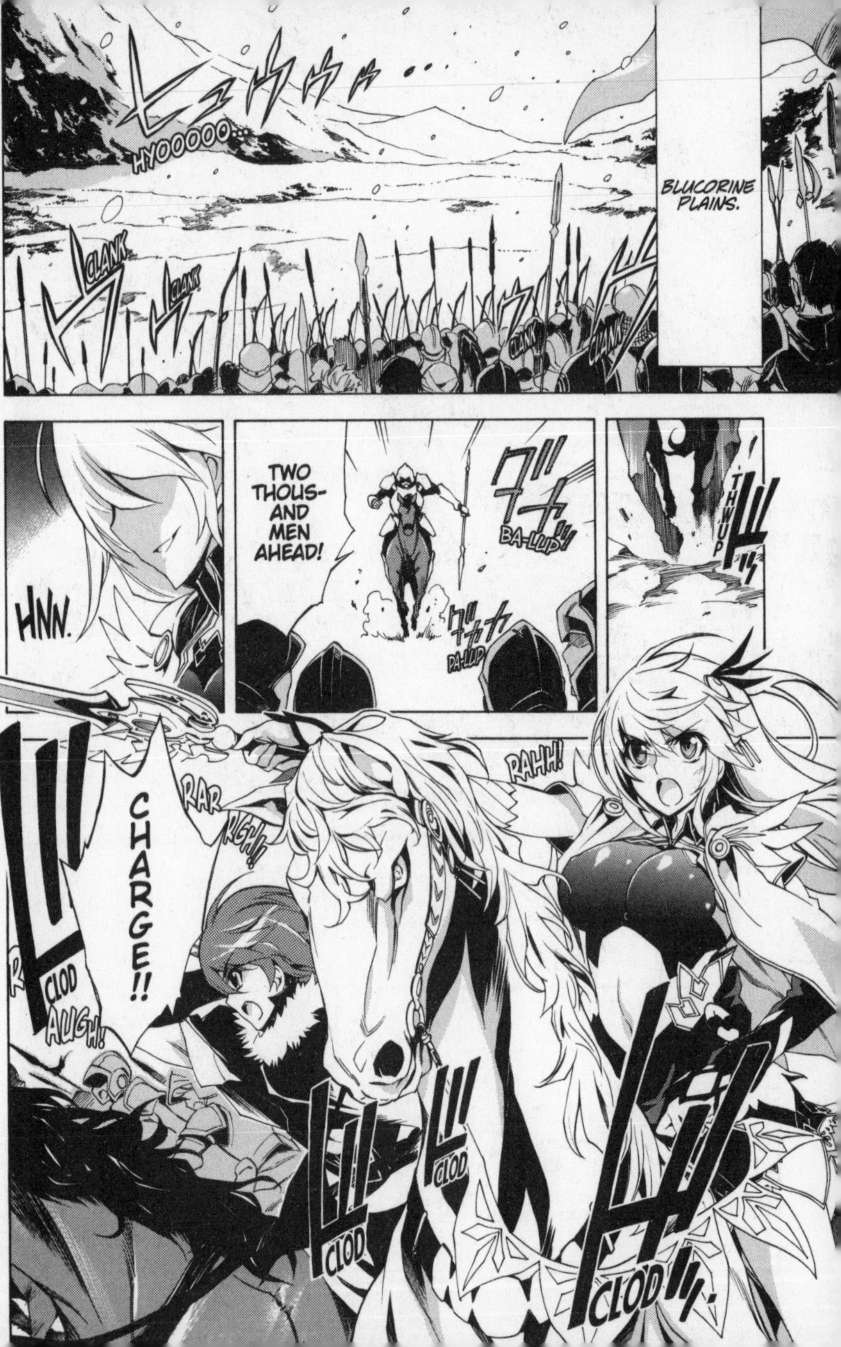
BLUCORINE PLAINS.
HYOOOOO...
CLANK
CLANK
CLANK
CLANK
THWUP
TWO THOUS-AND MEN AHEAD!
BA-LUP!!
PA-LUP
HNN.
RAHH!
CHARGE!!
RARRIGH!!
CLOD
AUGH!
CLOD
CLOD
CLOD...

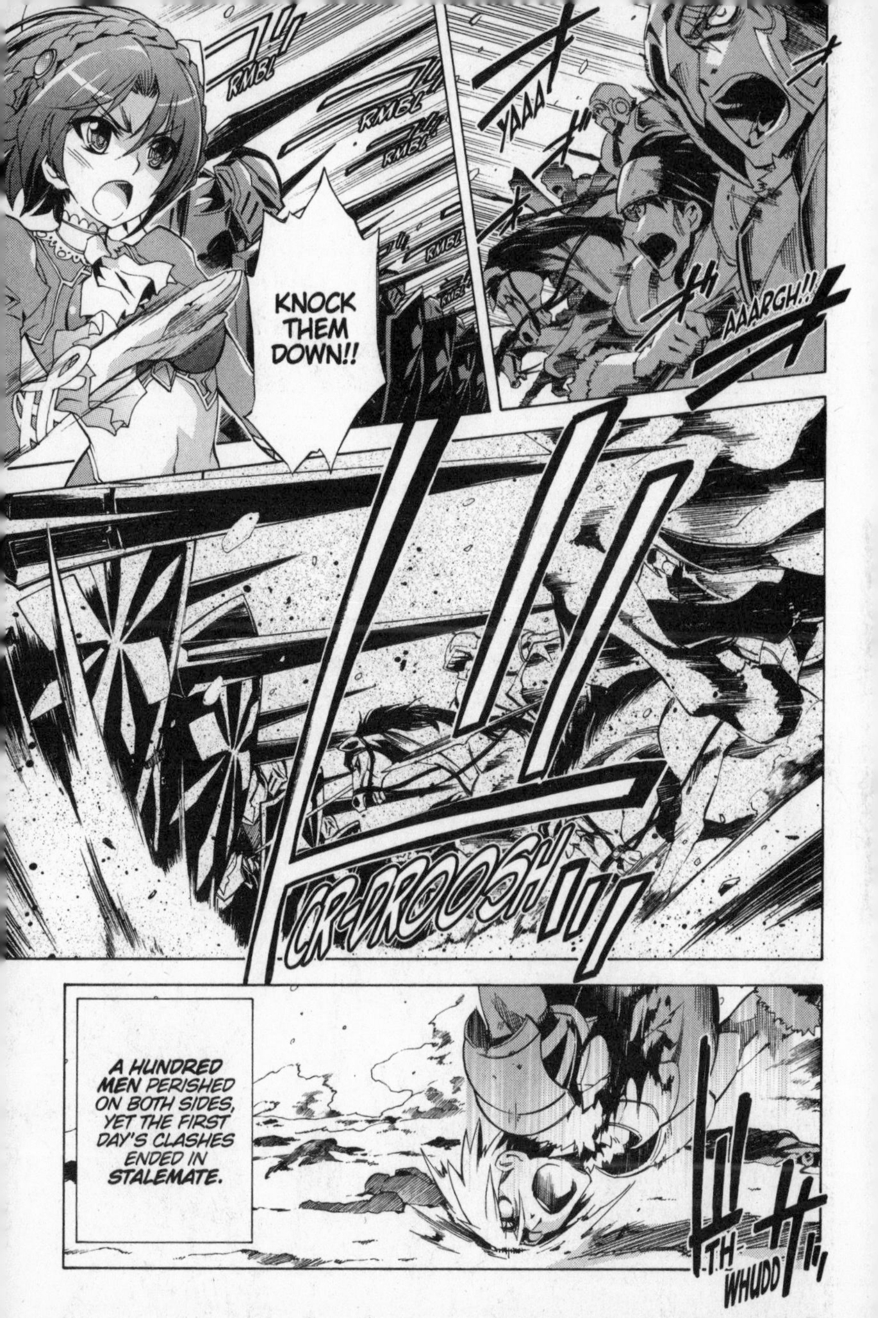
YAAA!
AAARGH!!
RMBL
RMBL
RMBL
RMBL
RMBL
KNOCK THEM DOWN!!
CR-RROOSH!!
T.H
WHUDD
A HUNDRED MEN PERISHED ON BOTH SIDES, YET THE FIRST DAY'S CLASHES ENDED IN STALEMATE.

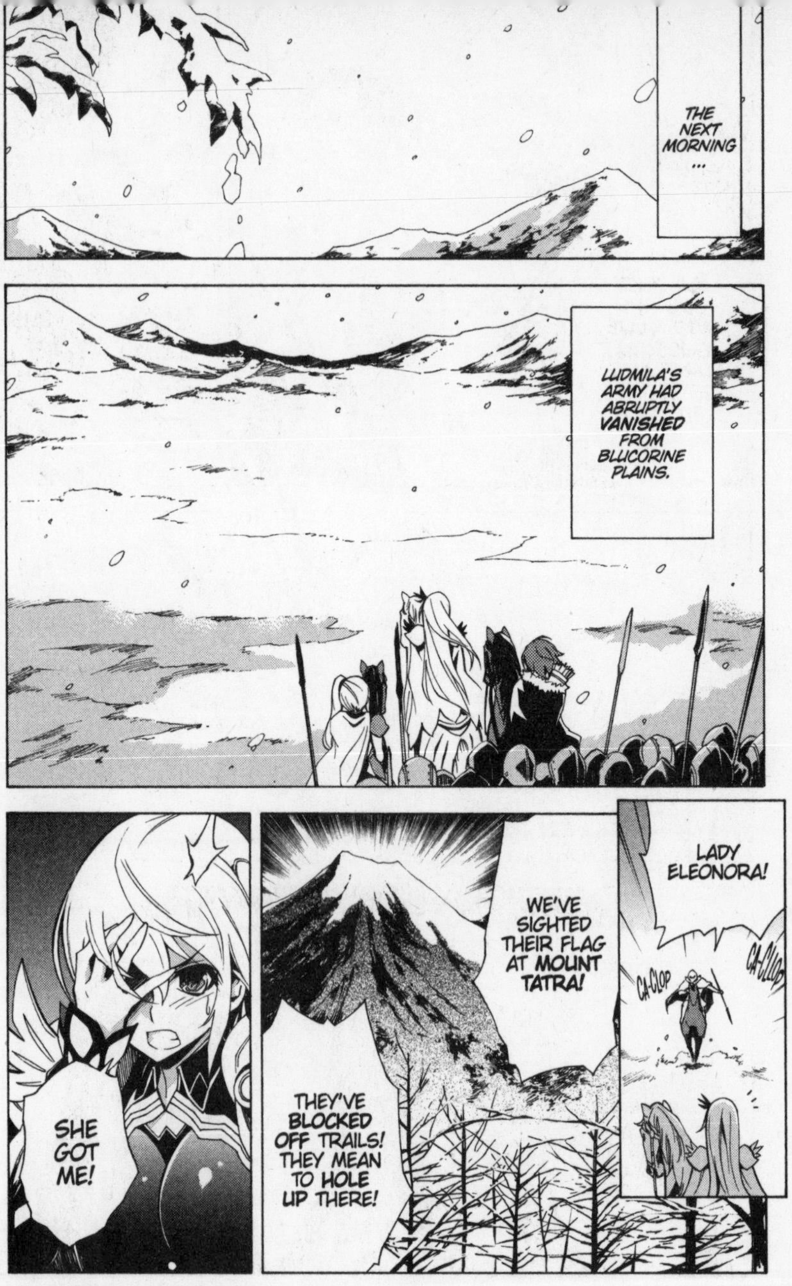
THE NEXT MORNING ...
LUDMILA'S ARMY HAD ABRUPTLY VANISHED FROM BLUCORINE PLAINS.
LADY ELEONORA!
CA-CLOP
CA-CLOP
WE'VE SIGHTED THEIR FLAG AT MOUNT TATRA!
THEY'VE BLOCKED OFF TRAILS! THEY MEAN TO HOLE UP THERE!
SHE GOT ME!

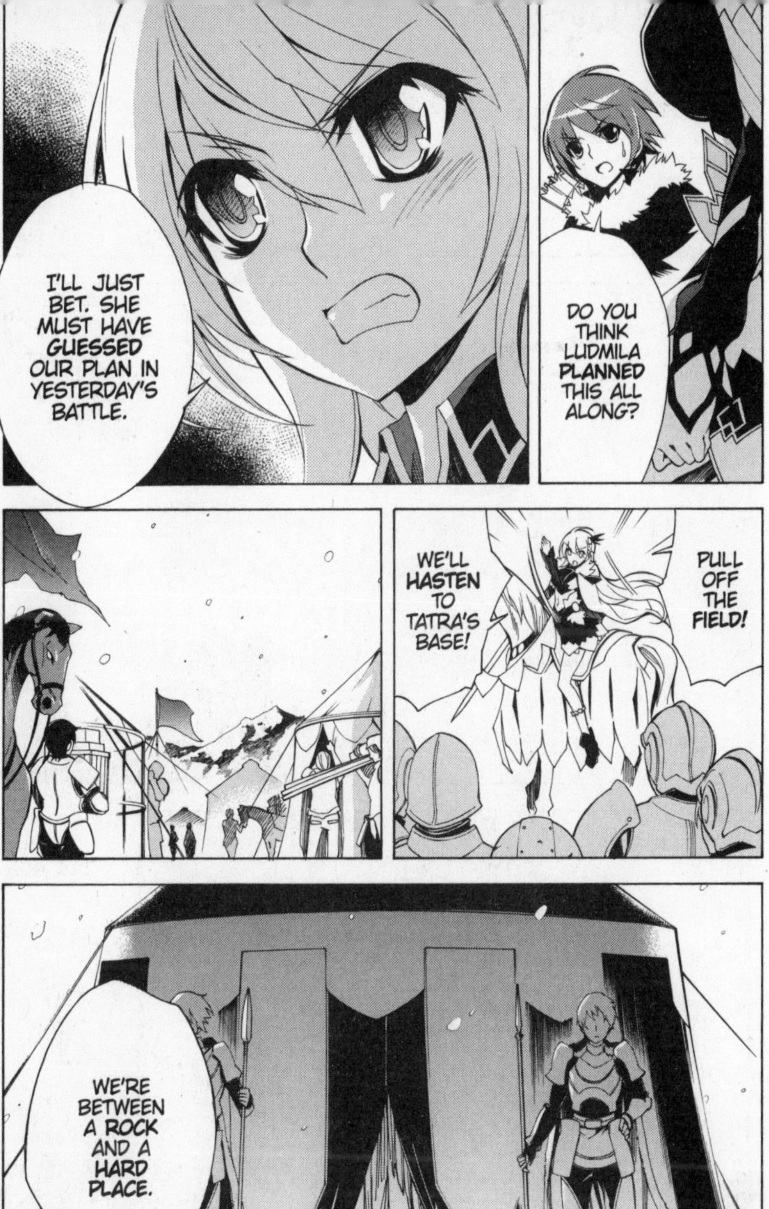
DO YOU THINK LUDMILA PLANNED THIS ALL ALONG?
I'LL JUST BET. SHE MUST HAVE GUESSED OUR PLAN IN YESTERDAY'S BATTLE.
PULL OFF THE FIELD!
WE'LL HASTEN TO TATRA'S BASE!
WE'RE BETWEEN A ROCK AND A HARD PLACE.

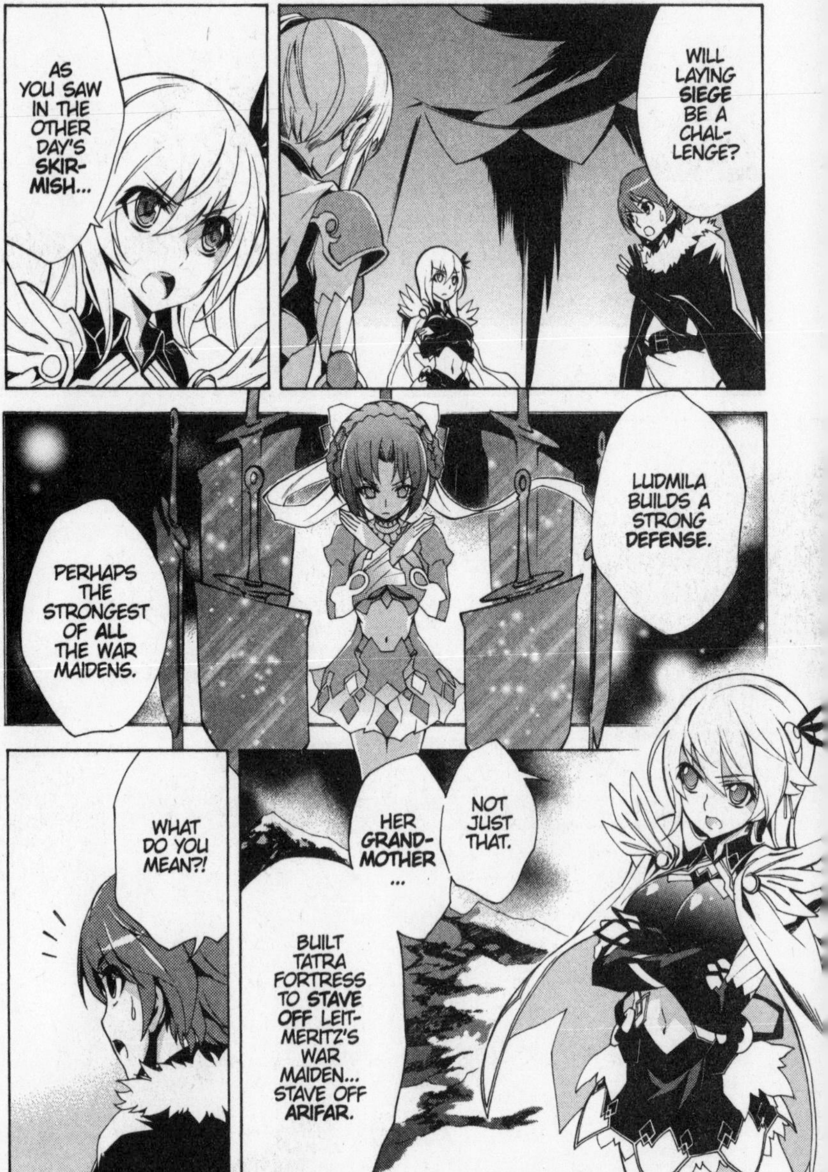
WILL LAYING SIEGE BE A CHALLENGE?
AS YOU SAW IN THE OTHER DAY'S SKIRMISH...
LUDMILA BUILDS A STRONG DEFENSE.
PERHAPS THE STRONGEST OF ALL THE WAR MAIDENS.
NOT JUST THAT.
HER GRANDMOTHER...
BUILT TATRA FORTRESS TO STAVE OFF LEITMERITZ'S WAR MAIDEN... STAVE OFF ARIFAR.
WHAT DO YOU MEAN?!

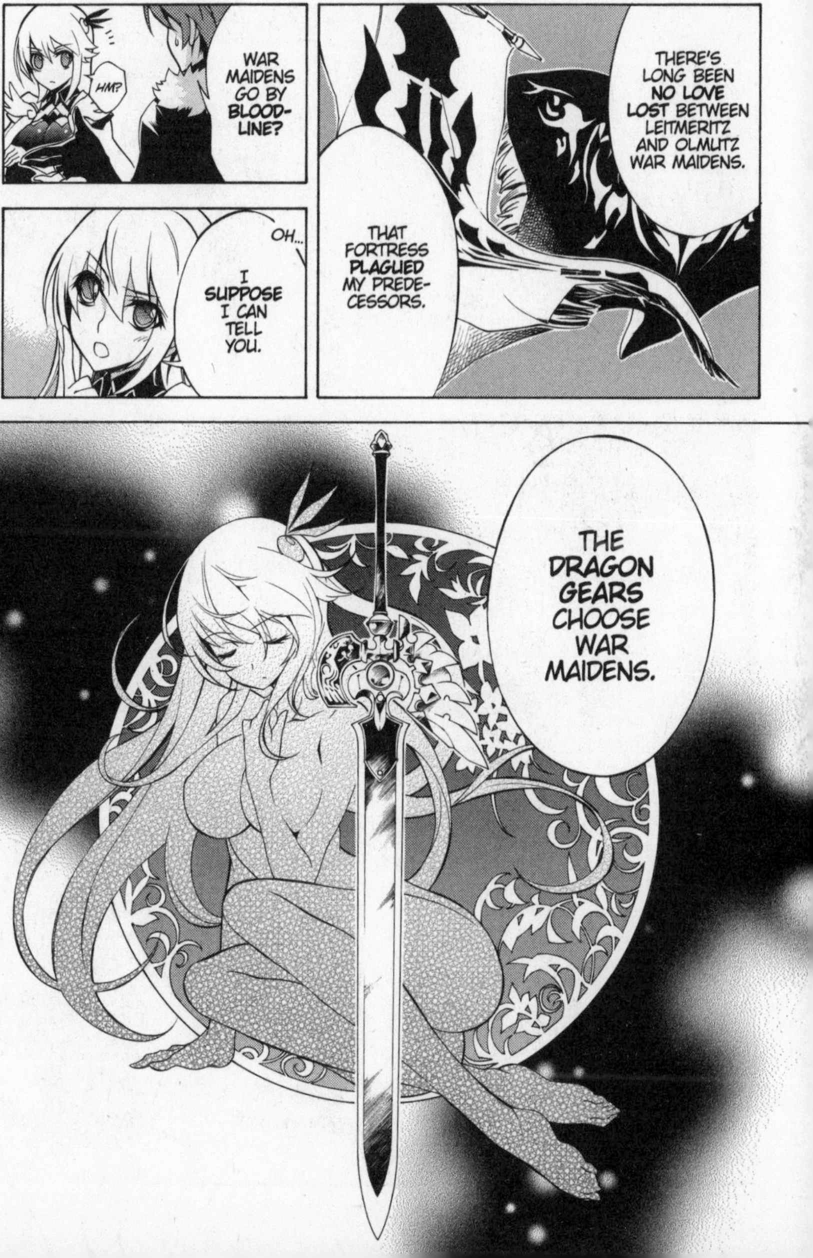
THERE'S LONG BEEN NO LOVE LOST BETWEEN LEITMERITZ AND OLMUTZ WAR MAIDENS.
THAT FORTRESS PLAGUED MY PREDECESSORS.
WAR MAIDENS GO BY BLOOD-LINE?
HM?
OH...
I SUPPOSE I CAN TELL YOU.
THE DRAGON GEARS CHOOSE WAR MAIDENS.

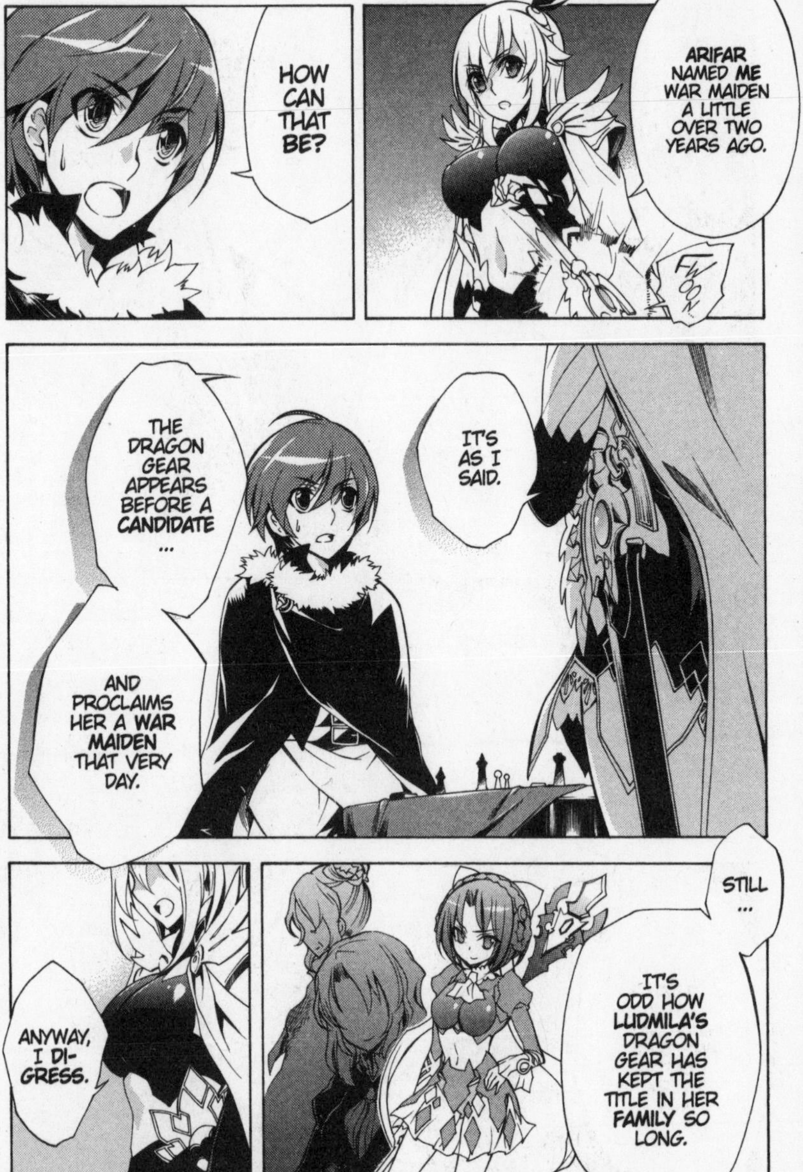
ARIFAR NAMED ME WAR MAIDEN A LITTLE OVER TWO YEARS AGO.
FWOON...
HOW CAN THAT BE?
IT'S AS I SAID.
THE DRAGON GEAR APPEARS BEFORE A CANDIDATE...
AND PROCLAIMS HER A WAR MAIDEN THAT VERY DAY.
STILL...
IT'S ODD HOW LUDMILA'S DRAGON GEAR HAS KEPT THE TITLE IN HER FAMILY SO LONG.
ANYWAY, I DIGRESS.

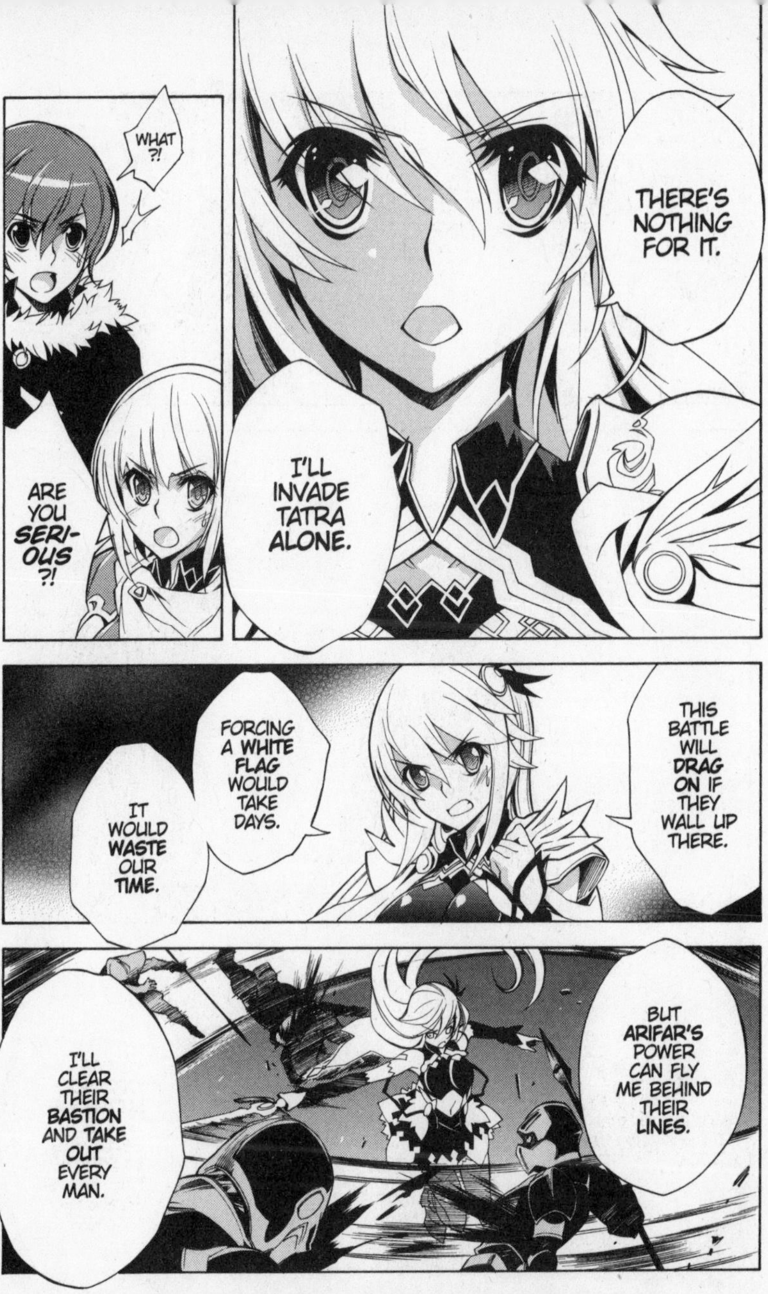
THERE'S NOTHING FOR IT.
I'LL INVADE TATRA ALONE.
WHAT?!
ARE YOU SERIOUS?!
THIS BATTLE WILL DRAG ON IF THEY WALL UP THERE.
FORCING A WHITE FLAG WOULD TAKE DAYS.
IT WOULD WASTE OUR TIME.
BUT ARIFAR'S POWER CAN FLY ME BEHIND THEIR LINES.
I'LL CLEAR THEIR BASTION AND TAKE OUT EVERY MAN.

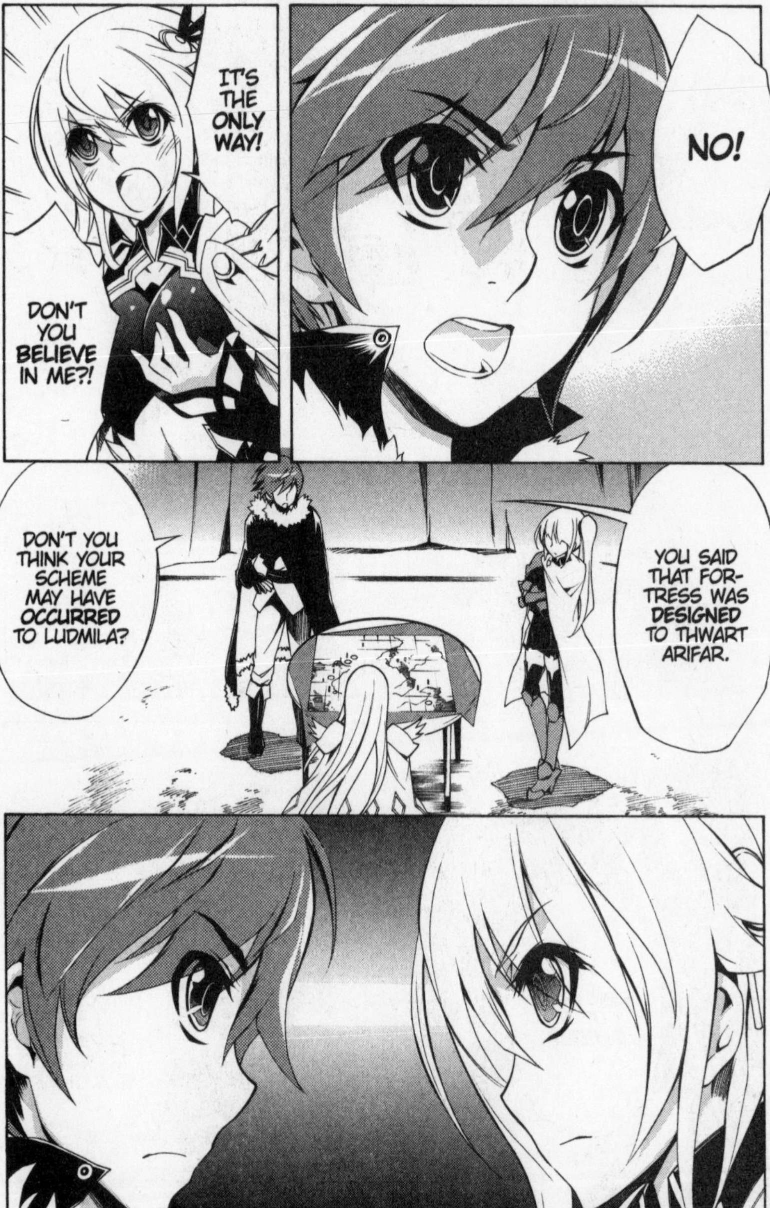
NO!
IT'S THE ONLY WAY!
DON'T YOU BELIEVE IN ME?!
YOU SAID THAT FOR-TRESS WAS DESIGNED TO THWART ARIFAR.
DON'T YOU THINK YOUR SCHEME MAY HAVE OCCURRED TO LUDMILA?

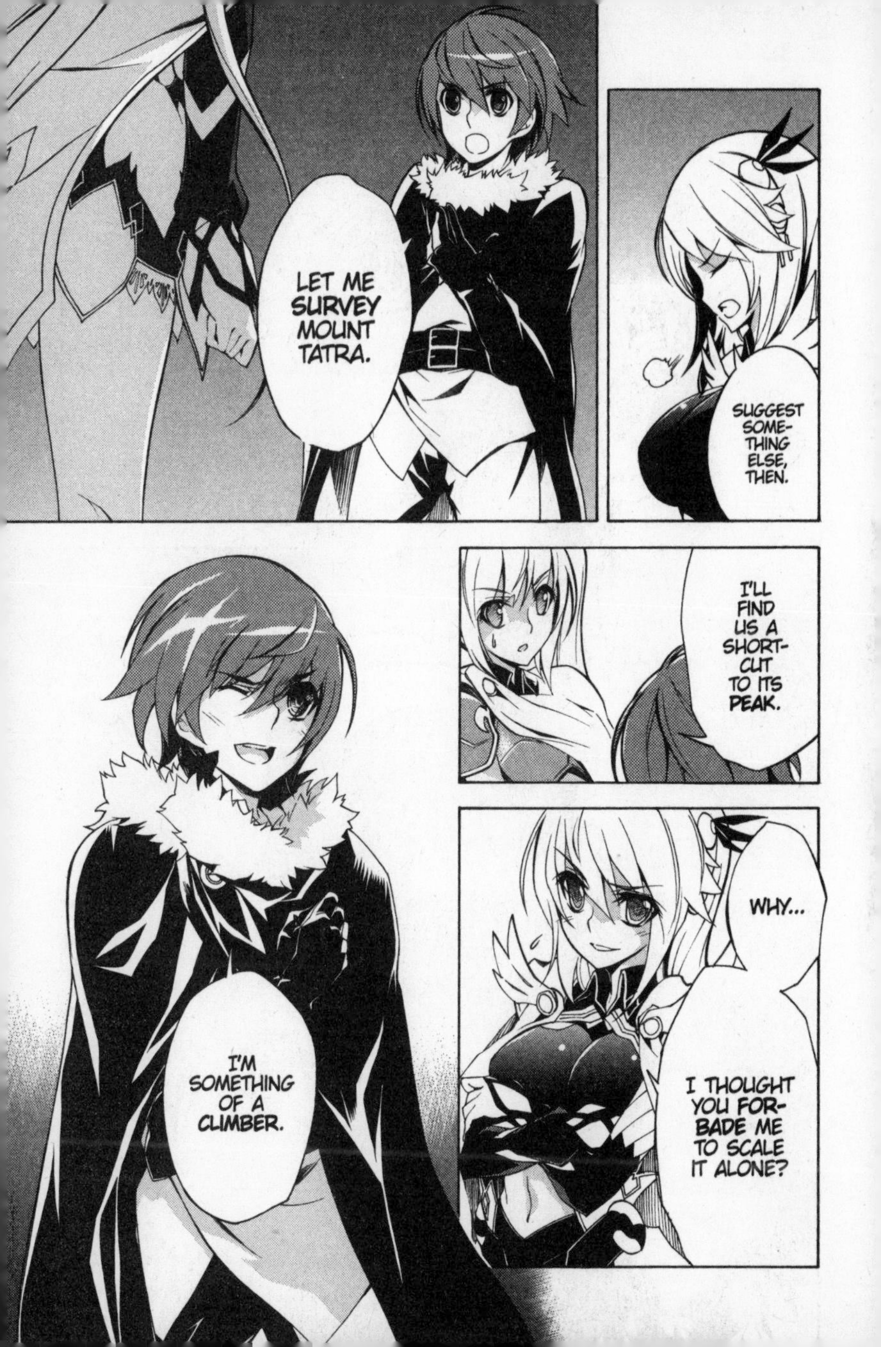
SUGGEST SOMETHING ELSE, THEN.
LET ME SURVEY MOUNT TATRA.
I'LL FIND US A SHORTCUT TO ITS PEAK.
WHY...
I THOUGHT YOU FORBADE ME TO SCALE IT ALONE?
I'M SOMETHING OF A CLIMBER.

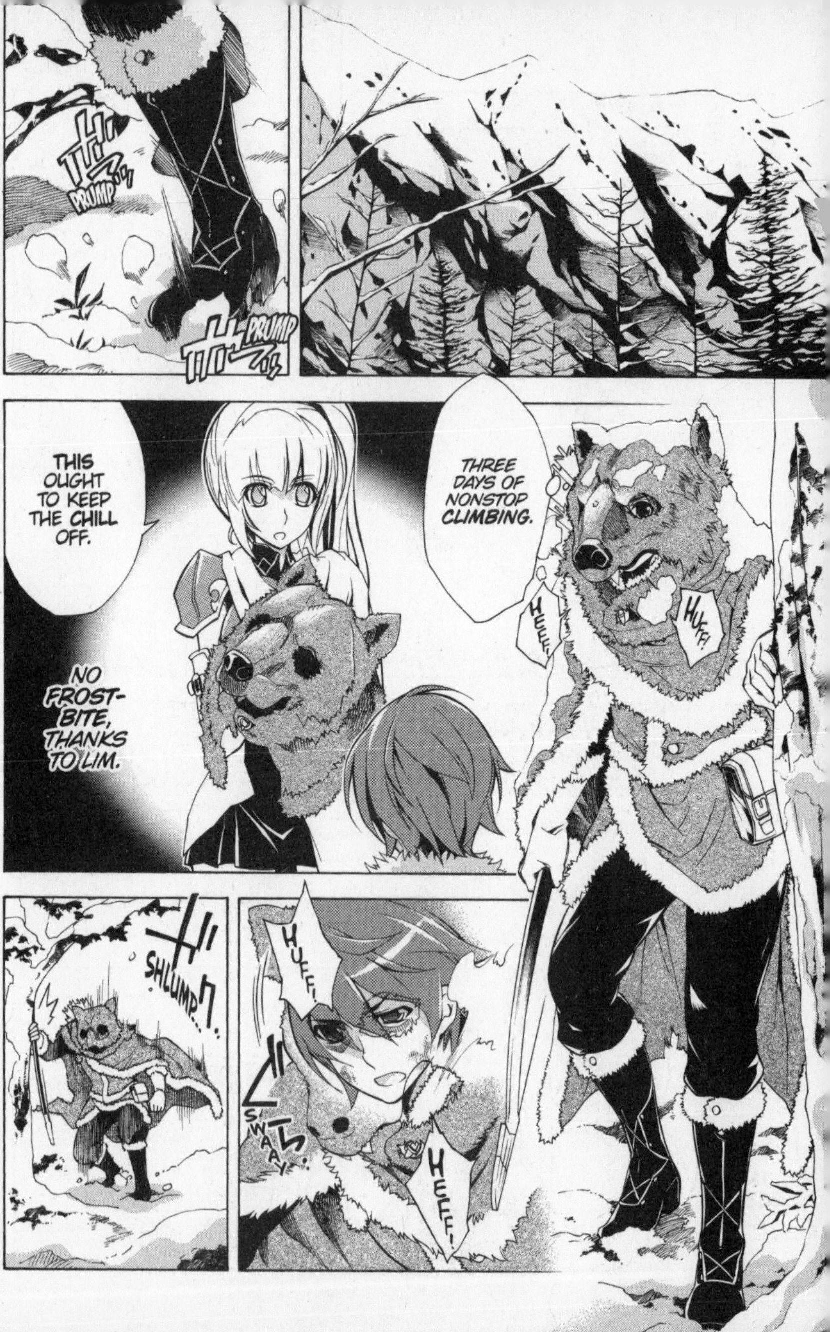
PRUMP
PRUMP
THREE DAYS OF NONSTOP CLIMBING.
HUFF!
HEFF!
THIS OUGHT TO KEEP THE CHILL OFF.
NO FROST-BITE, THANKS TO LIM.
HUFF!
HEFF!
SWAAAY...
SHLUMP...

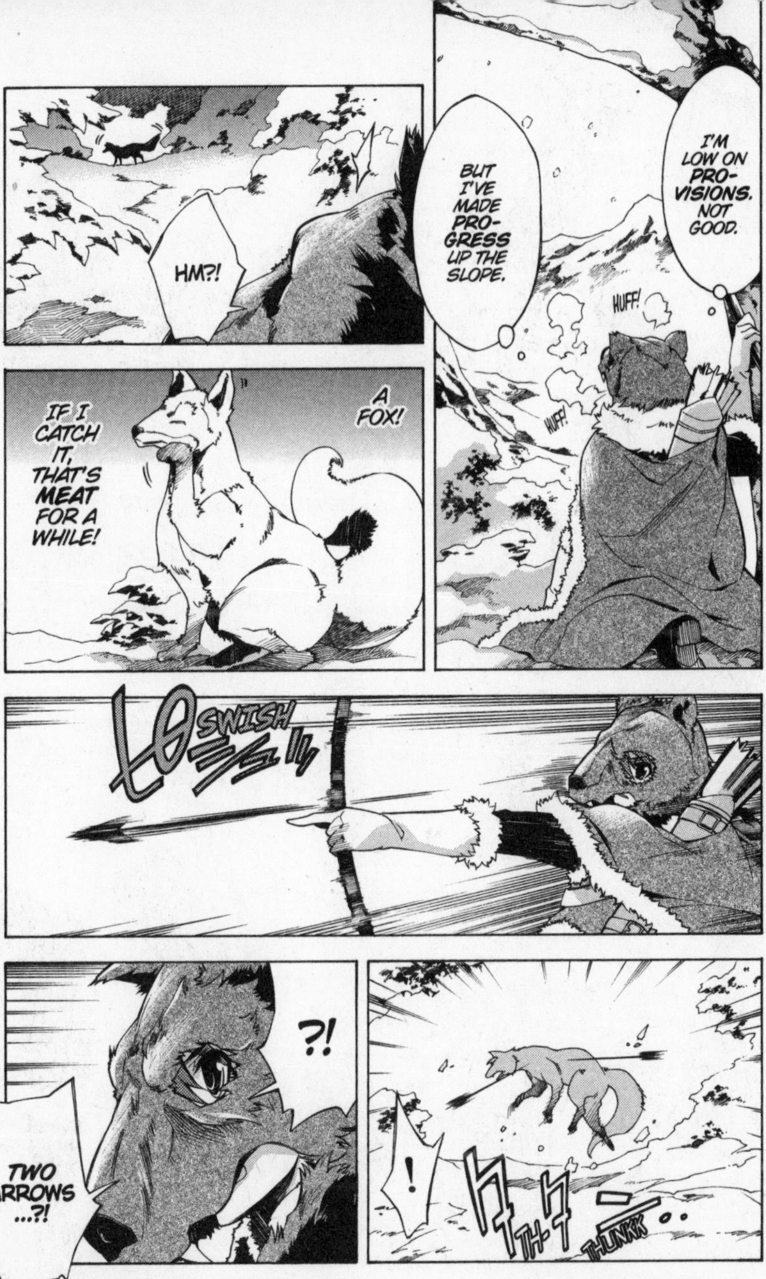

I'M LOW ON PROVISIONS. NOT GOOD.
BUT I'VE MADE PROGRESS UP THE SLOPE.
HUFF!
HUFF!
HM?!
A FOX!
IF I CATCH IT, THAT'S MEAT FOR A WHILE!
SWISH
!
THUNKK
?!
TWO ARROWS ...?!

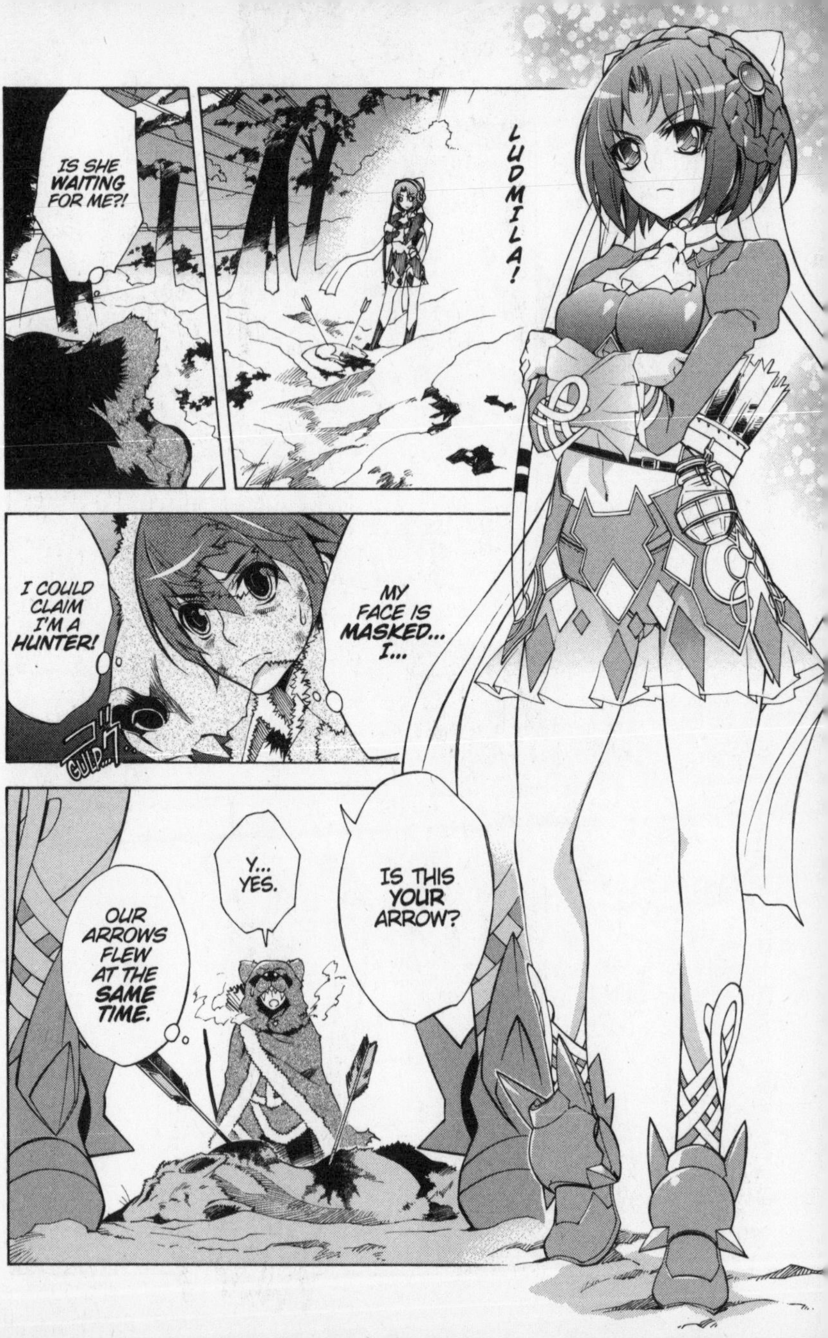
LUDMILA!
IS SHE WAITING FOR ME?!
MY FACE IS MASKED... I...
I COULD CLAIM I'M A HUNTER!
GULP...
IS THIS YOUR ARROW?
Y... YES.
OUR ARROWS FLEW AT THE SAME TIME.

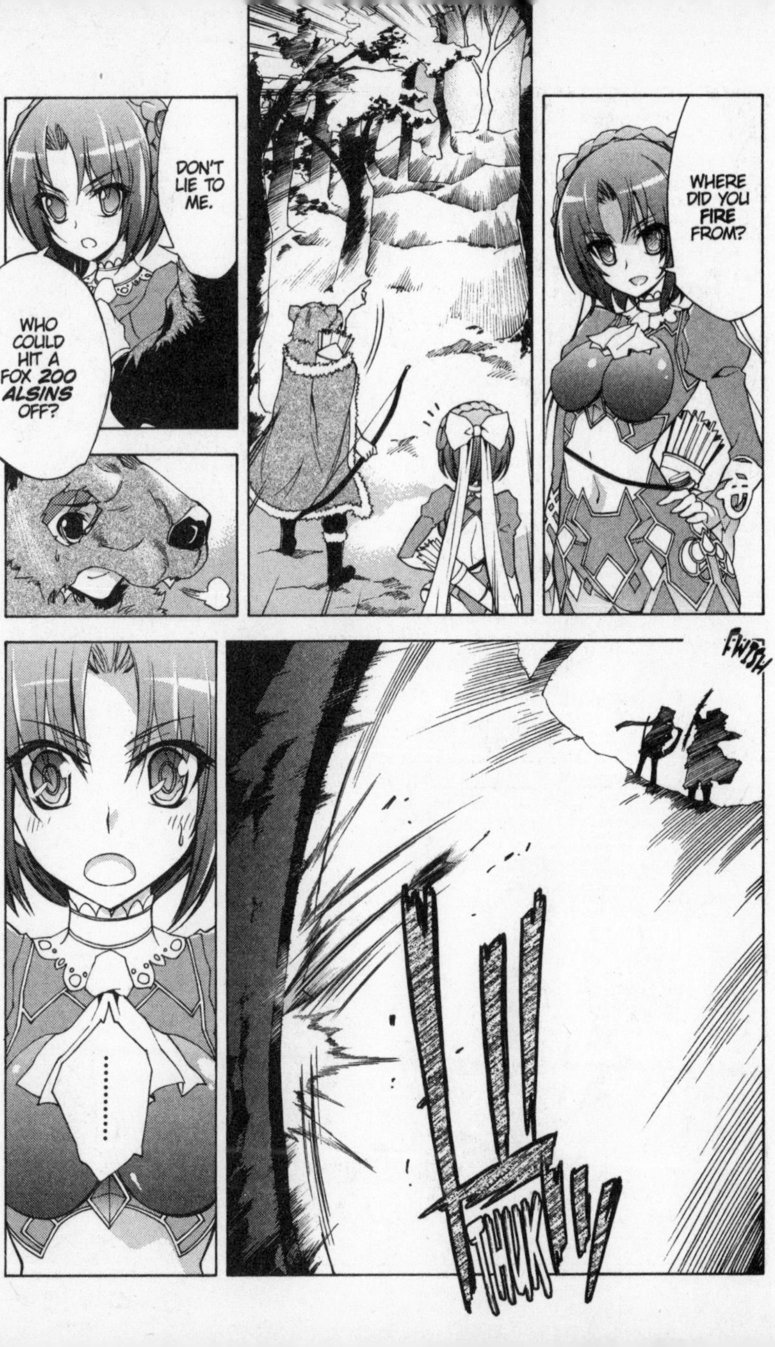

WHERE DID YOU FIRE FROM?
DON'T LIE TO ME.
WHO COULD HIT A FOX 200 ALSINS OFF?
FWISH
THUNK
......

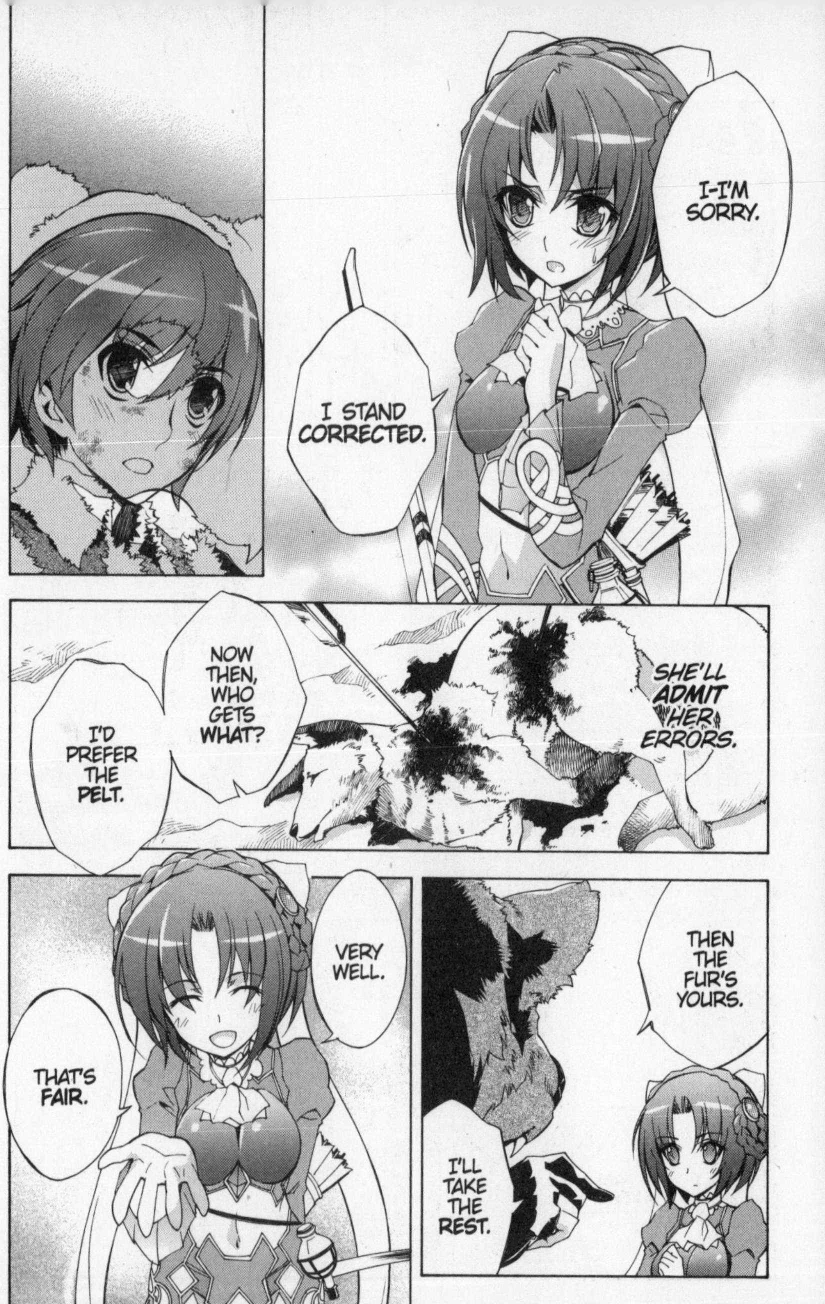
I-I'M SORRY.
I STAND CORRECTED.
SHE'LL ADMIT HER ERRORS.
NOW THEN, WHO GETS WHAT?
I'D PREFER THE PELT.
THEN THE FUR'S YOURS.
I'LL TAKE THE REST.
VERY WELL.
THAT'S FAIR.

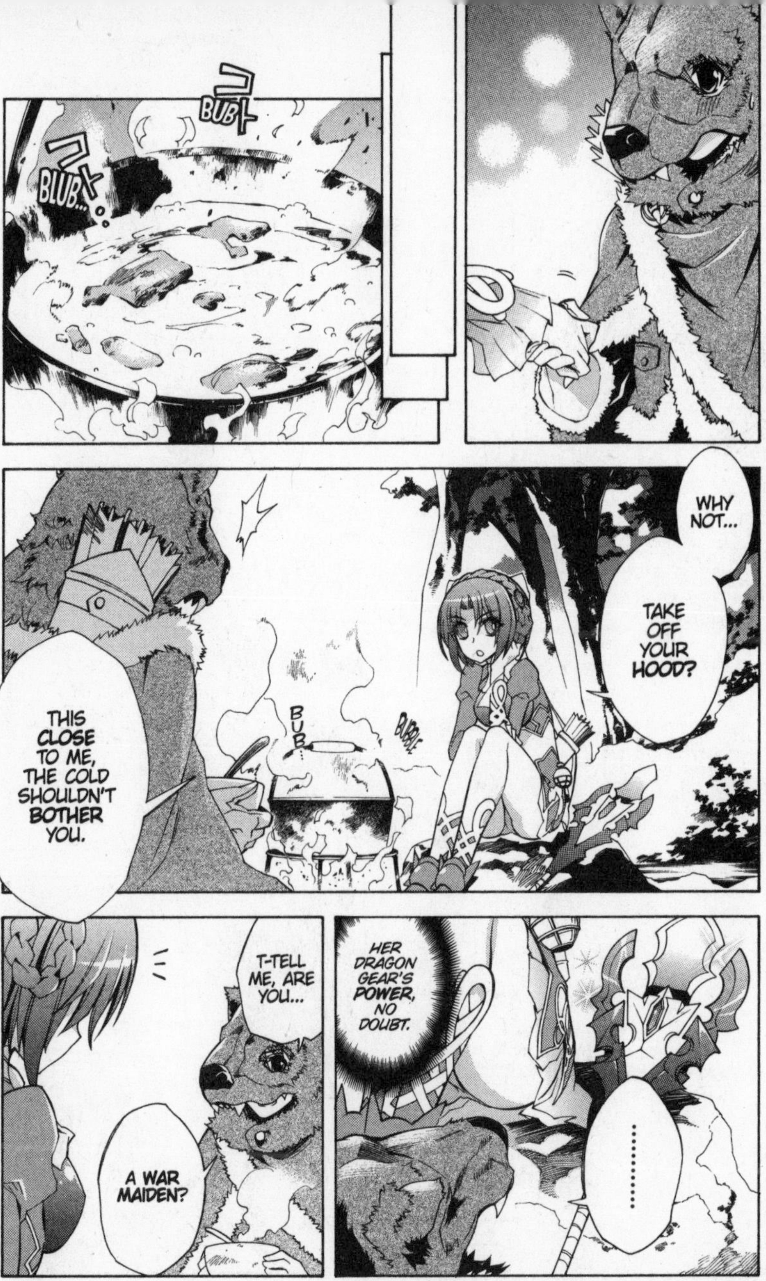
BUB
BLUB...
WHY NOT...
TAKE OFF YOUR HOOD?
BUBBLE
BUB...
THIS CLOSE TO ME, THE COLD SHOULDN'T BOTHER YOU.
HER DRAGON GEAR'S POWER, NO DOUBT.
......
T-TELL ME, ARE YOU...
A WAR MAIDEN?

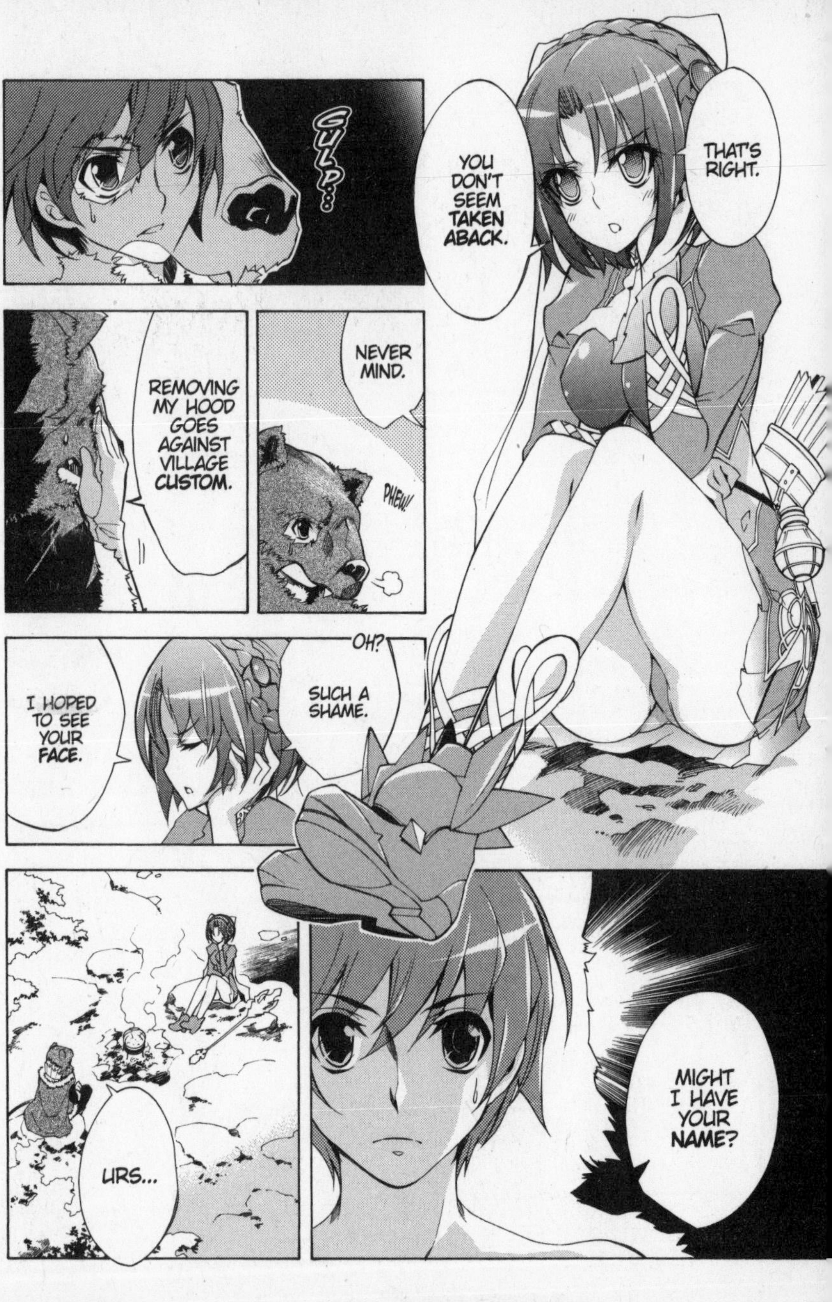
THAT'S RIGHT.
YOU DON'T SEEM TAKEN ABACK.
GULP...
NEVER MIND.
PHEW!
REMOVING MY HOOD GOES AGAINST VILLAGE CUSTOM.
OH?
SUCH A SHAME.
I HOPED TO SEE YOUR FACE.
MIGHT I HAVE YOUR NAME?
URS...

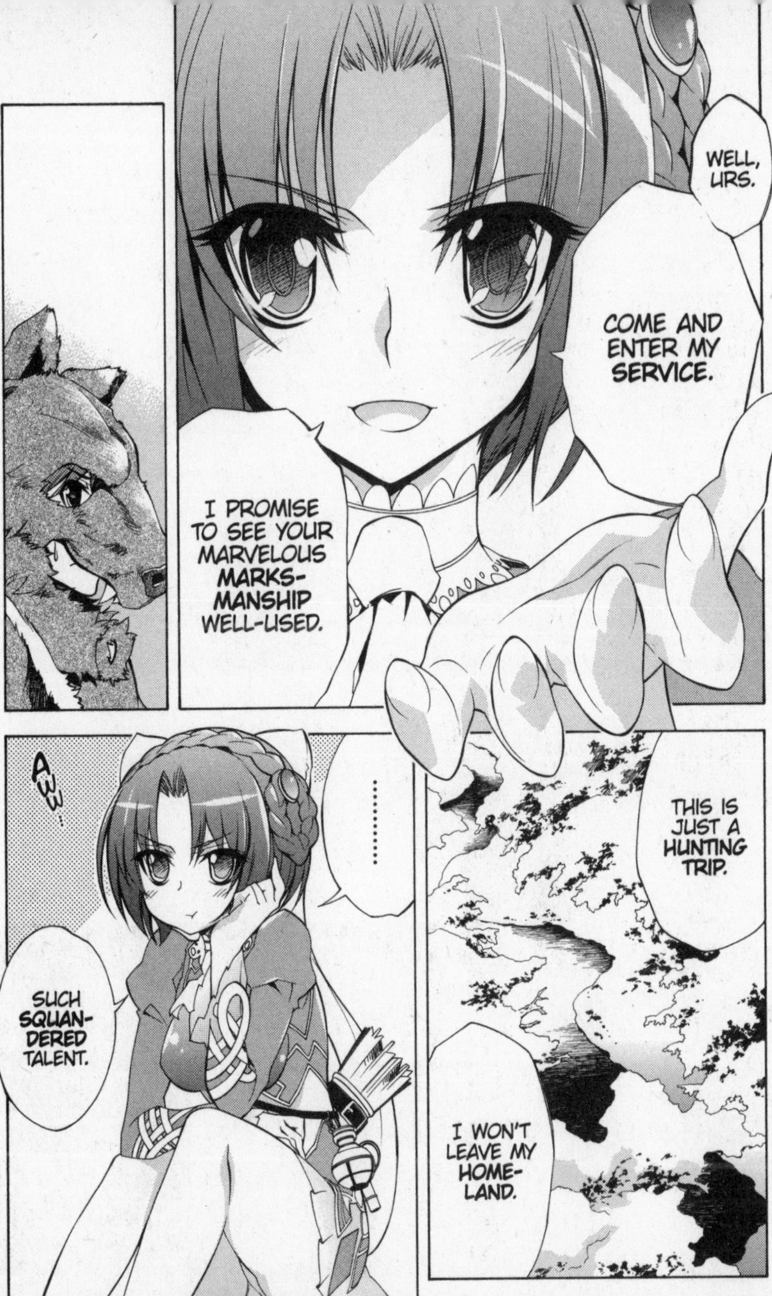
WELL, URS.
COME AND ENTER MY SERVICE.
I PROMISE TO SEE YOUR MARVELOUS MARKS-MANSHIP WELL-USED.
THIS IS JUST A HUNTING TRIP.
I WON'T LEAVE MY HOME-LAND.
......
AWW...
SUCH SQUAN-DERED TALENT.

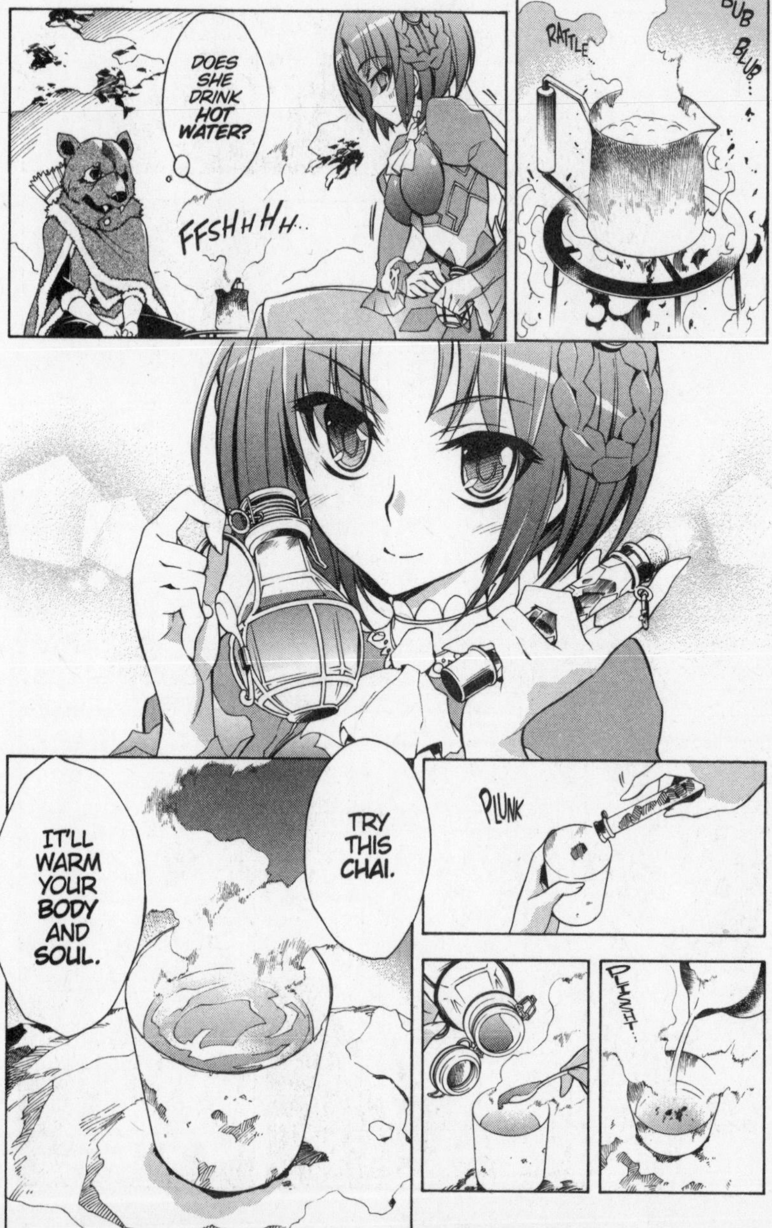

RATTLE...
BUB BLUB...
DOES SHE DRINK HOT WATER?
FFSHHHH...
PLUNK
TRY THIS CHAI.
IT'LL WARM YOUR BODY AND SOUL.

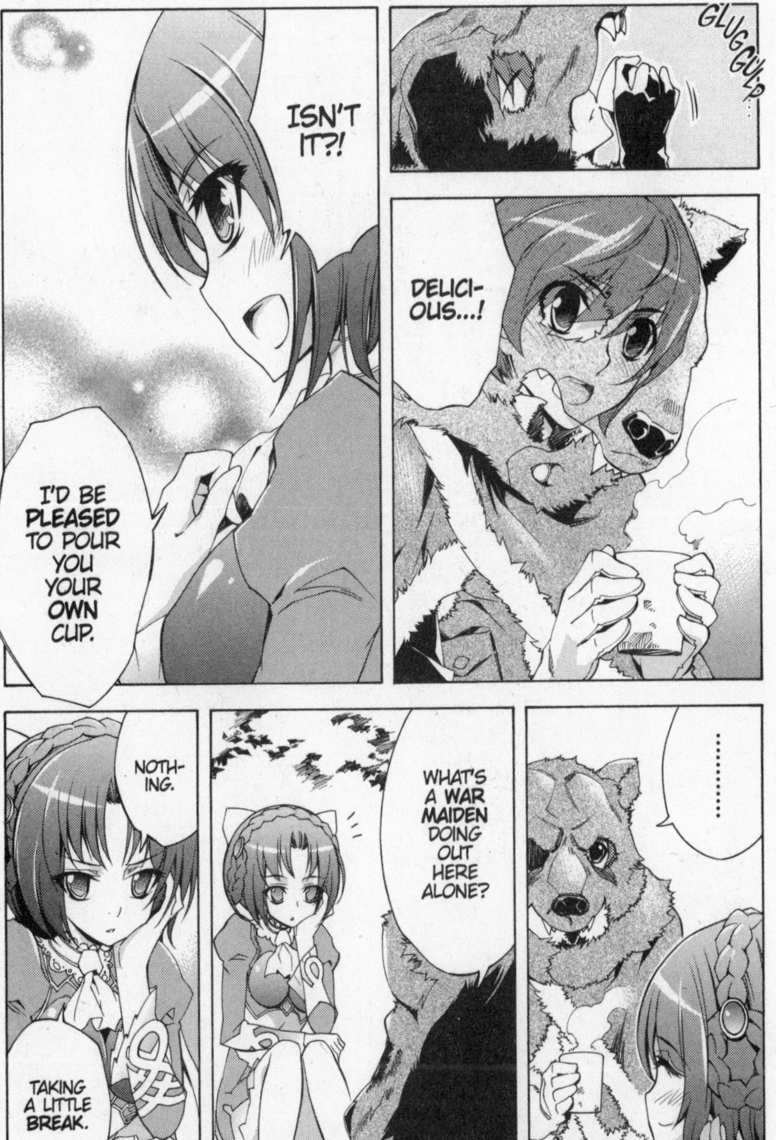
GLUGGULP
DELICI-OUS...!
ISN'T IT?!
I'D BE PLEASED TO POUR YOU YOUR OWN CUP.
....
WHAT'S A WAR MAIDEN DOING OUT HERE ALONE?
NOTH-ING.
TAKING A LITTLE BREAK.

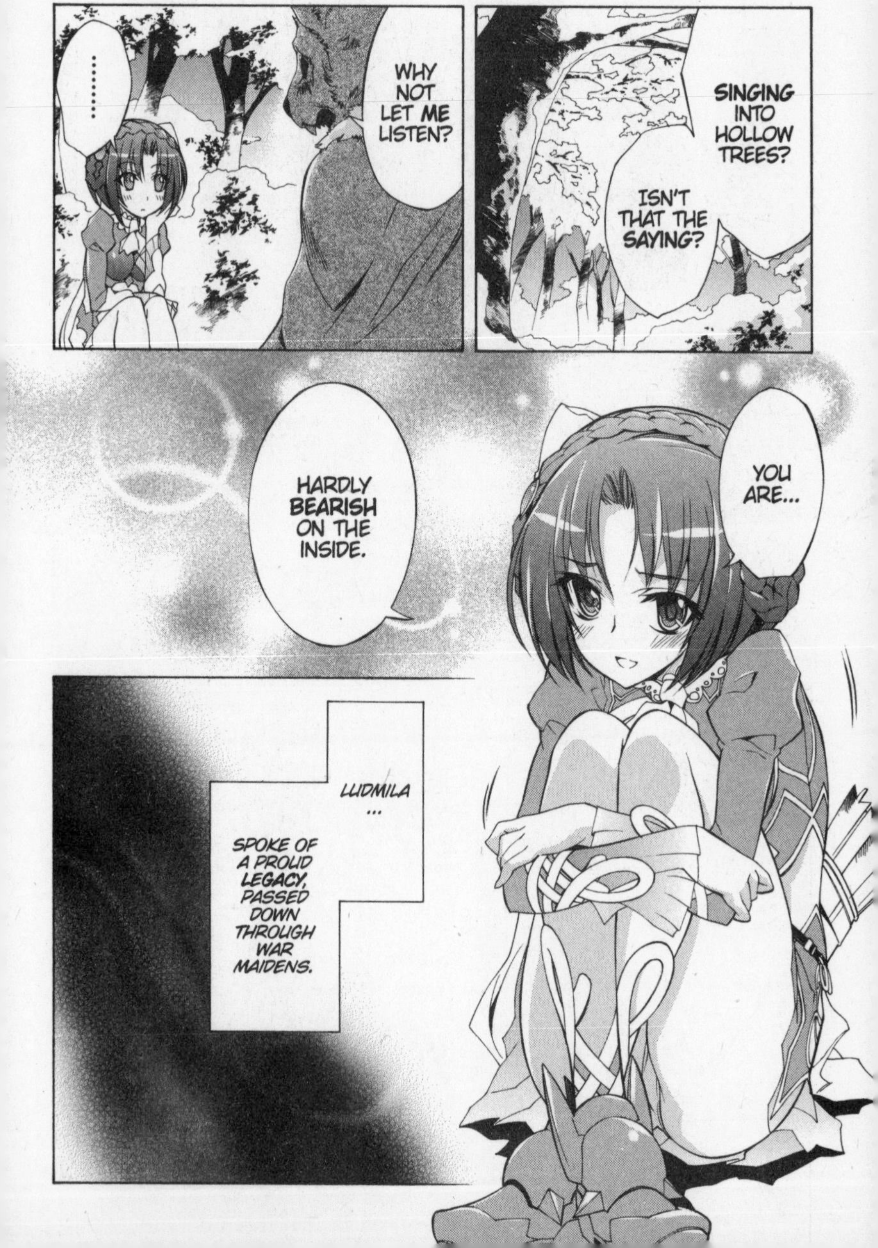
SINGING INTO HOLLOW TREES?
ISN'T THAT THE SAYING?
WHY NOT LET ME LISTEN?
......
YOU ARE...
HARDLY BEARISH ON THE INSIDE.
LUDMILA ...
SPOKE OF A PROUD LEGACY, PASSED DOWN THROUGH WAR MAIDENS.

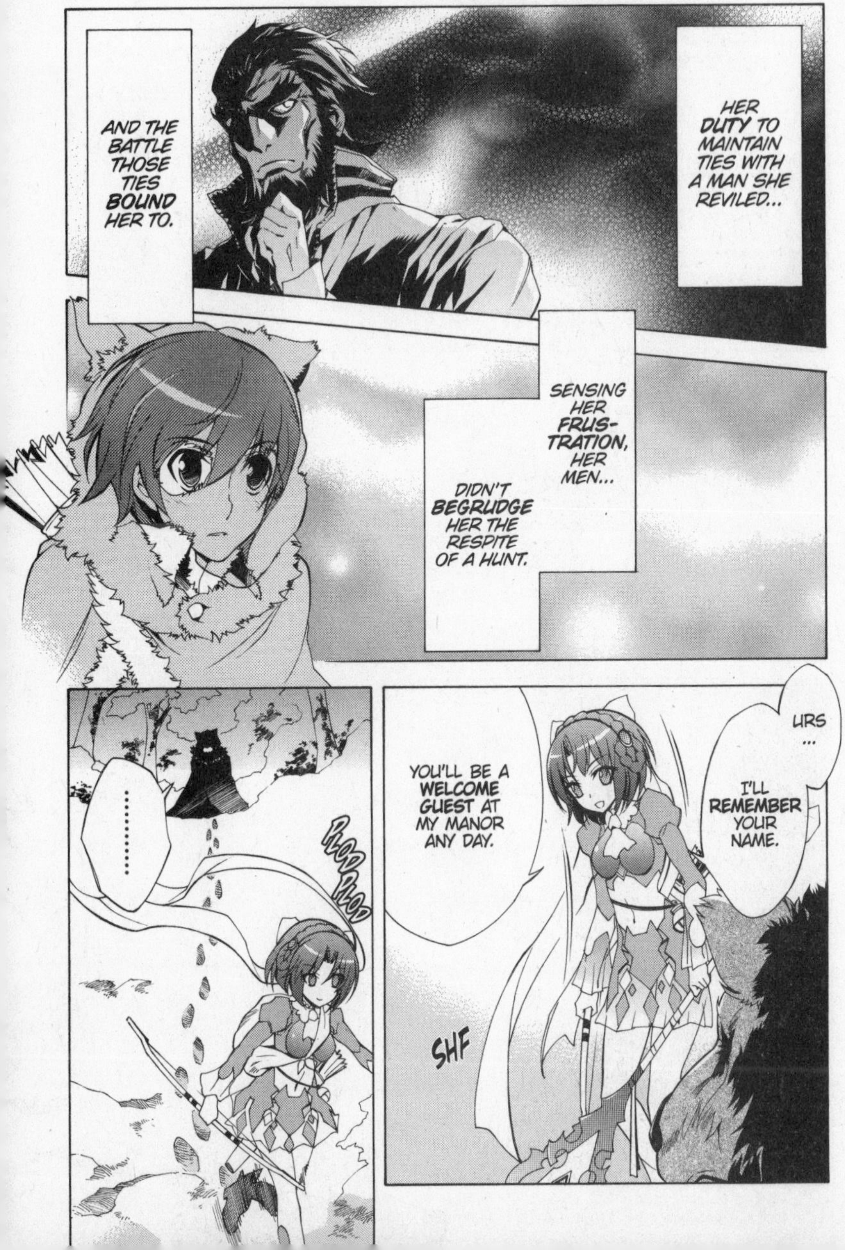
HER DUTY TO MAINTAIN TIES WITH A MAN SHE REVILED...
AND THE BATTLE THOSE TIES BOUND HER TO.
SENSING HER FRUS-TRATION, HER MEN...
DIDN'T BEGRUDGE HER THE RESPITE OF A HUNT.
URS ... I'LL REMEMBER YOUR NAME.
YOU'LL BE A WELCOME GUEST AT MY MANOR ANY DAY.
SHF
....
PLOD PLOD

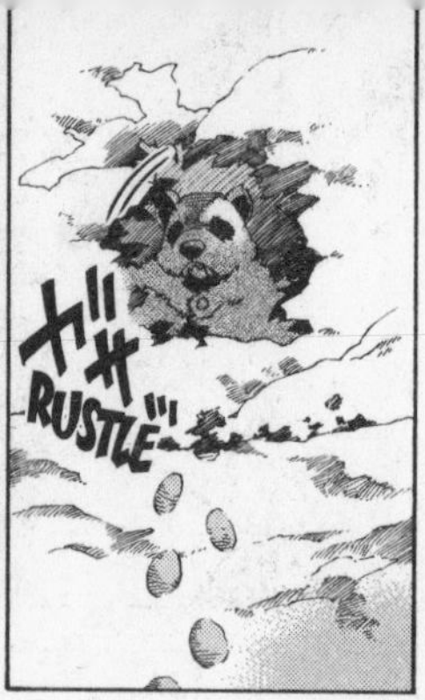
RUSTLE

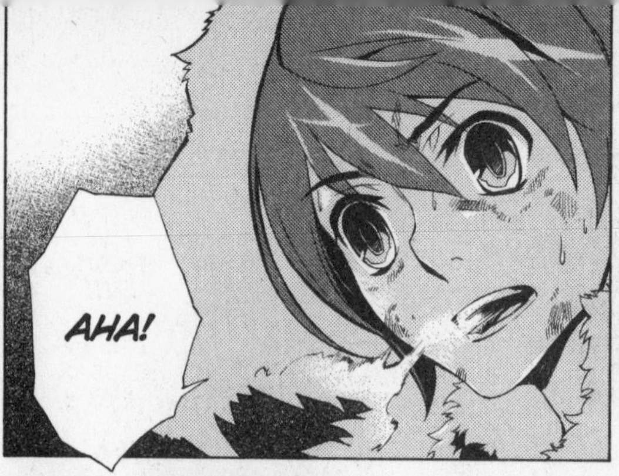
AHA!

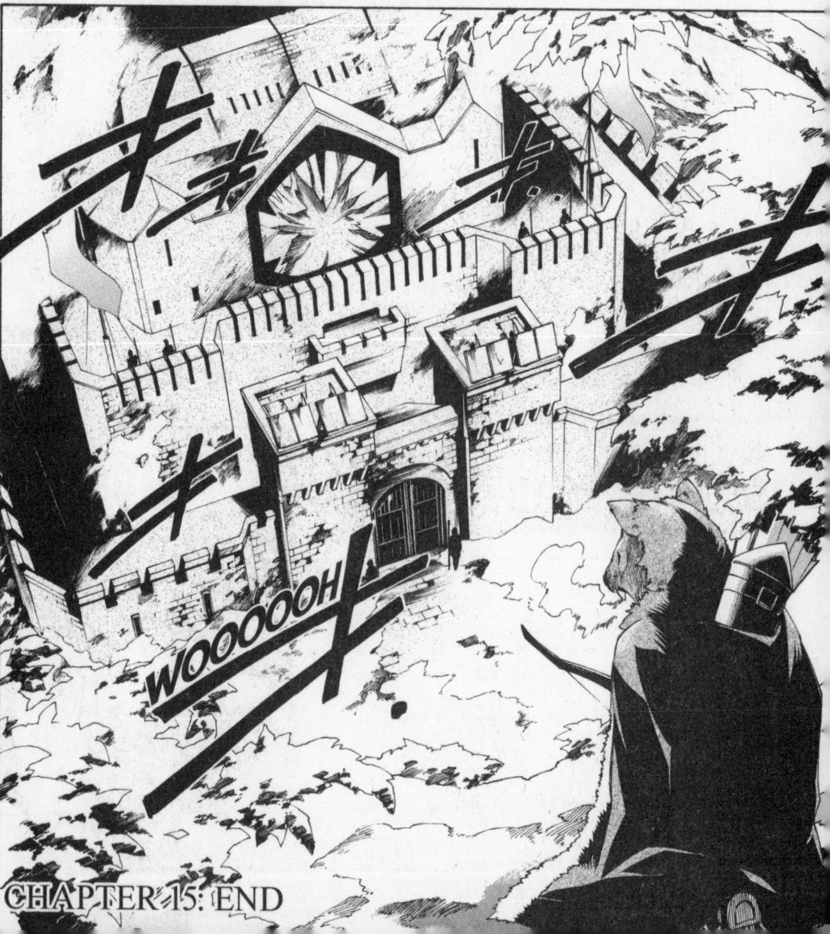
WOOOOOH
CHAPTER 15: END

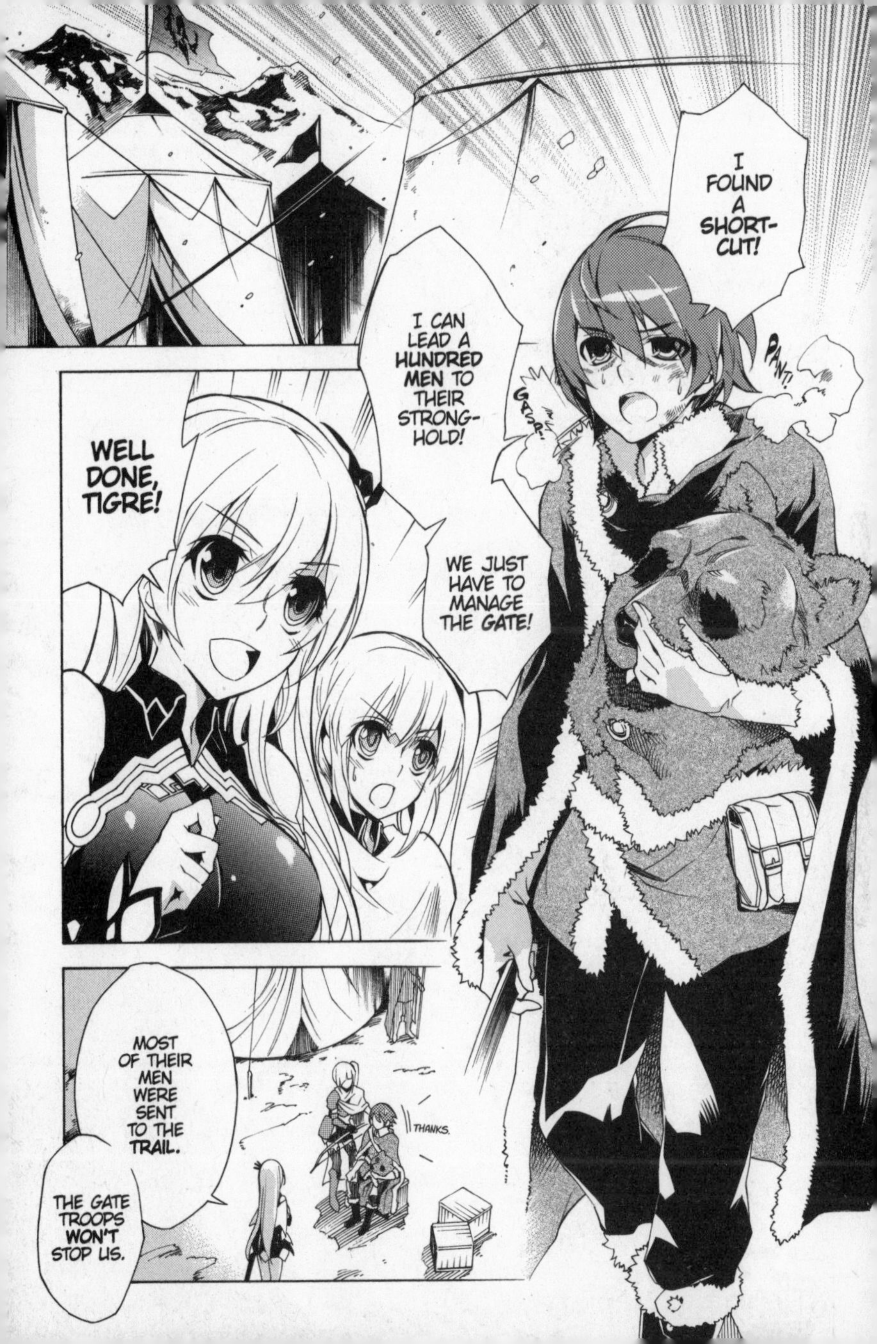
I FOUND A SHORT-CUT!
PANT!
GASP!
I CAN LEAD A HUNDRED MEN TO THEIR STRONG-HOLD!
WE JUST HAVE TO MANAGE THE GATE!
WELL DONE, TIGRE!
MOST OF THEIR MEN WERE SENT TO THE TRAIL.
THANKS.
THE GATE TROOPS WON'T STOP US.

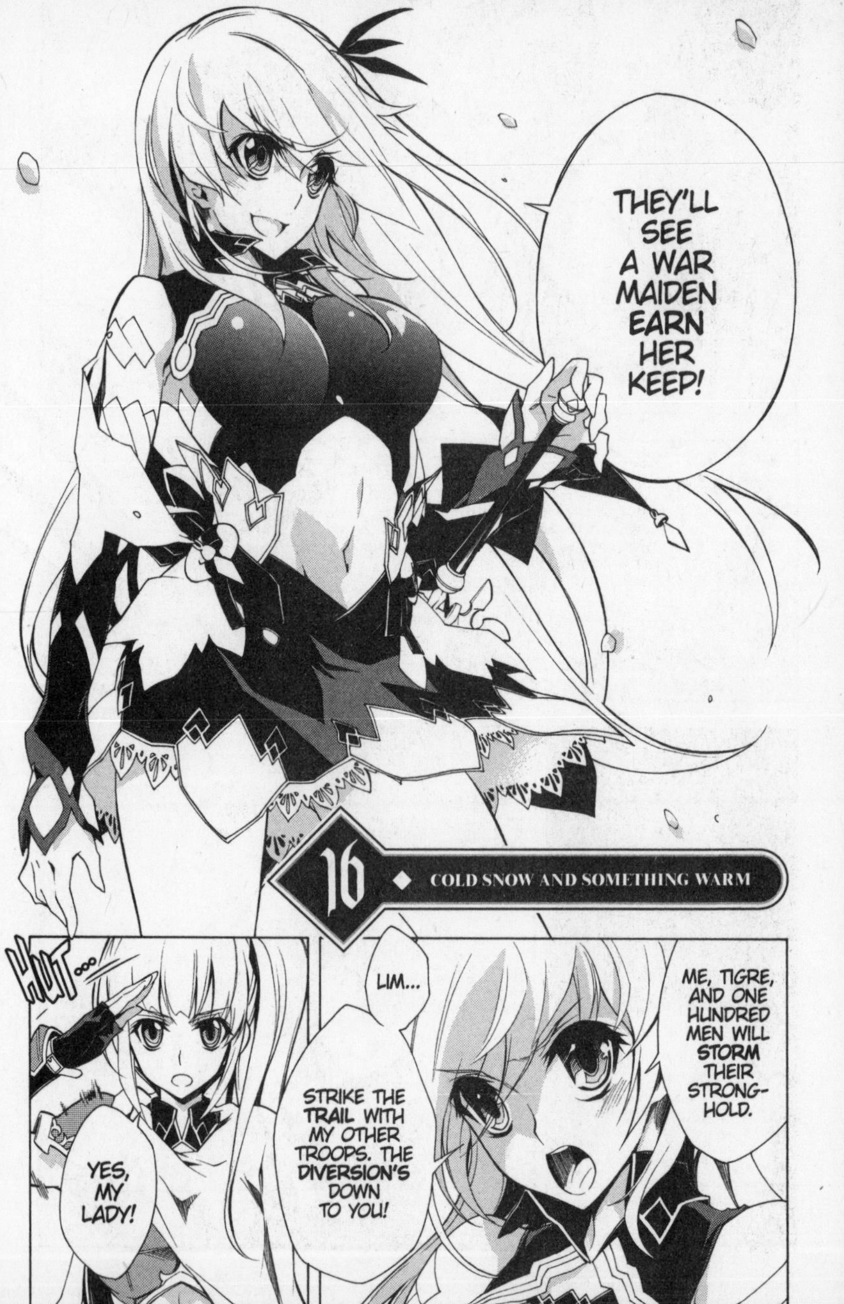
THEY'LL SEE A WAR MAIDEN EARN HER KEEP!
16 ◆ COLD SNOW AND SOMETHING WARM
LIM...
ME, TIGRE, AND ONE HUNDRED MEN WILL STORM THEIR STRONG-HOLD.
STRIKE THE TRAIL WITH MY OTHER TROOPS. THE DIVERSION'S DOWN TO YOU!
HUT...
YES, MY LADY!

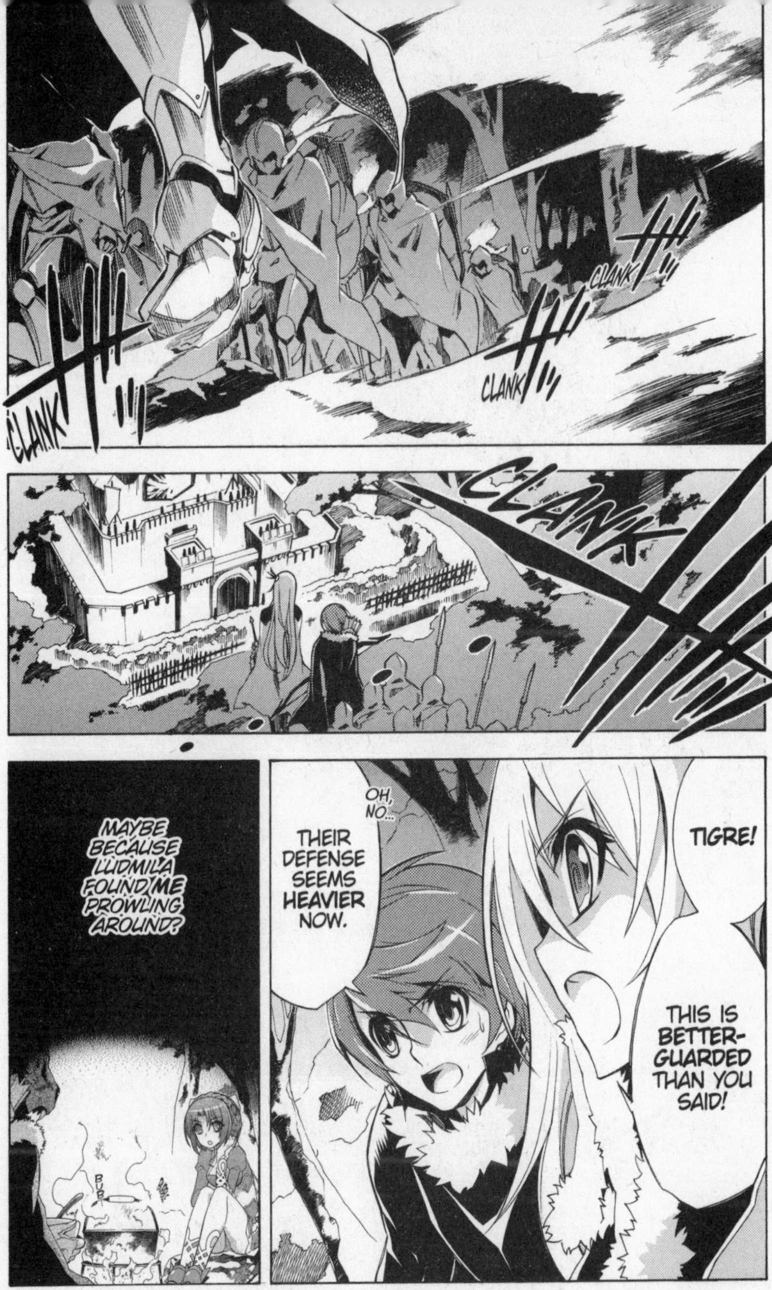
CLANK
CLANK
CLANK
CLANK
TIGRE!
THIS IS BETTER-GUARDED THAN YOU SAID!
OH, NO...
THEIR DEFENSE SEEMS HEAVIER NOW.
MAYBE BECAUSE LUDMILA FOUND ME PROWLING AROUND?
BUB

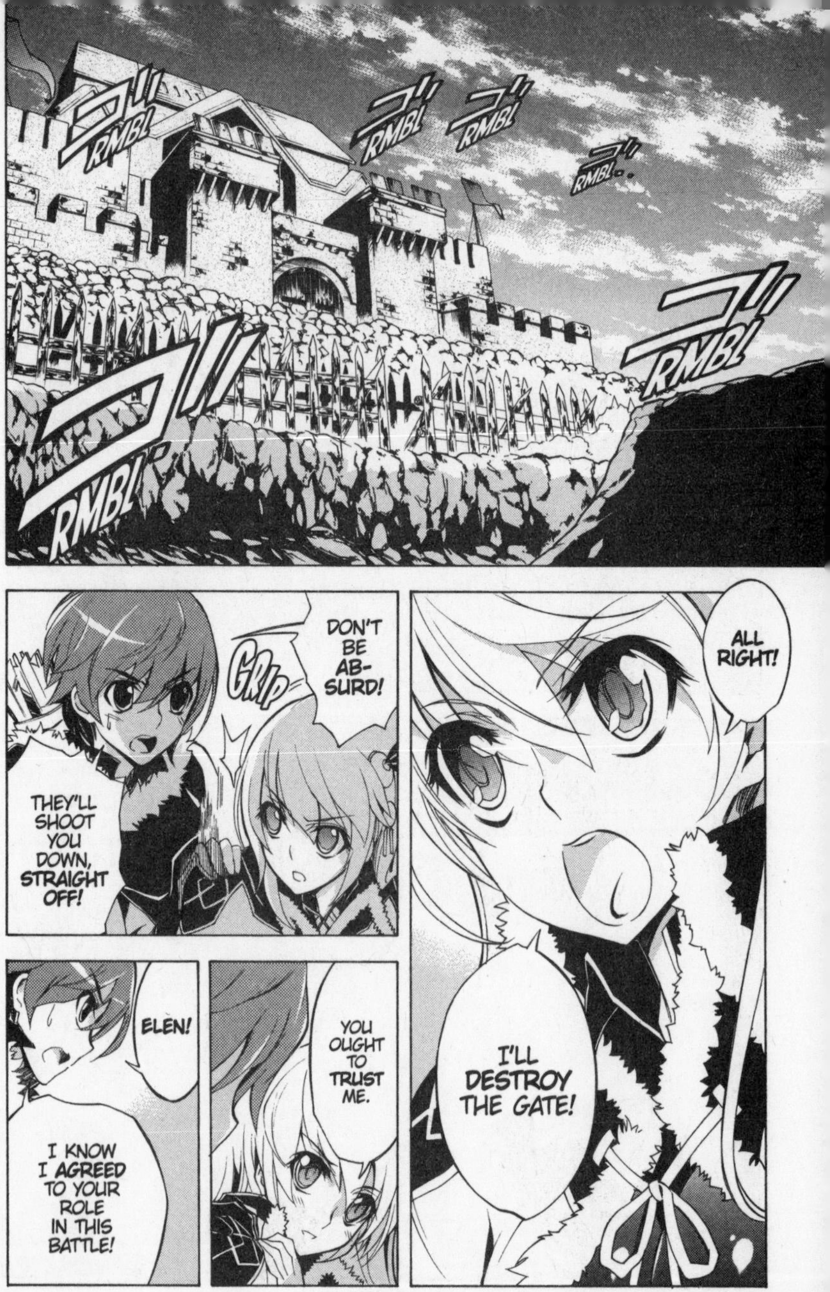
RMBL
RMBL
RMBL
RMBL..
RMBL
RMBL
ALL RIGHT!
I'LL DESTROY THE GATE!
GRIP
DON'T BE ABSURD!
THEY'LL SHOOT YOU DOWN, STRAIGHT OFF!
YOU OUGHT TO TRUST ME.
ELEN!
I KNOW I AGREED TO YOUR ROLE IN THIS BATTLE!

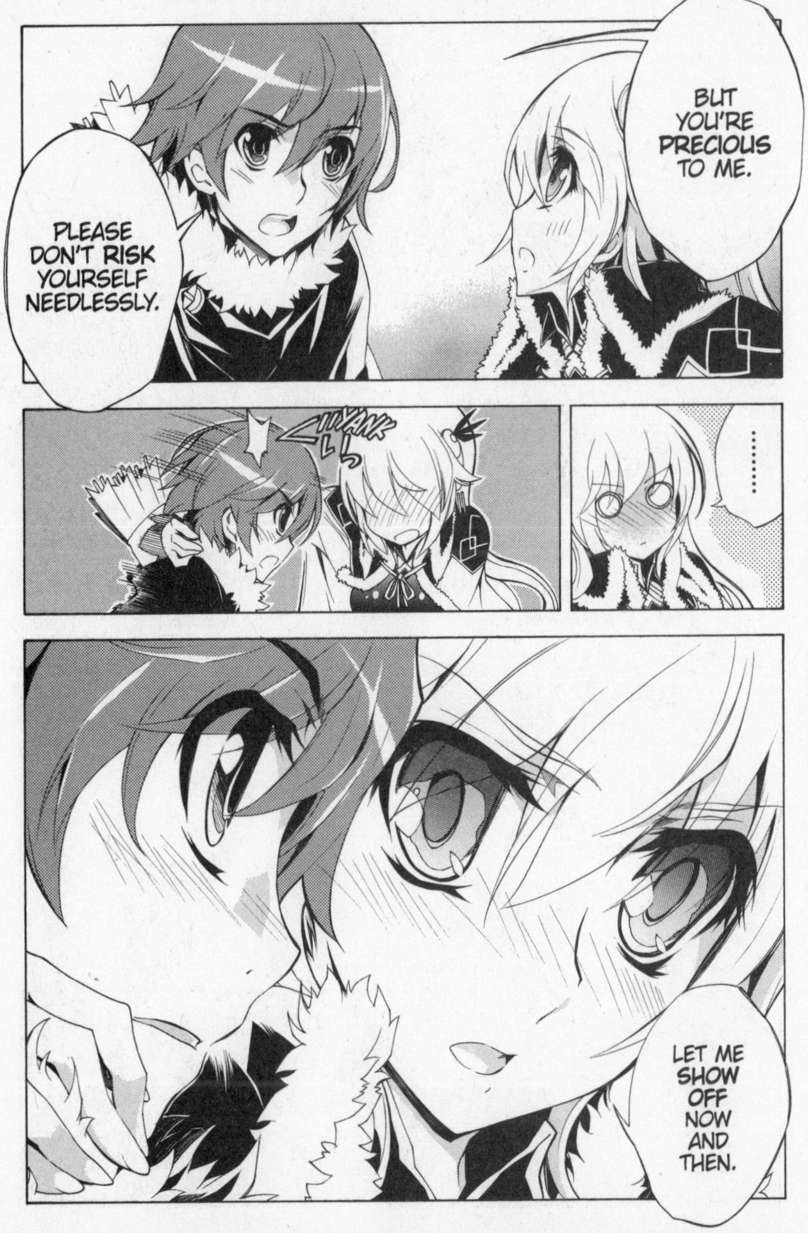
PLEASE DON'T RISK YOURSELF NEEDLESSLY.
BUT YOU'RE PRECIOUS TO ME.
CLIIYANK
......
LET ME SHOW OFF NOW AND THEN.

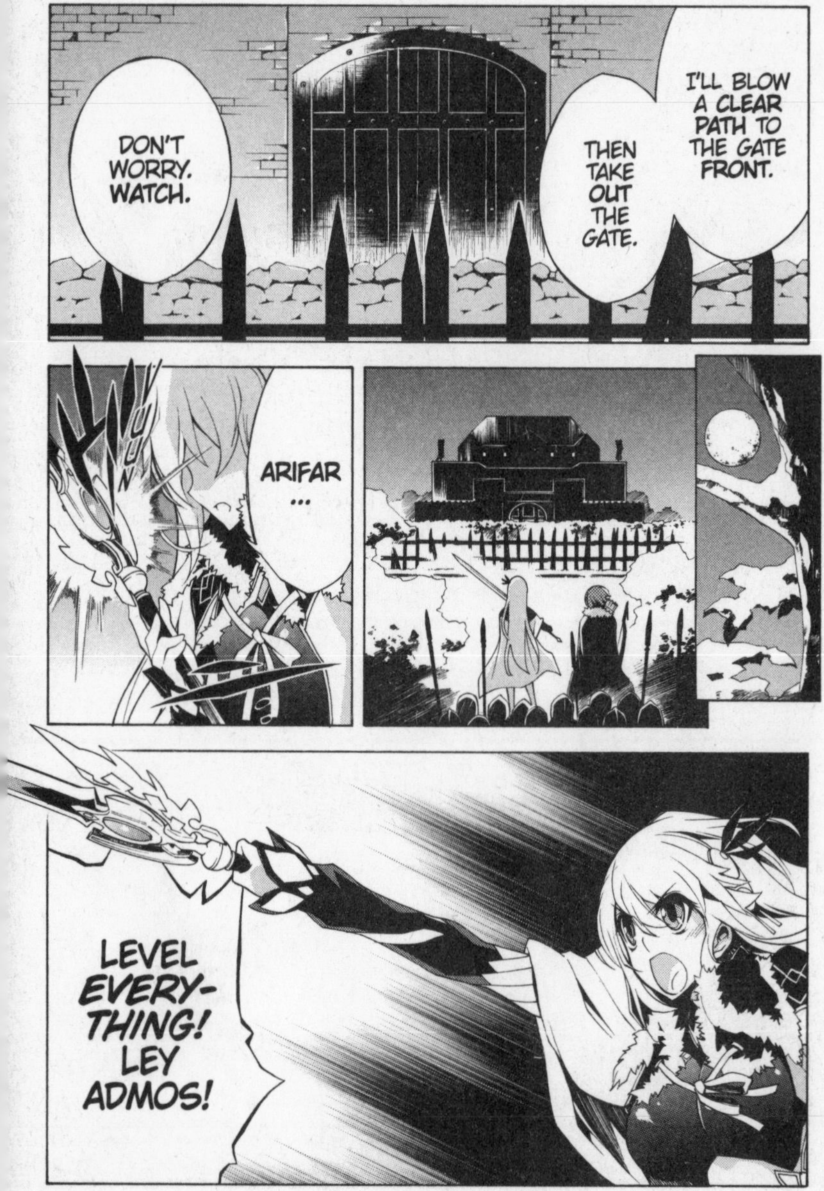
I'LL BLOW A CLEAR PATH TO THE GATE FRONT.
THEN TAKE OUT THE GATE.
DON'T WORRY. WATCH.
ARIFAR ...
LEVEL EVERYTHING! LEY ADMOS!

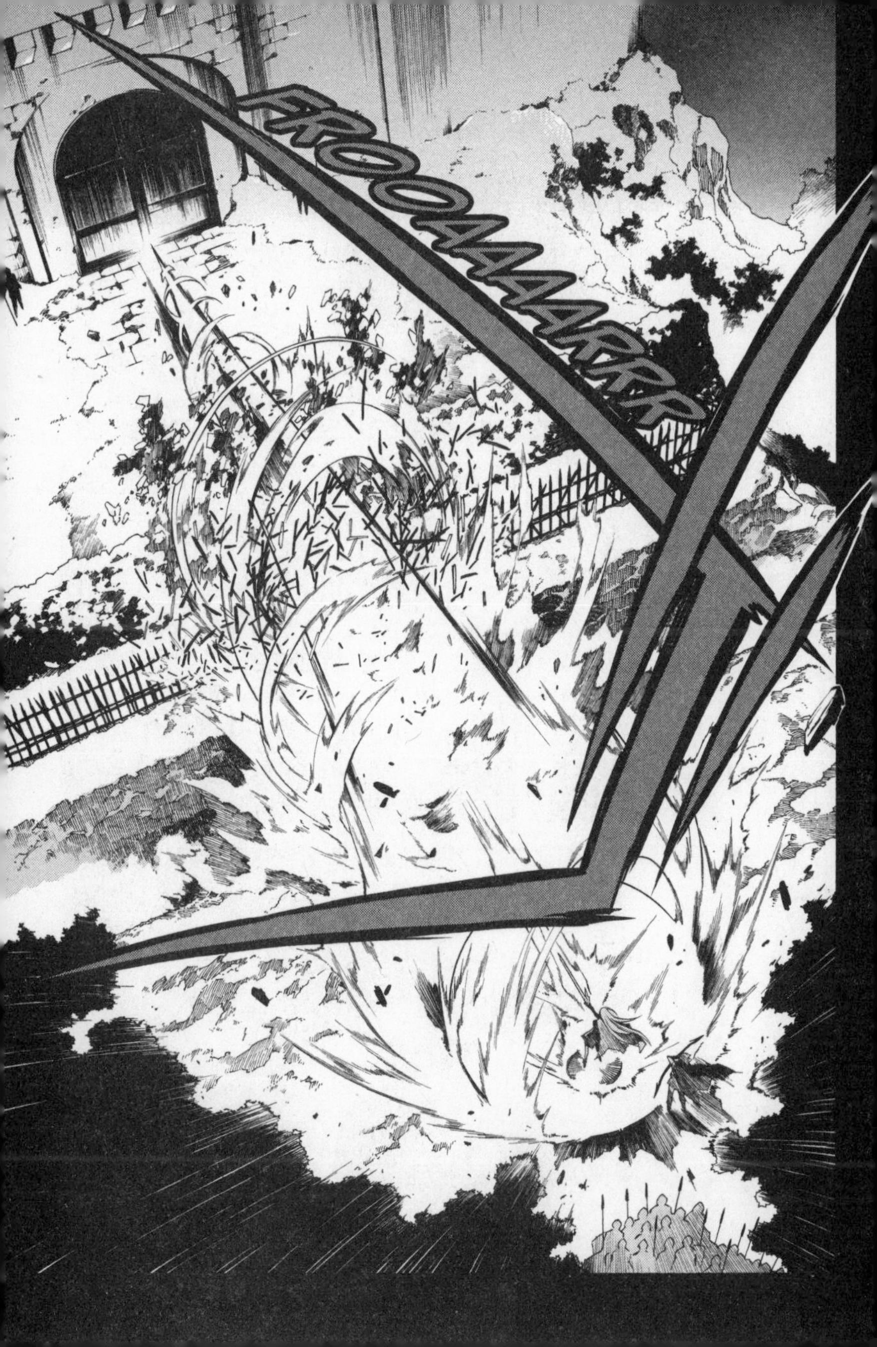
FROOAAAARRR

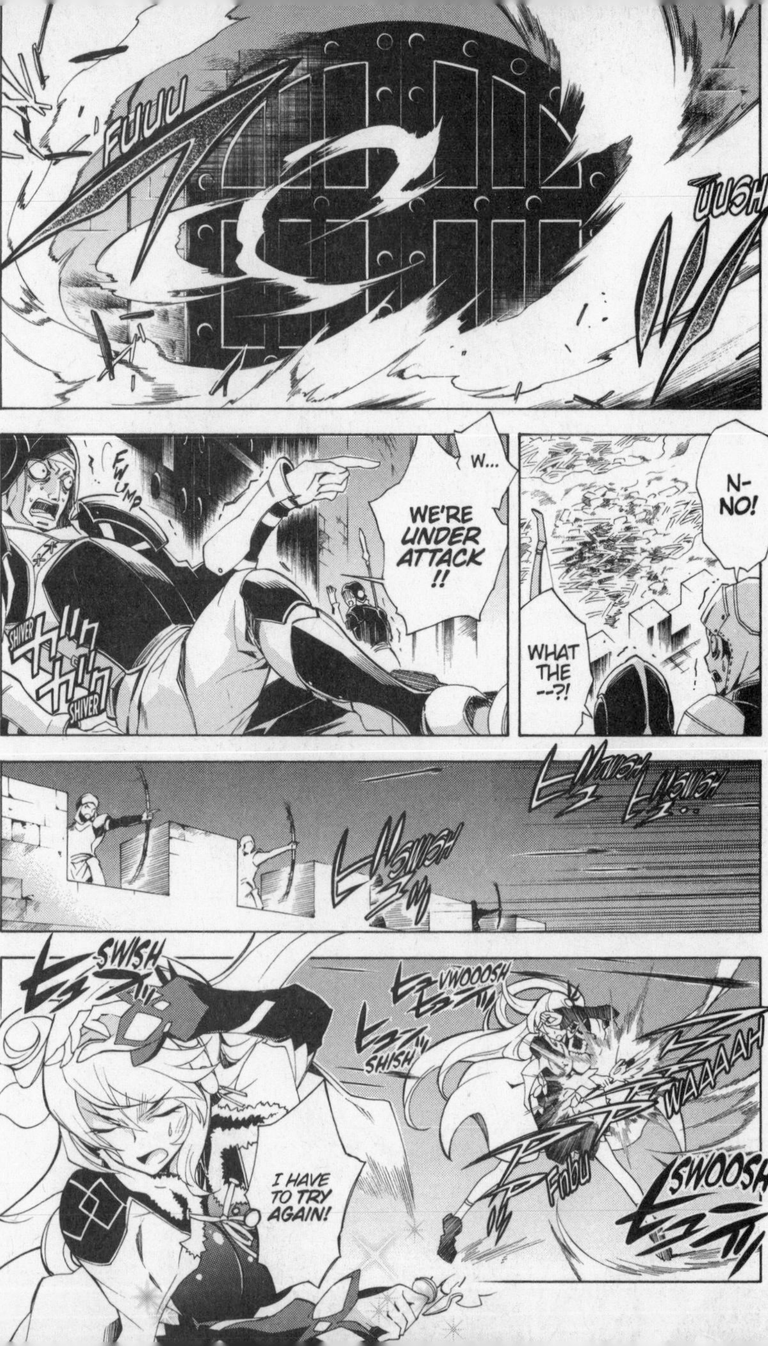
UUSH
FUUU
N-NO!
WHAT THE --?!
W...
WE'RE UNDER ATTACK !!
FWUMP
SHIVER
SHIVER
SWISH
WAAAAH
SWOOSH
VWOOOSH
SHISH
SWISH
I HAVE TO TRY AGAIN!

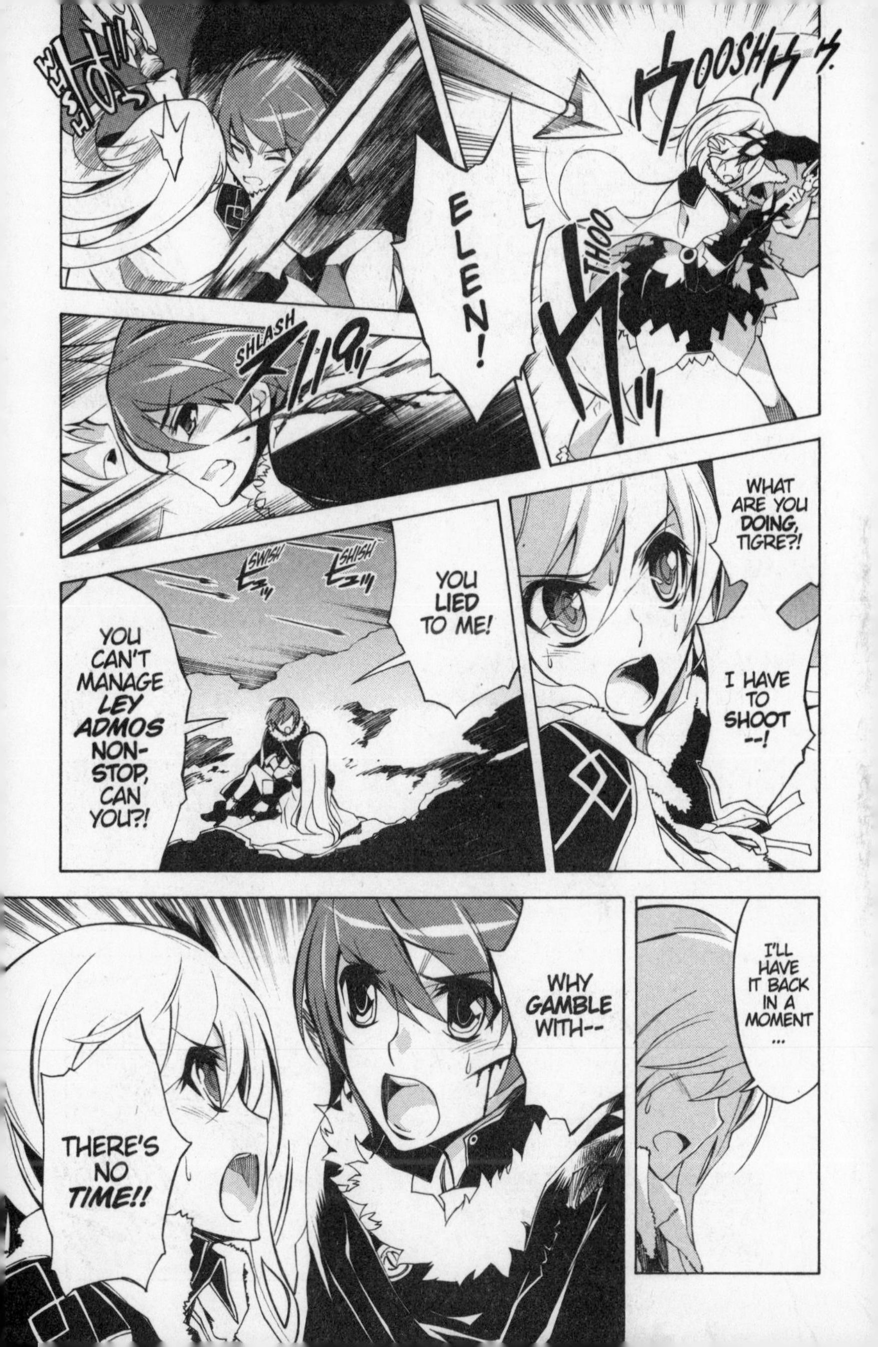
THOO
ELEN!
SHLASH
WHAT ARE YOU DOING, TIGRE?!
I HAVE TO SHOOT --!
YOU LIED TO ME!
SHISH
SWISH
YOU CAN'T MANAGE LEY ADMOS NON-STOP, CAN YOU?!
I'LL HAVE IT BACK IN A MOMENT ...
WHY GAMBLE WITH--
THERE'S NO TIME!!

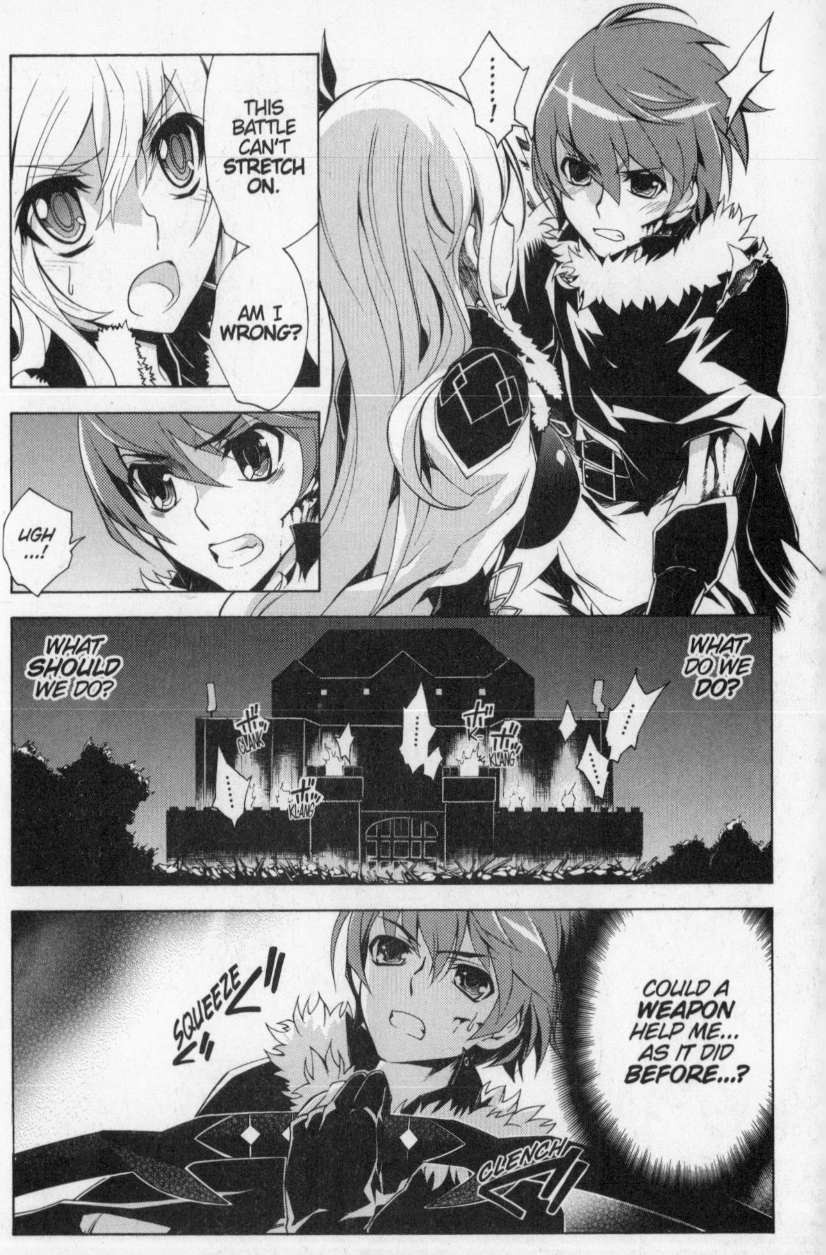
......!
THIS BATTLE CAN'T STRETCH ON.
AM I WRONG?
UGH ...!
WHAT DO WE DO?
WHAT SHOULD WE DO?
KLANG
CLANK
KLANG
COULD A WEAPON HELP ME... AS IT DID BEFORE...?
SQUEEZE
CLENCH

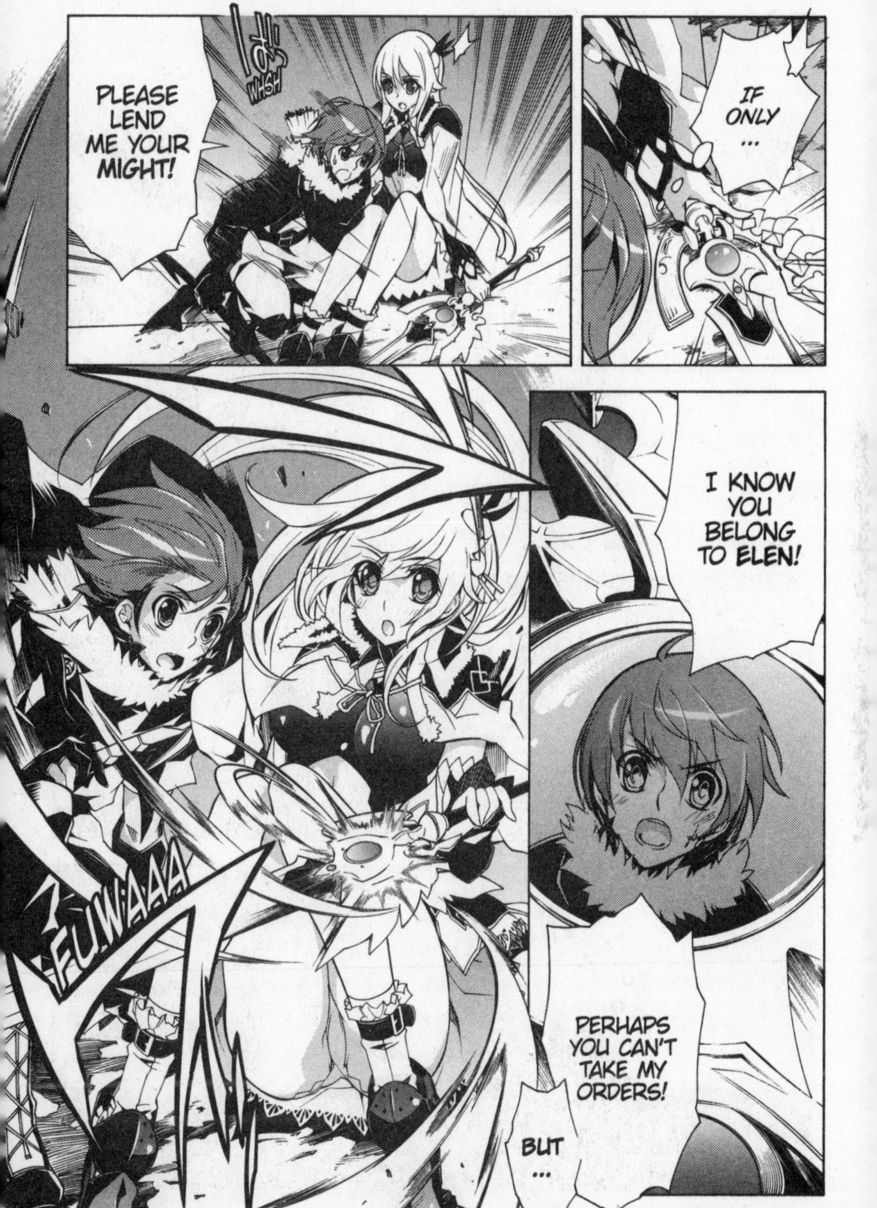
IF ONLY ...
PLEASE LEND ME YOUR MIGHT!
WHSH
I KNOW YOU BELONG TO ELEN!
PERHAPS YOU CAN'T TAKE MY ORDERS!
BUT ...
FUWAAA

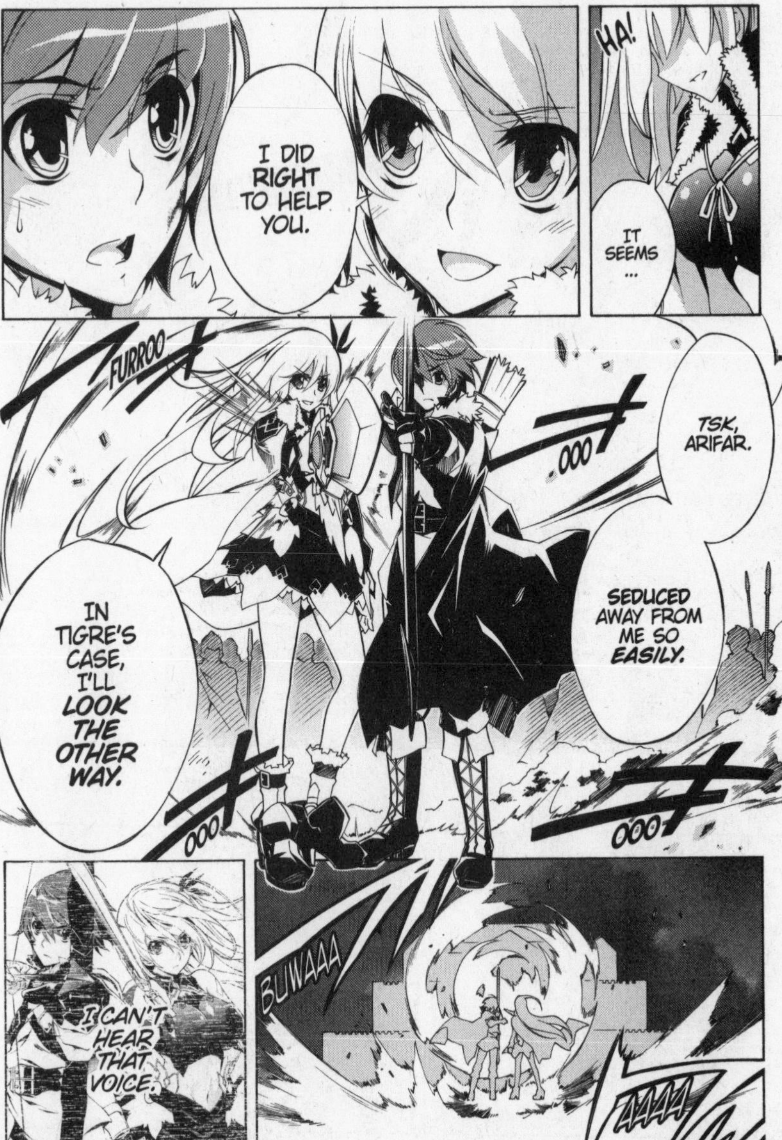
I DID RIGHT TO HELP YOU.
HA!
IT SEEMS ...
FURROO
TSK, ARIFAR.
OOO
SEDUCED AWAY FROM ME SO EASILY.
IN TIGRE'S CASE, I'LL LOOK THE OTHER WAY.
OOO
OOO
I CAN'T HEAR THAT VOICE.
BUWAAA
AAAA

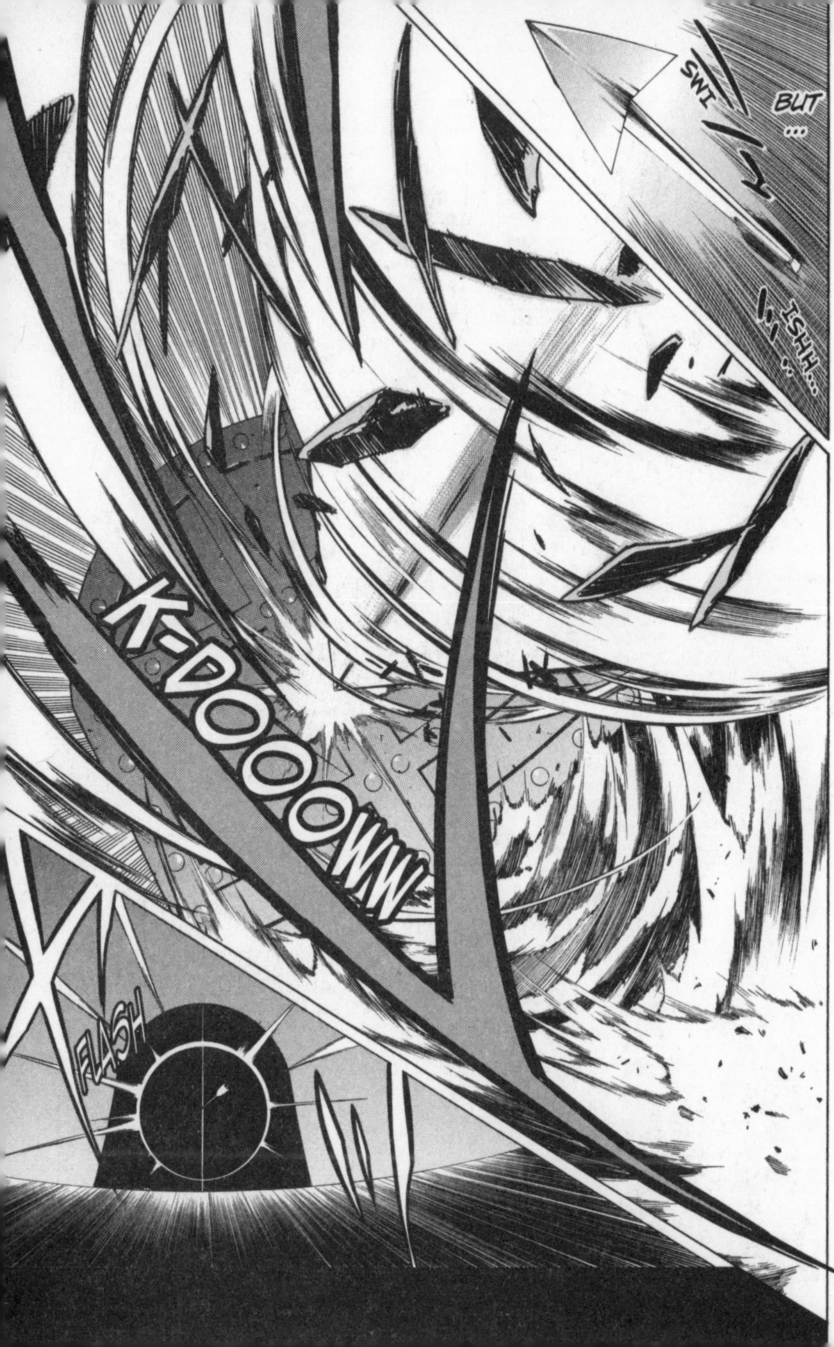
BUT ...
SWI
ISHH...
K-DOOOOWW
FLASH

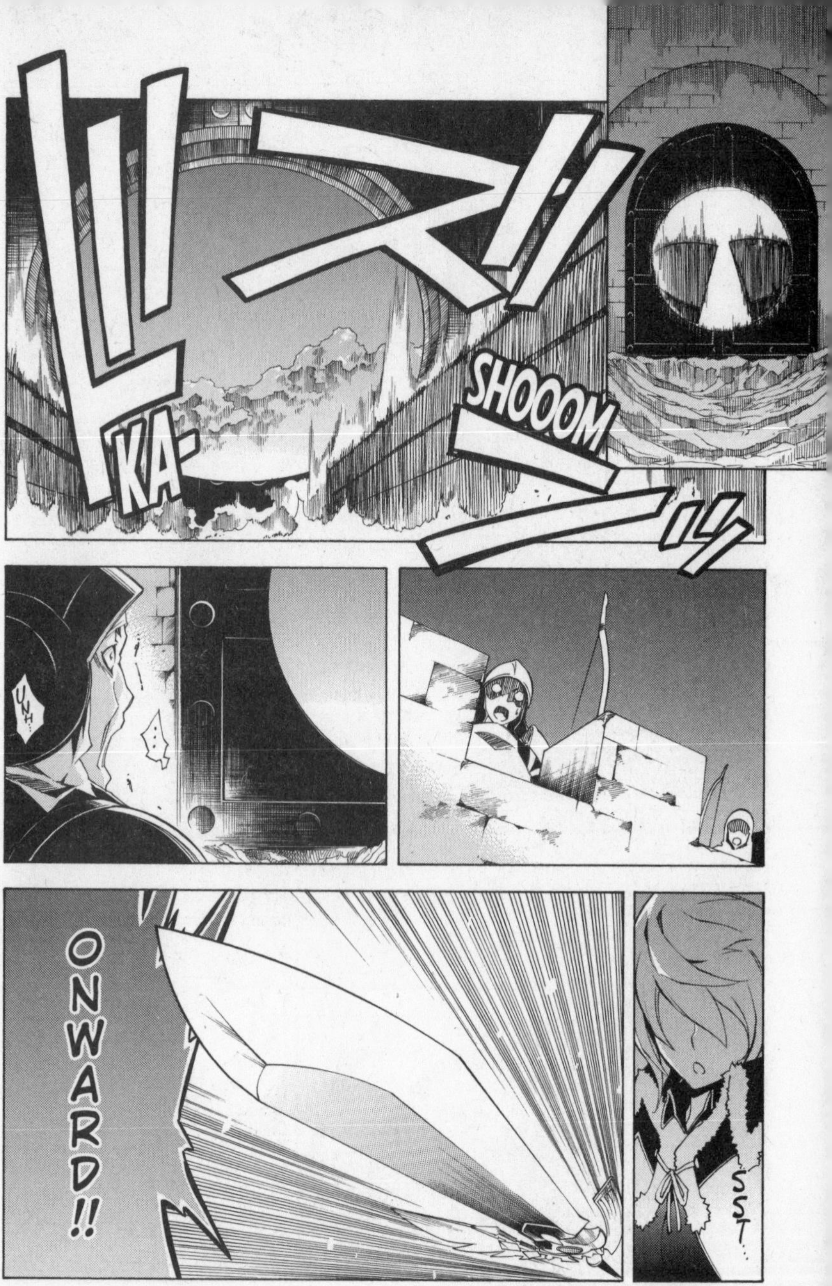
KA-
SHOOOM
UNH...
SST...
ONWARD!!

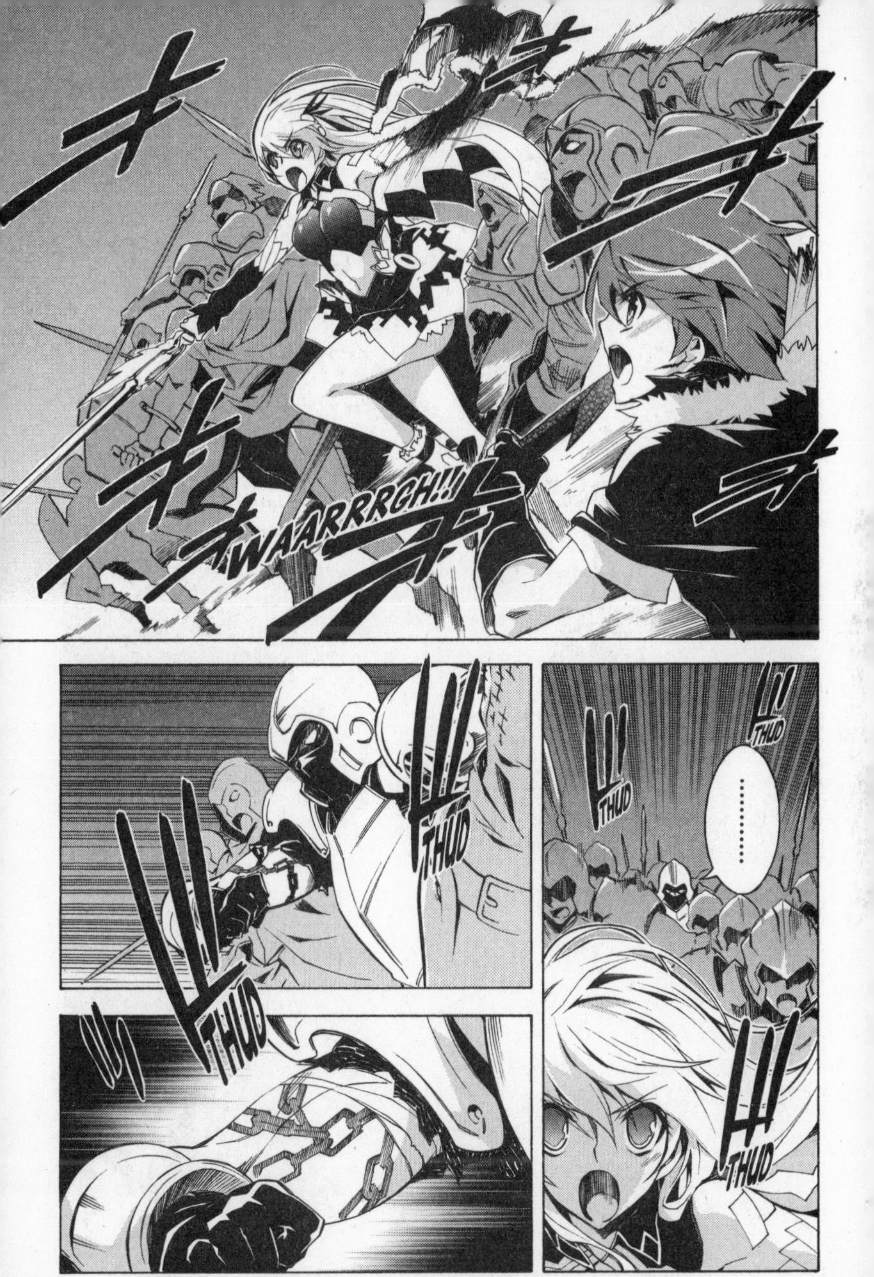
WAARRRGH!!
THUD
THUD
......
THUD
THUD
THUD

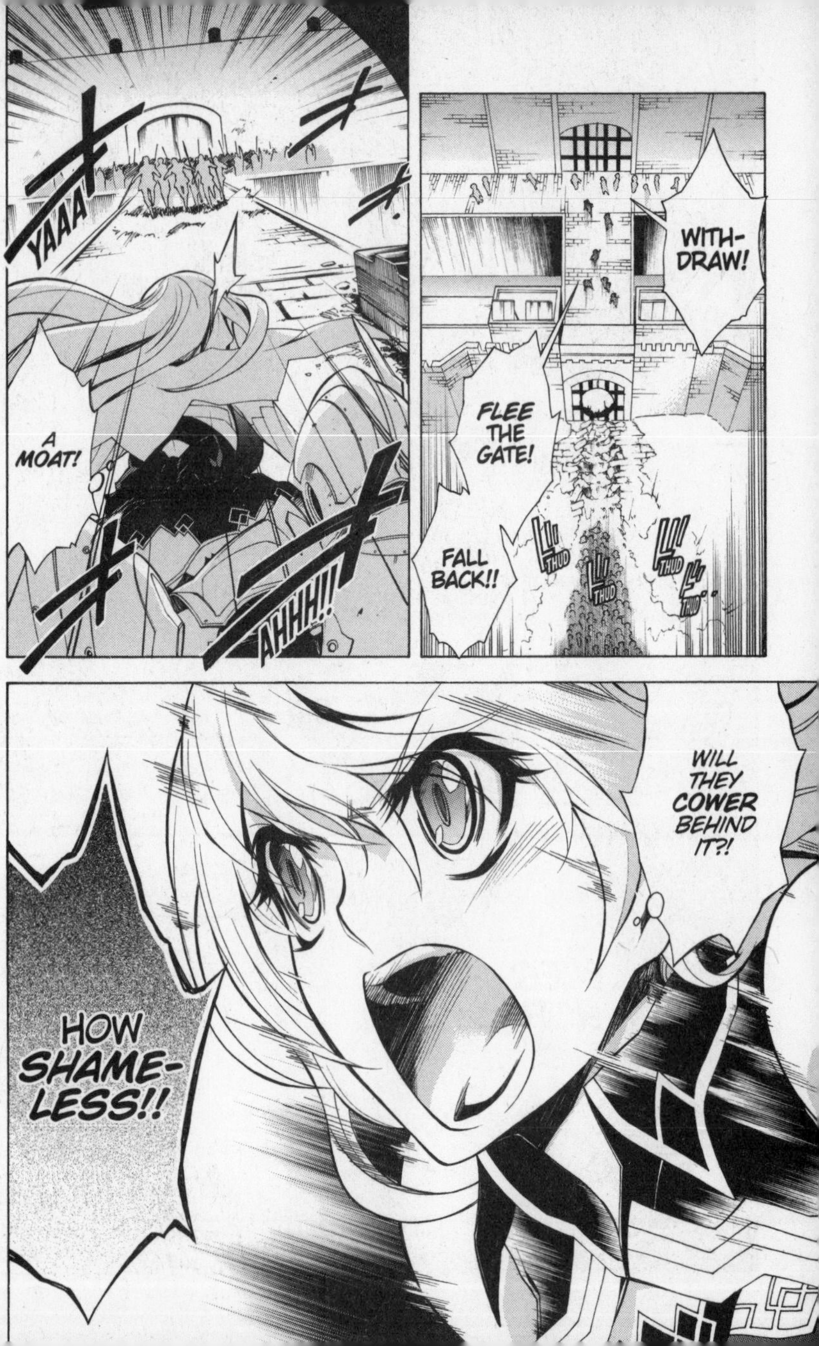
WITH-DRAW!
FLEE THE GATE!
FALL BACK!!
THUD
THUD
THUD
THUD
YAAA
A MOAT!
AHHH!!
WILL THEY COWER BEHIND IT?!
HOW SHAME-LESS!!

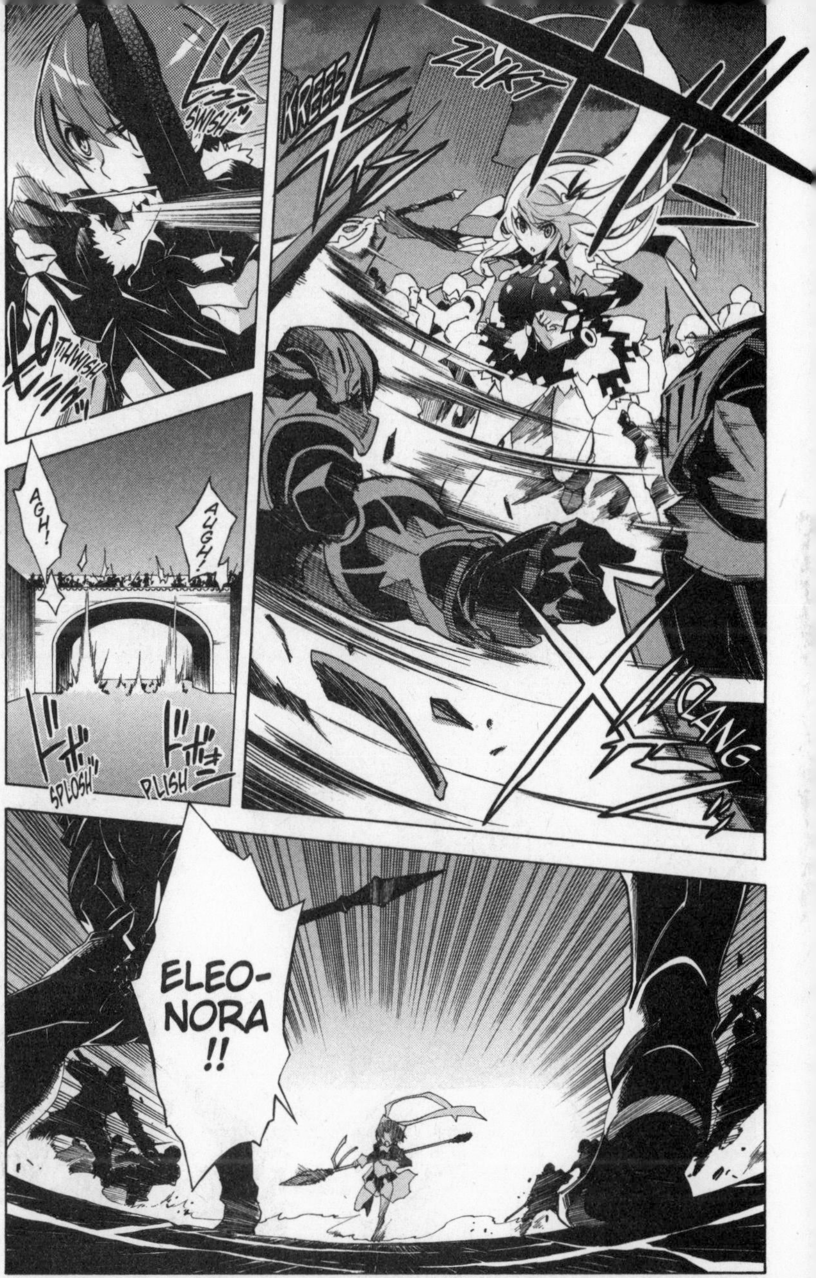
ZLIKT
KREEE
CLANG
SWISH
THWISH
AUGH!
AGH!
PLISH
SPLOSH
ELEO-
NORA
!!

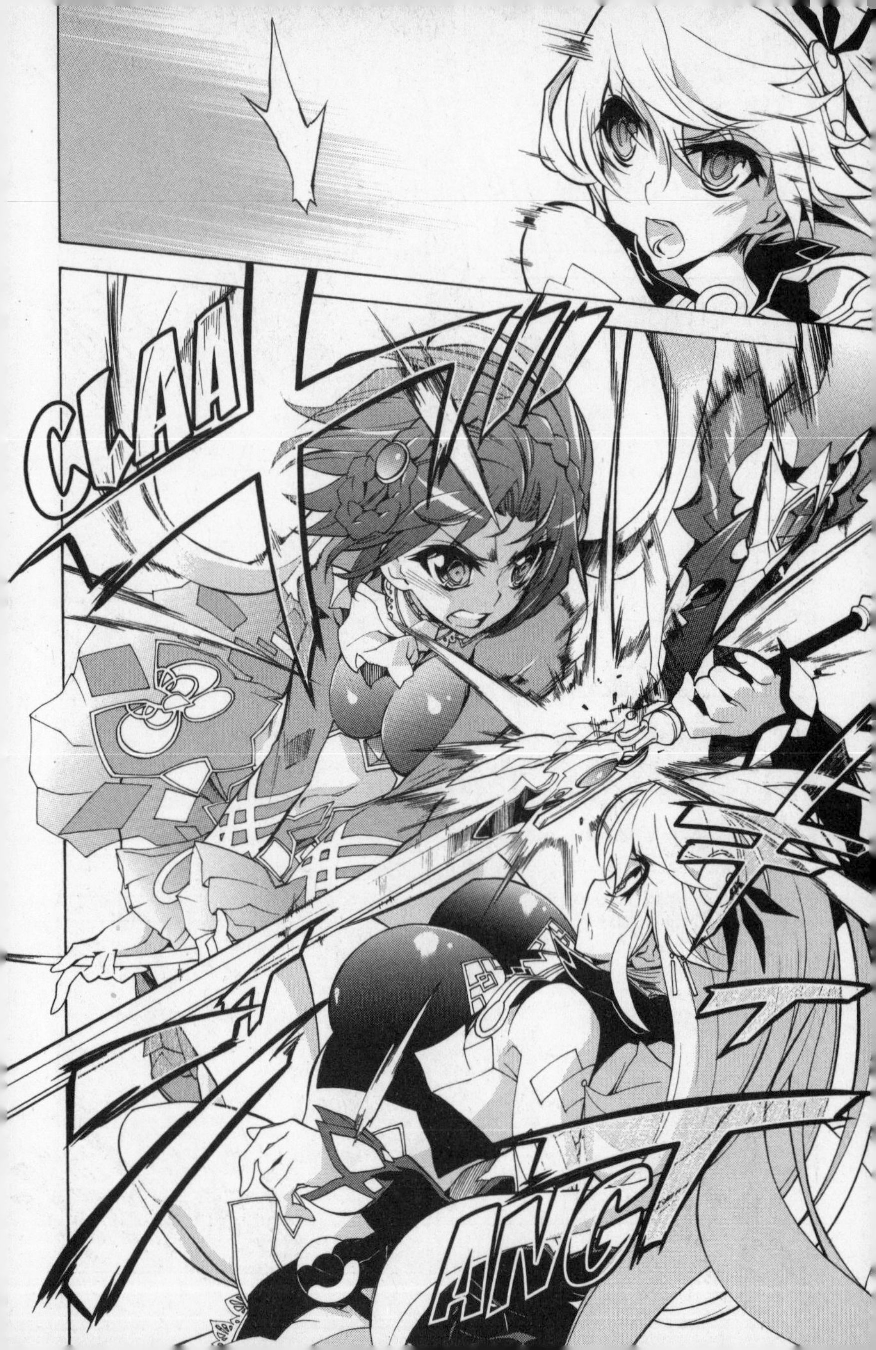
CLAA
ANG

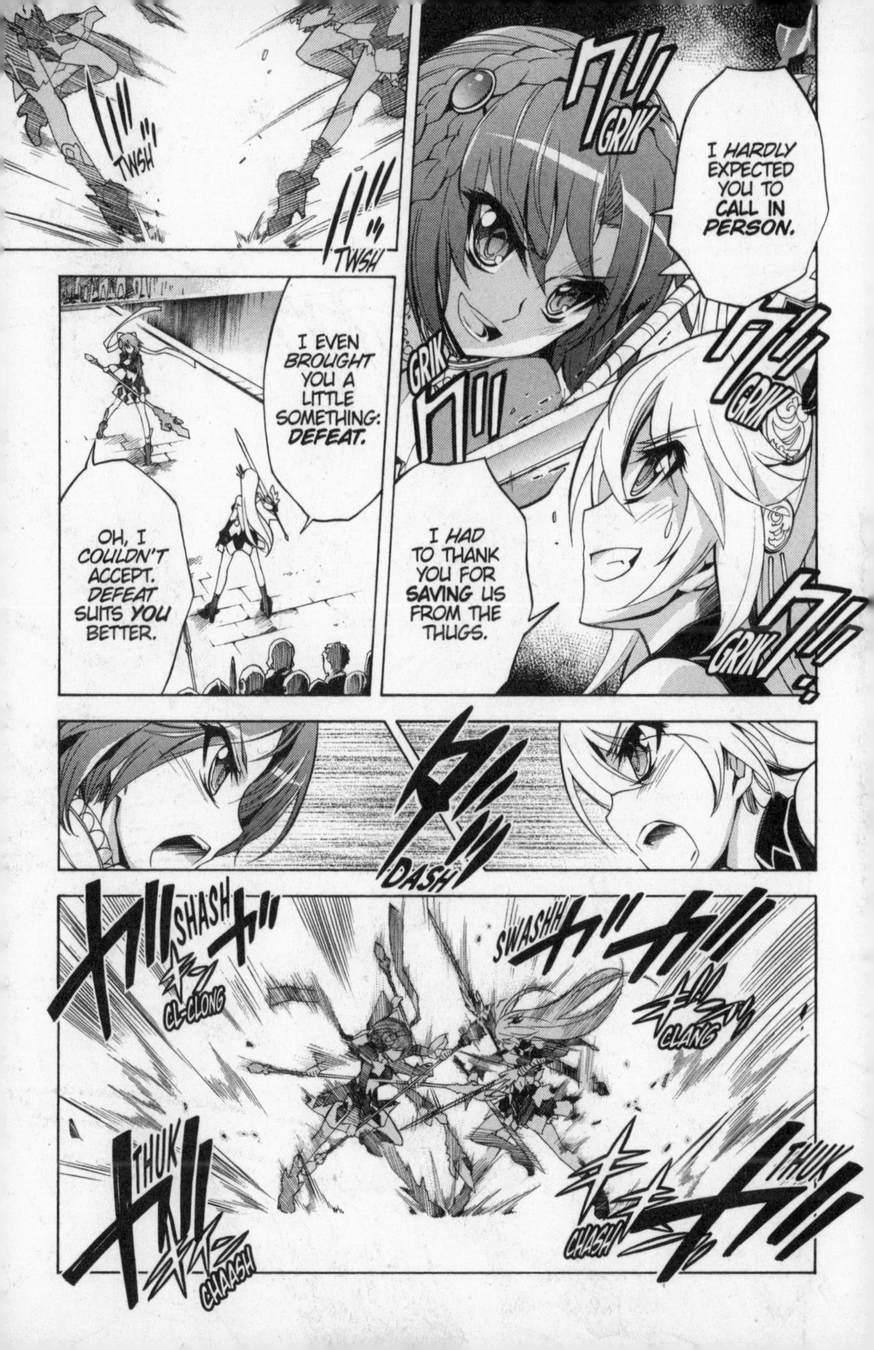
GRIK
I HARDLY EXPECTED YOU TO CALL IN PERSON.
GRIK
GRIK
I HAD TO THANK YOU FOR SAVING US FROM THE THUGS.
GRIK
TWSH
TWSH
I EVEN BROUGHT YOU A LITTLE SOMETHING: DEFEAT.
OH, I COULDN'T ACCEPT. DEFEAT SUITS YOU BETTER.
DASH
SWASHH
CLANG
SHASH
CL-CLONG
THUK
CHASH
THUK
CHAASH

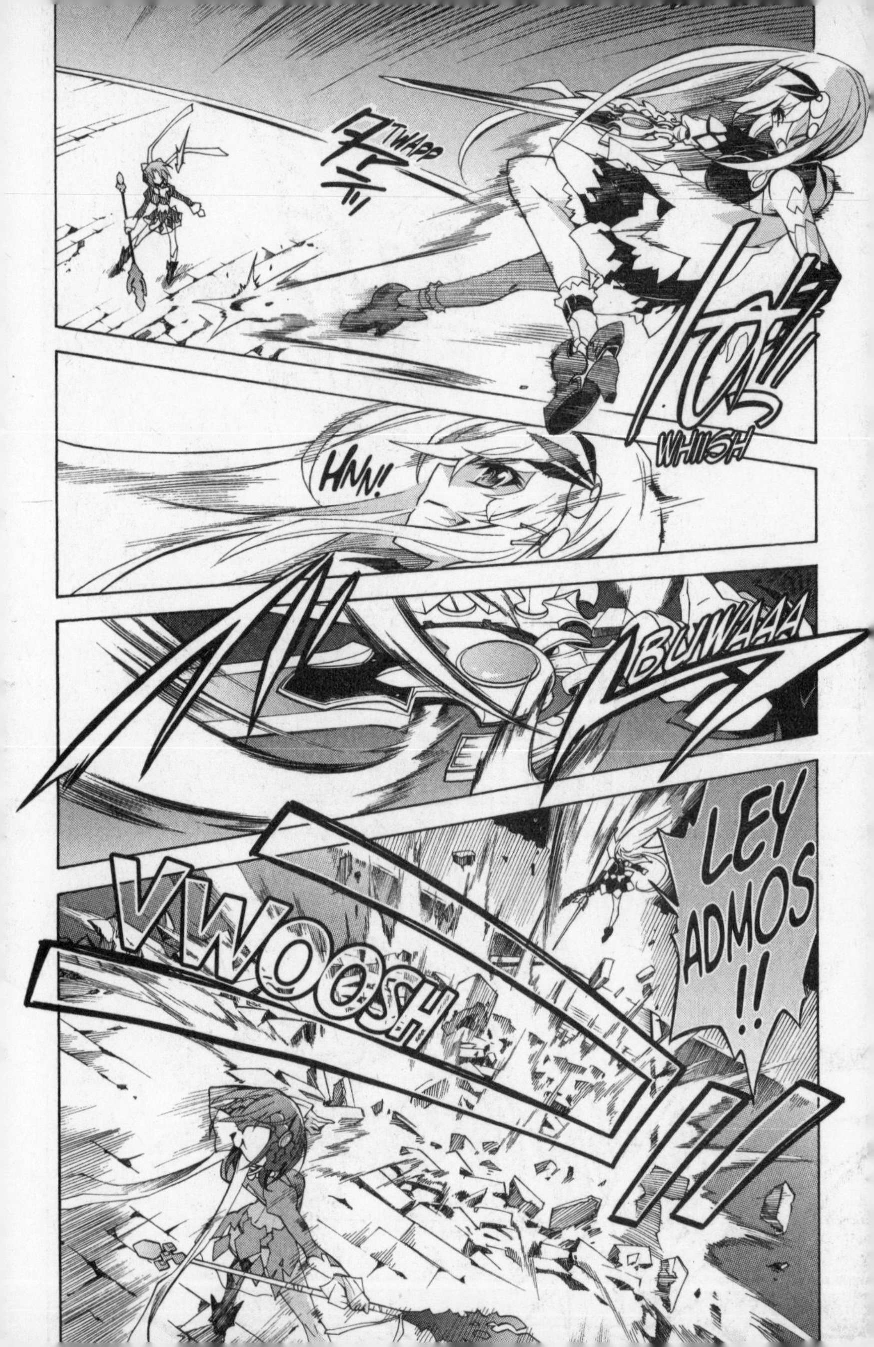
TWAPP
WHIISH
HNN!
BUWAAA
LEY ADMOS!!
VWOOSH

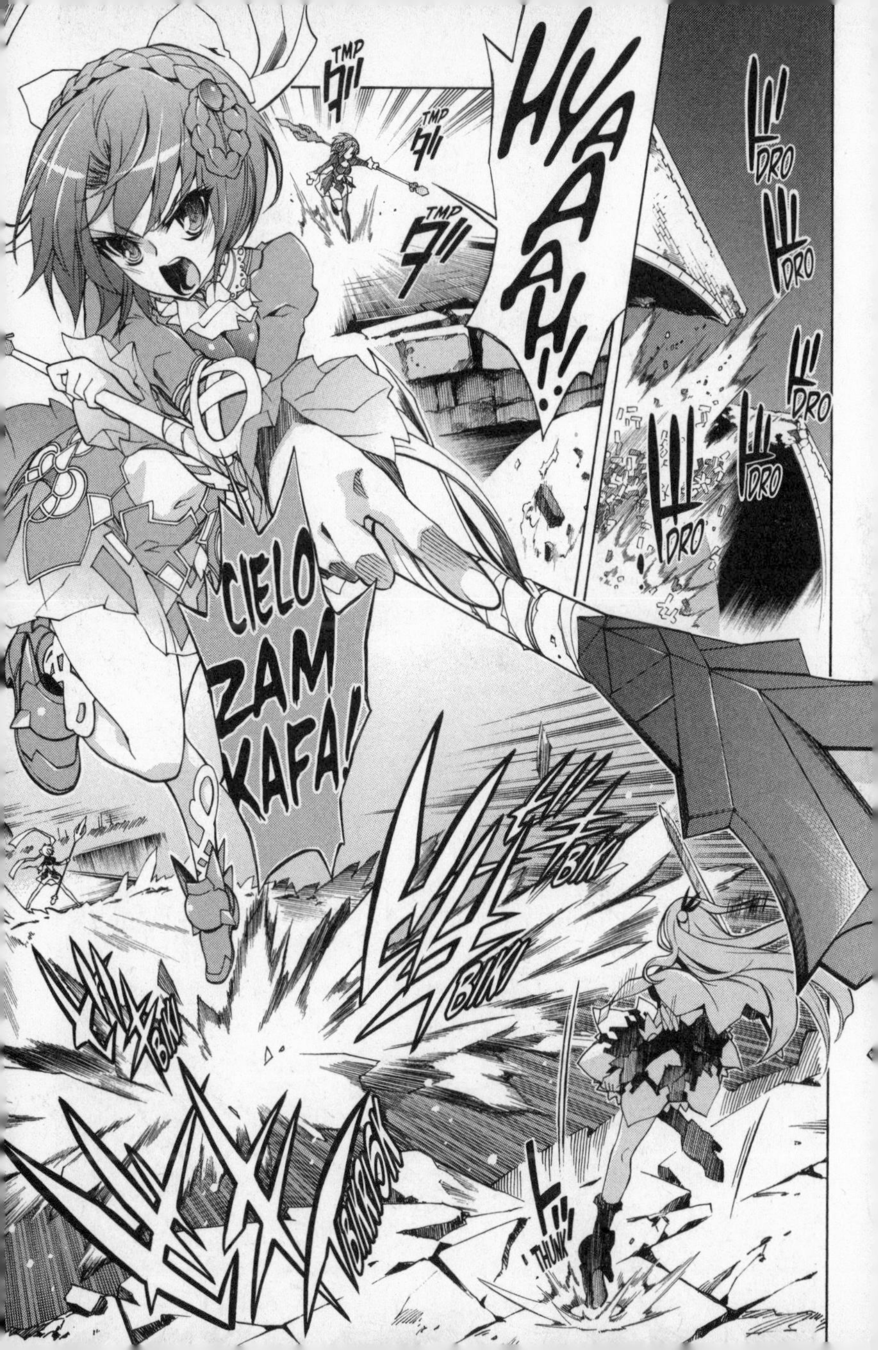

DRO
DRO
DRO
DRO
DRO
HYAAAAH!!
TMP
TMP
TMP
CIELO ZAMKAFA!
BKI
BKI
BKI
THUNK

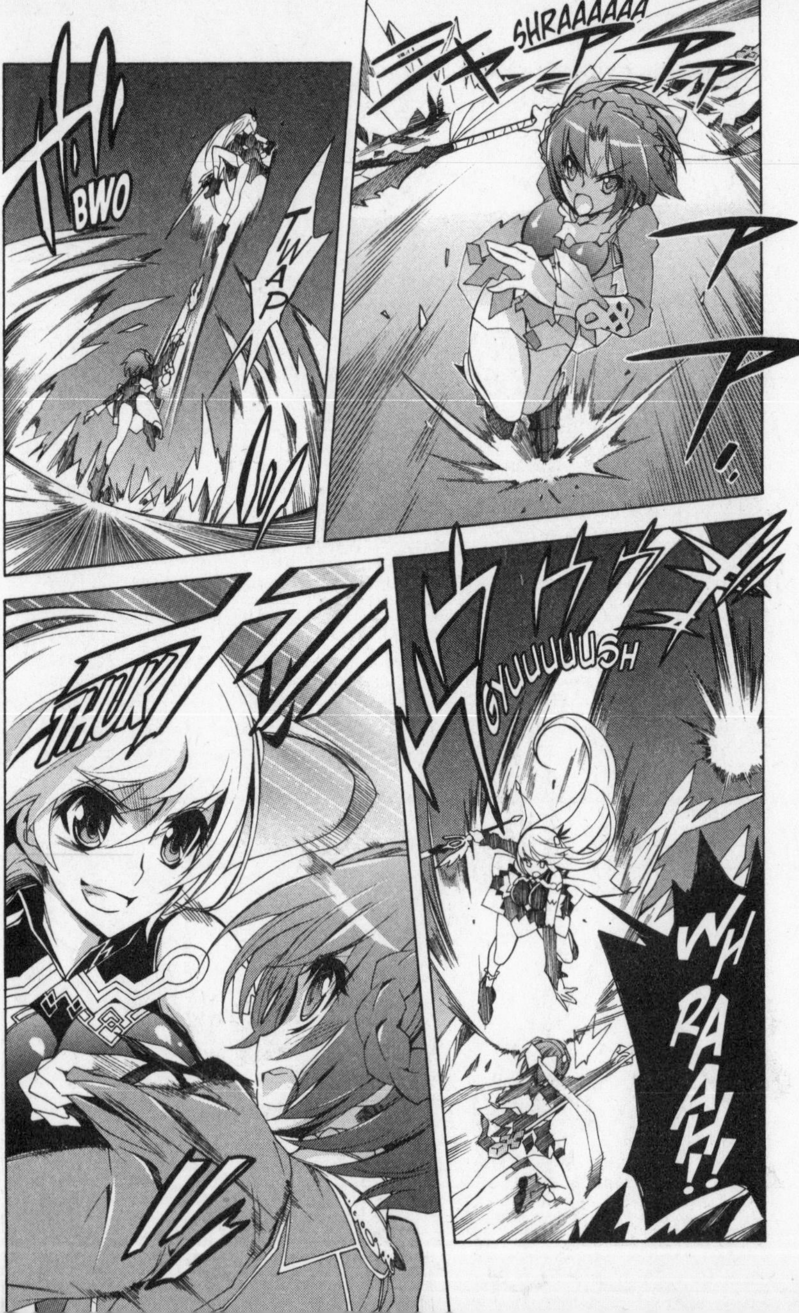
SHRAAAAAA
BWO
TWAP
GYUUUUUSH
WHRAAH!!
THUK!

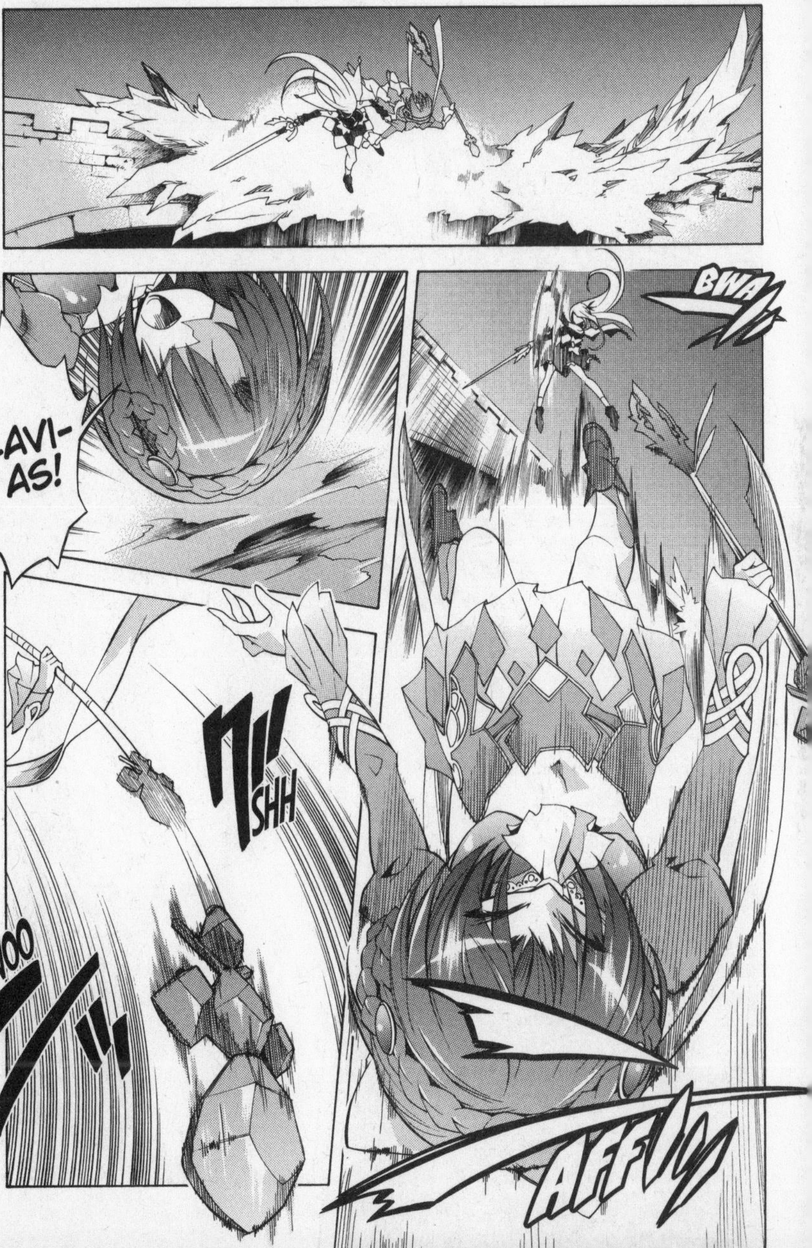
BWA
AFF
LAVI-AS!
SHH
WOO

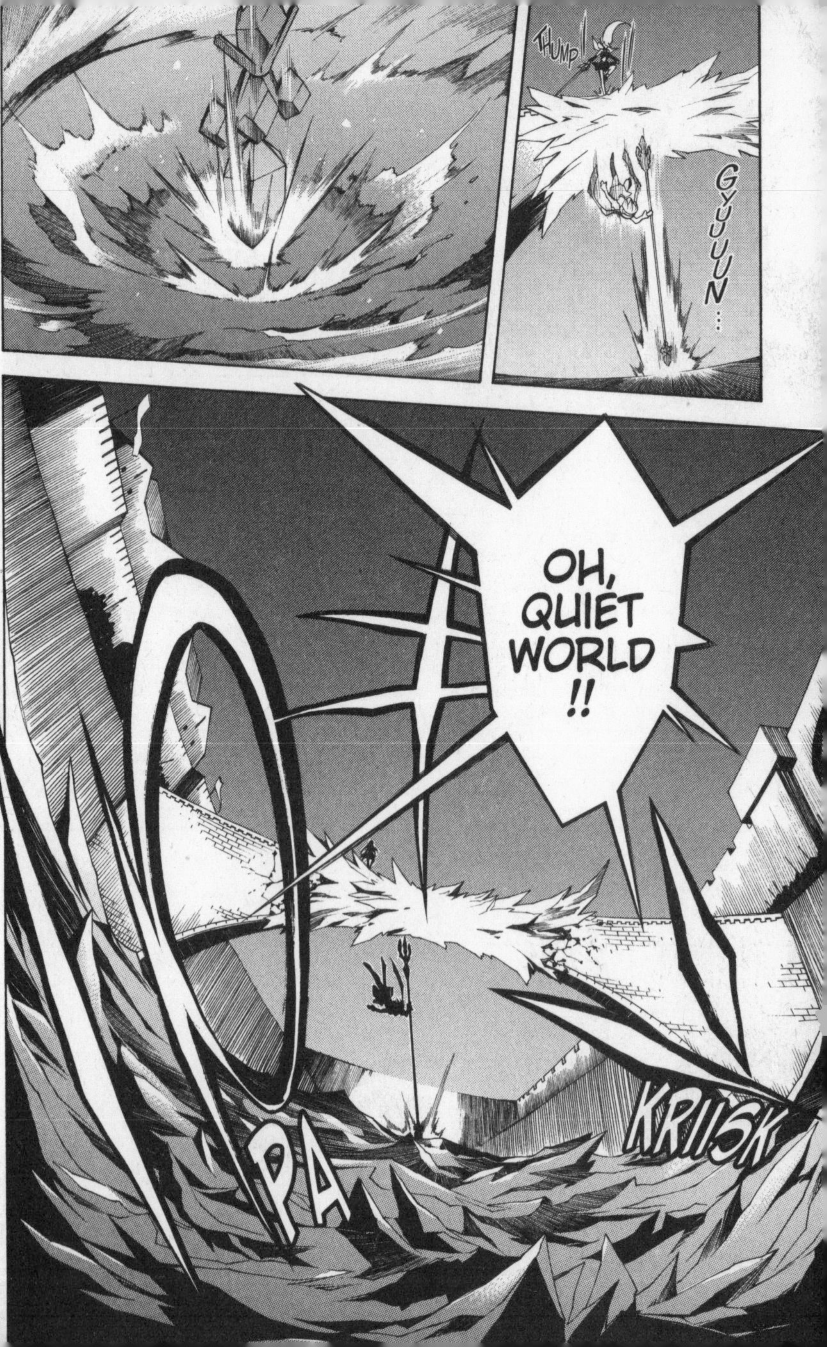
THUMP!
GYUUUUN...
OH, QUIET WORLD!!
KRIISK
PA

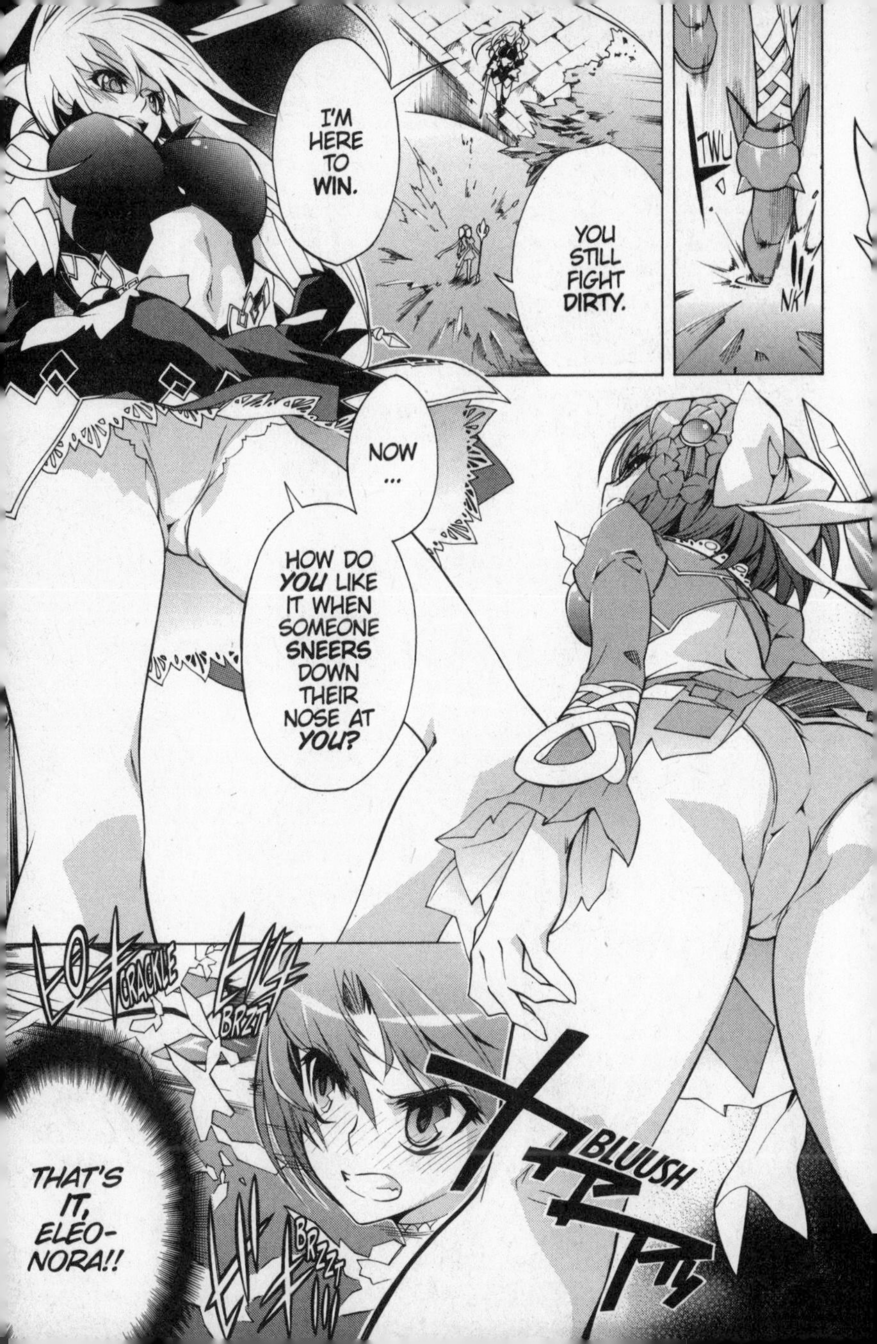
TWU
NK
YOU STILL FIGHT DIRTY.
I'M HERE TO WIN.
NOW ...
HOW DO YOU LIKE IT WHEN SOMEONE SNEERS DOWN THEIR NOSE AT YOU?
BLUUSH
CRACKLE
BRZZT
BRZZT
THAT'S IT, ELEO-NORA!!

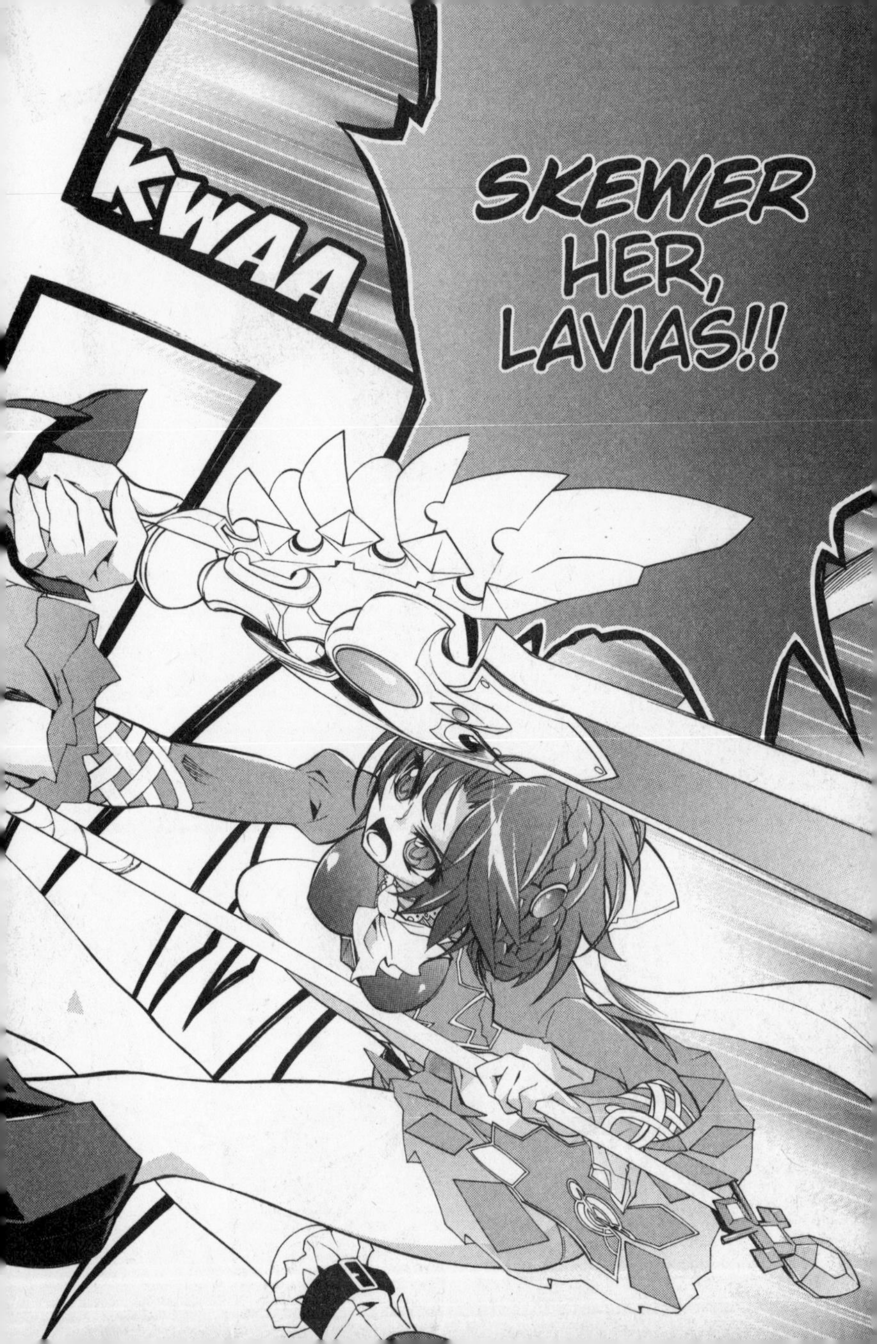
SKEWER HER, LAVIAS!!
KWAA

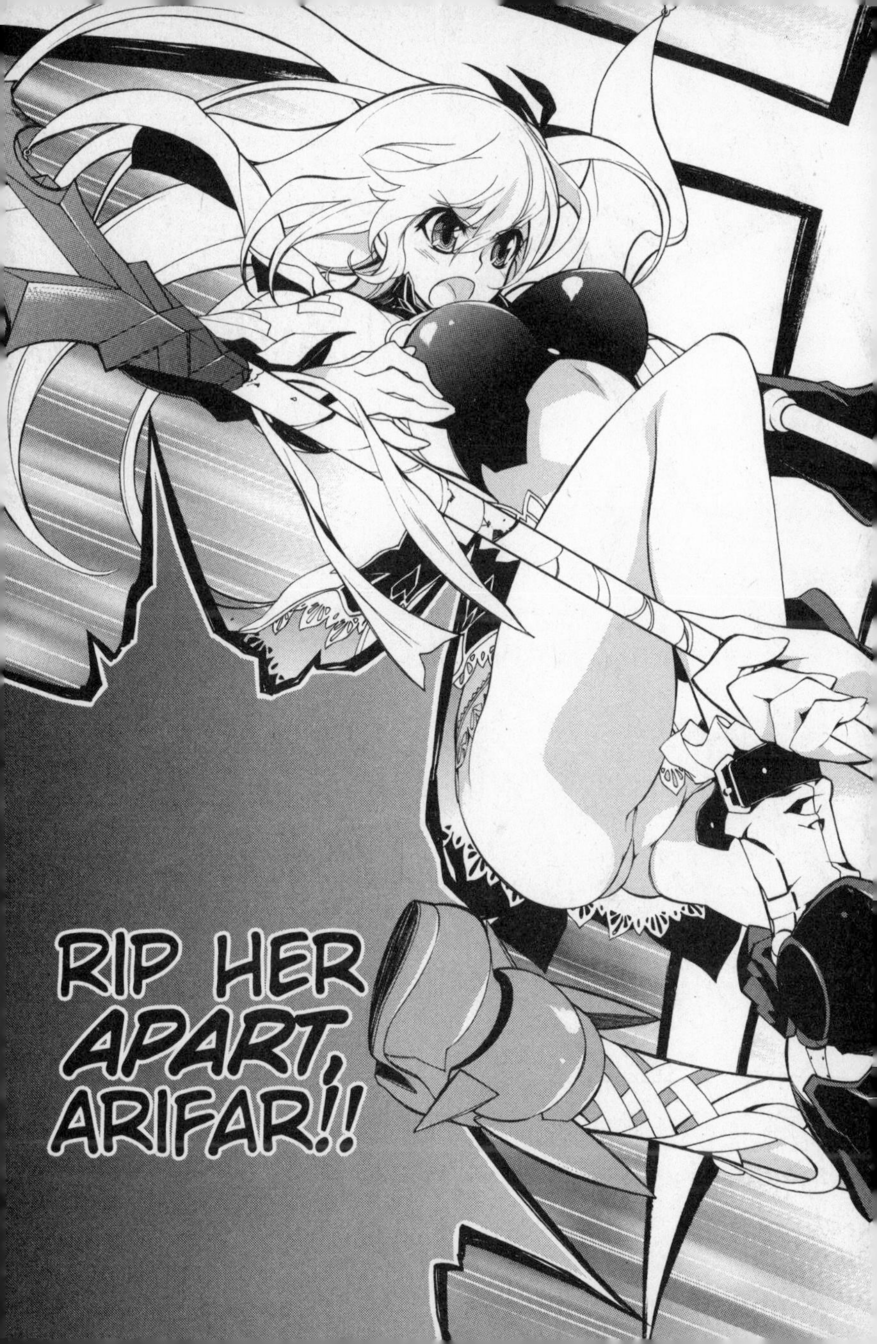
RIP HER APART, ARIFAR!!

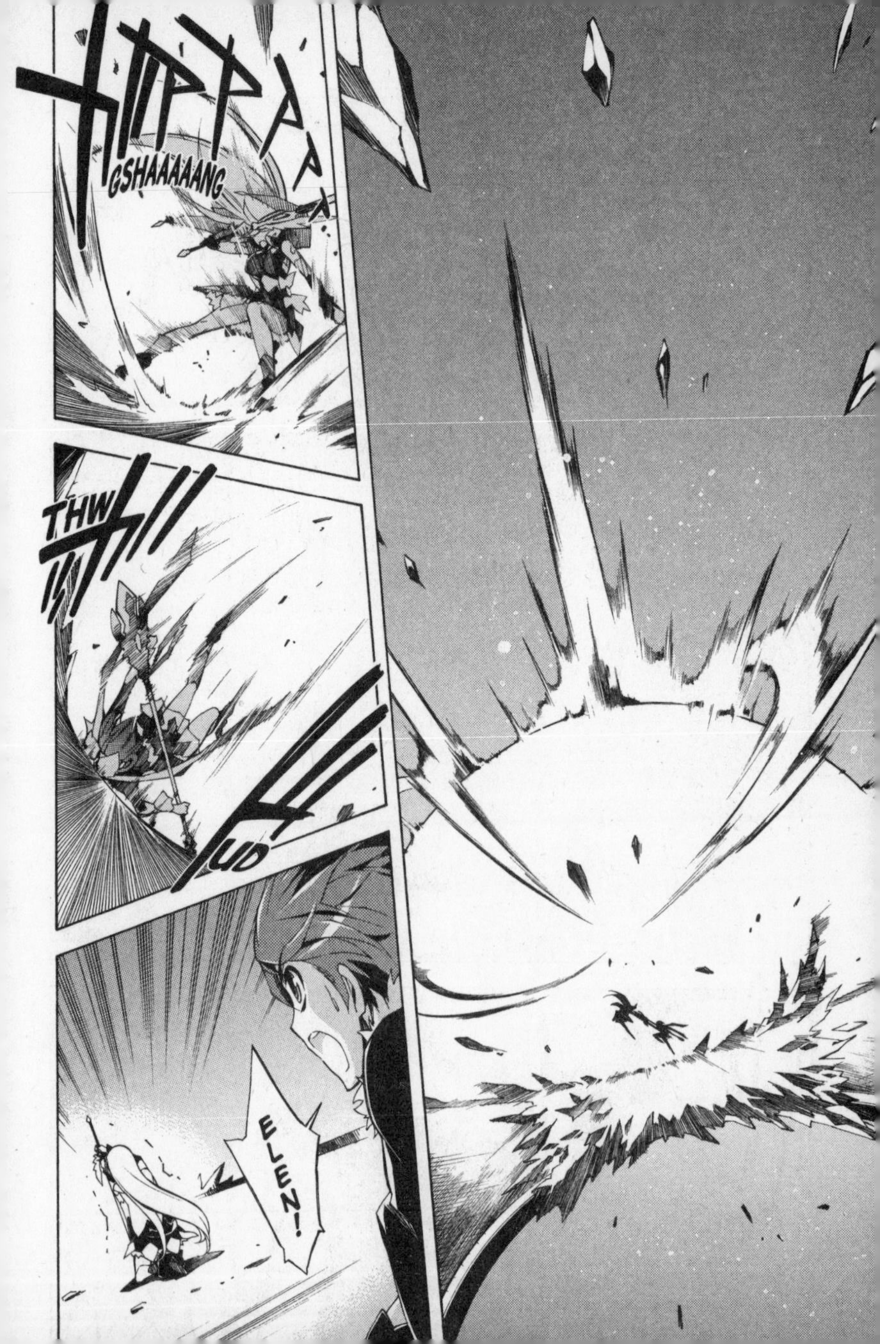

HIPPPAPT
GSHAAAAANG
THWISH
FUD
ELEN!

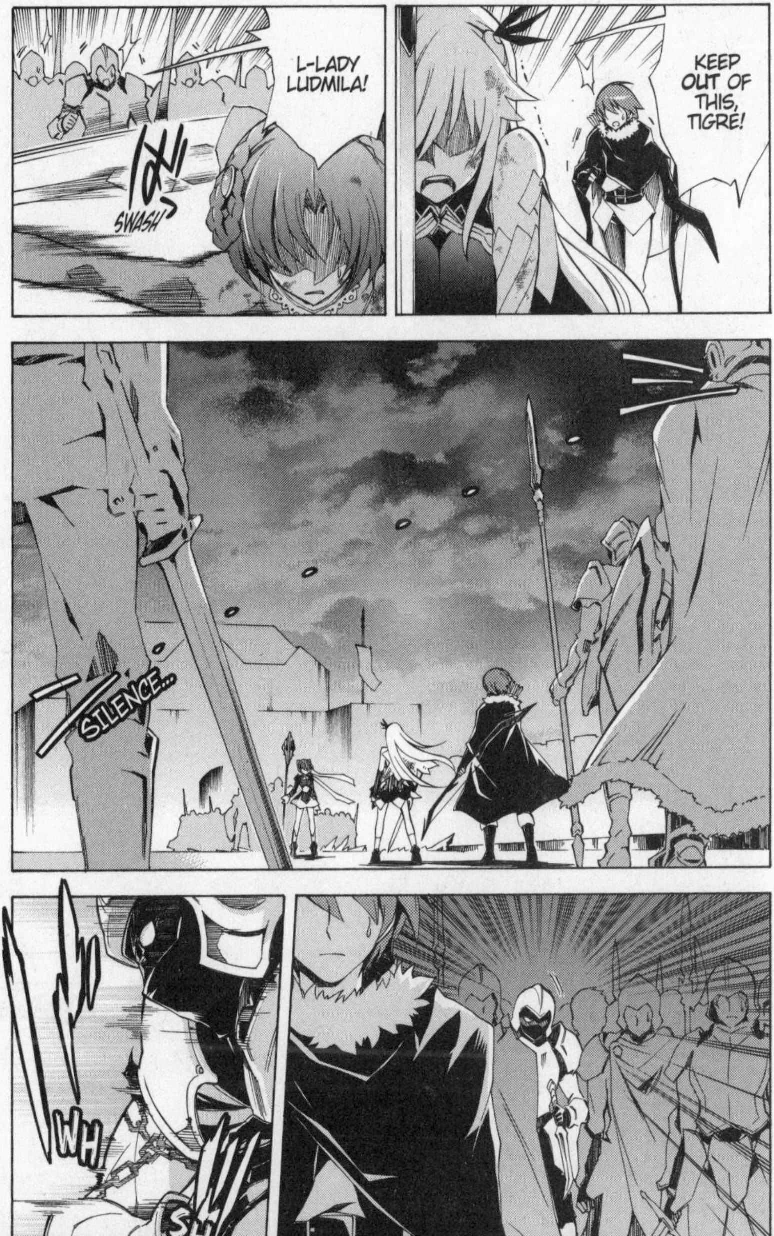
KEEP OUT OF THIS, TIGRE!
L-LADY LUDMILA!
は
SWASH
SILENCE...
WH
SH

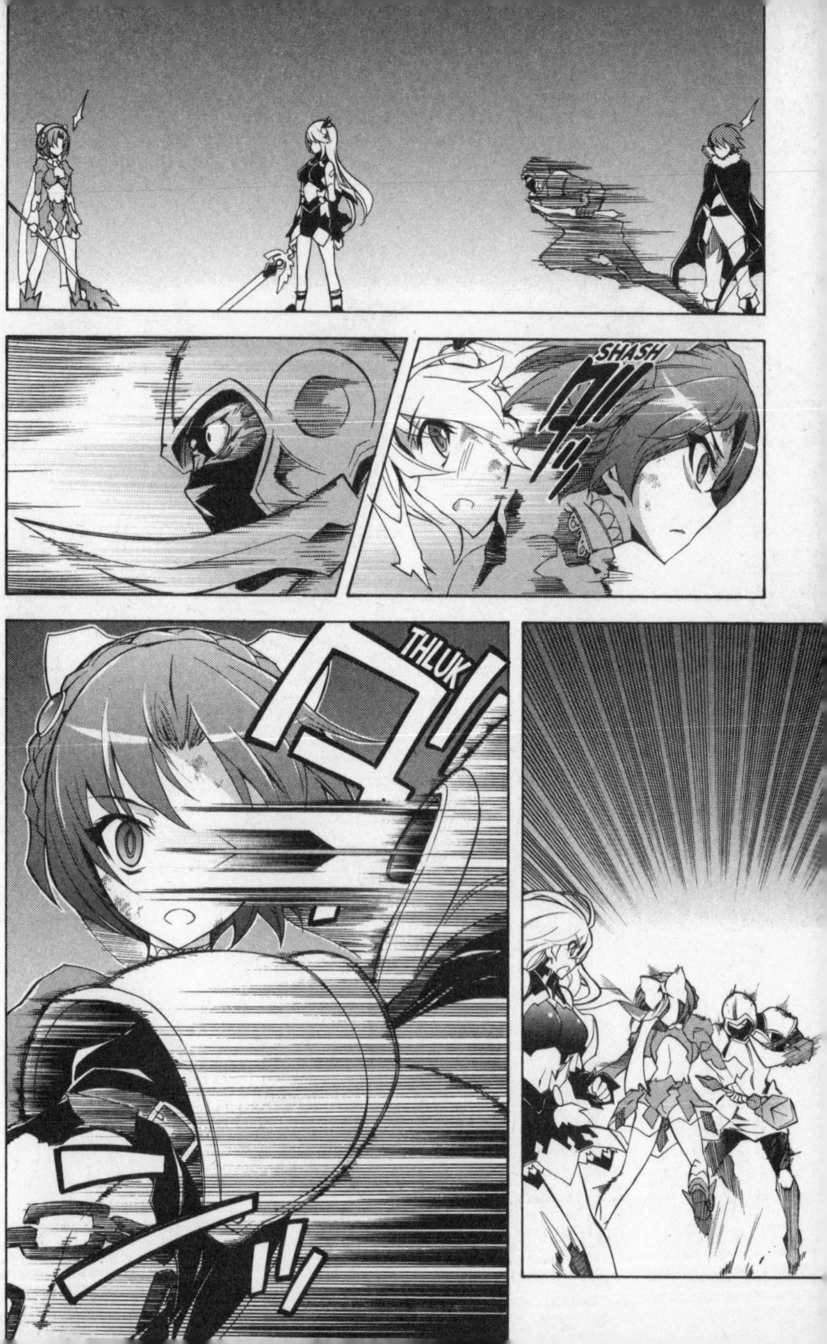
SHASH
THLUK

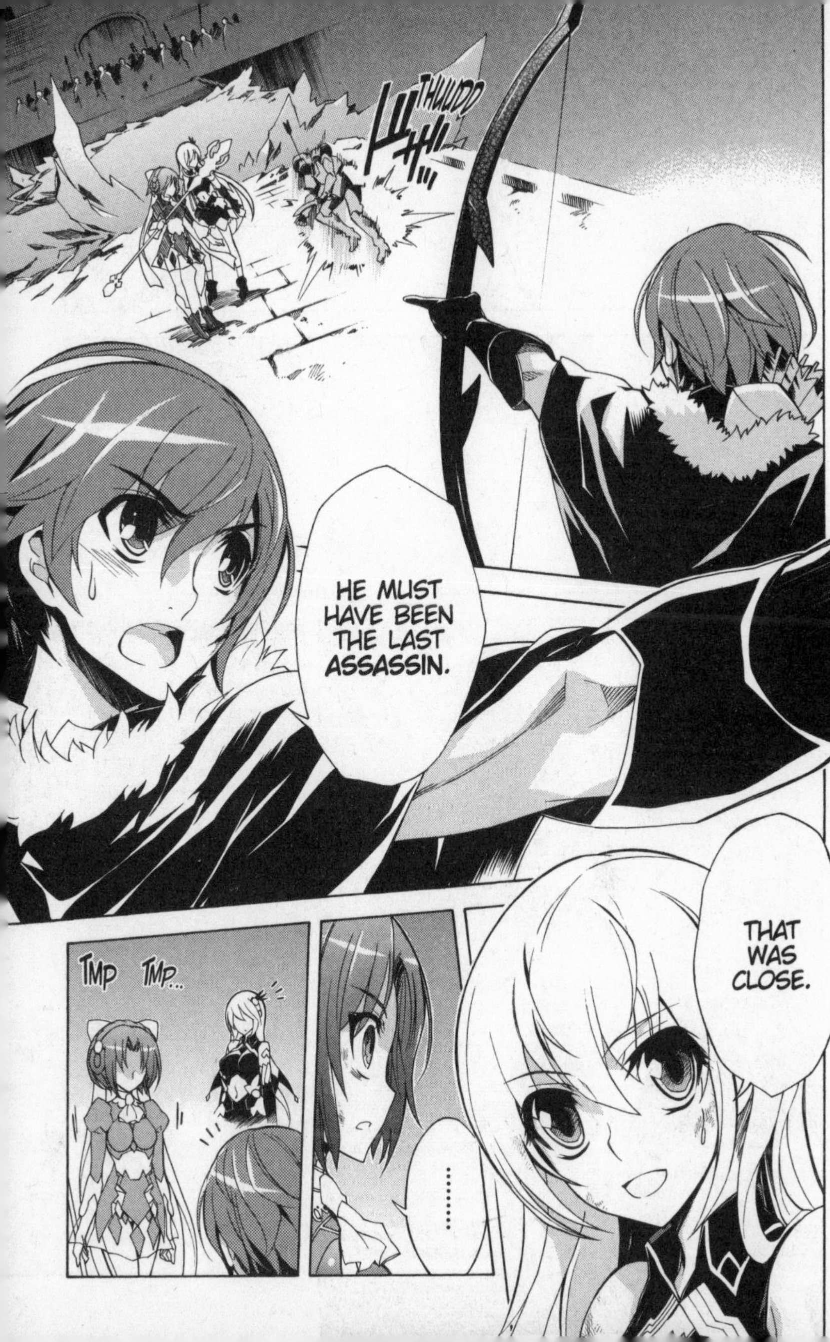
THUUDD
HE MUST HAVE BEEN THE LAST ASSASSIN.
THAT WAS CLOSE.
......
TMP TMP...

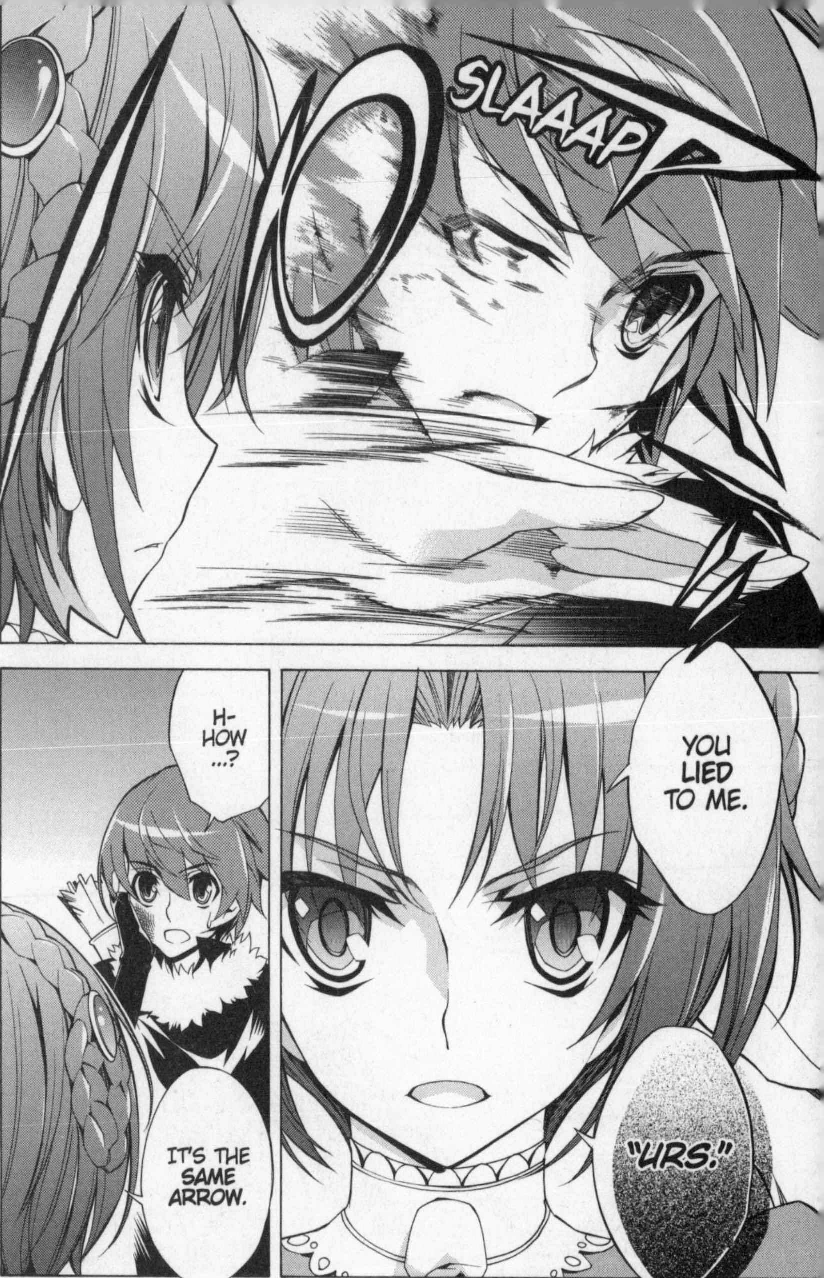
SLAAAP
YOU LIED TO ME.
"URS."
H-HOW ...?
IT'S THE SAME ARROW.

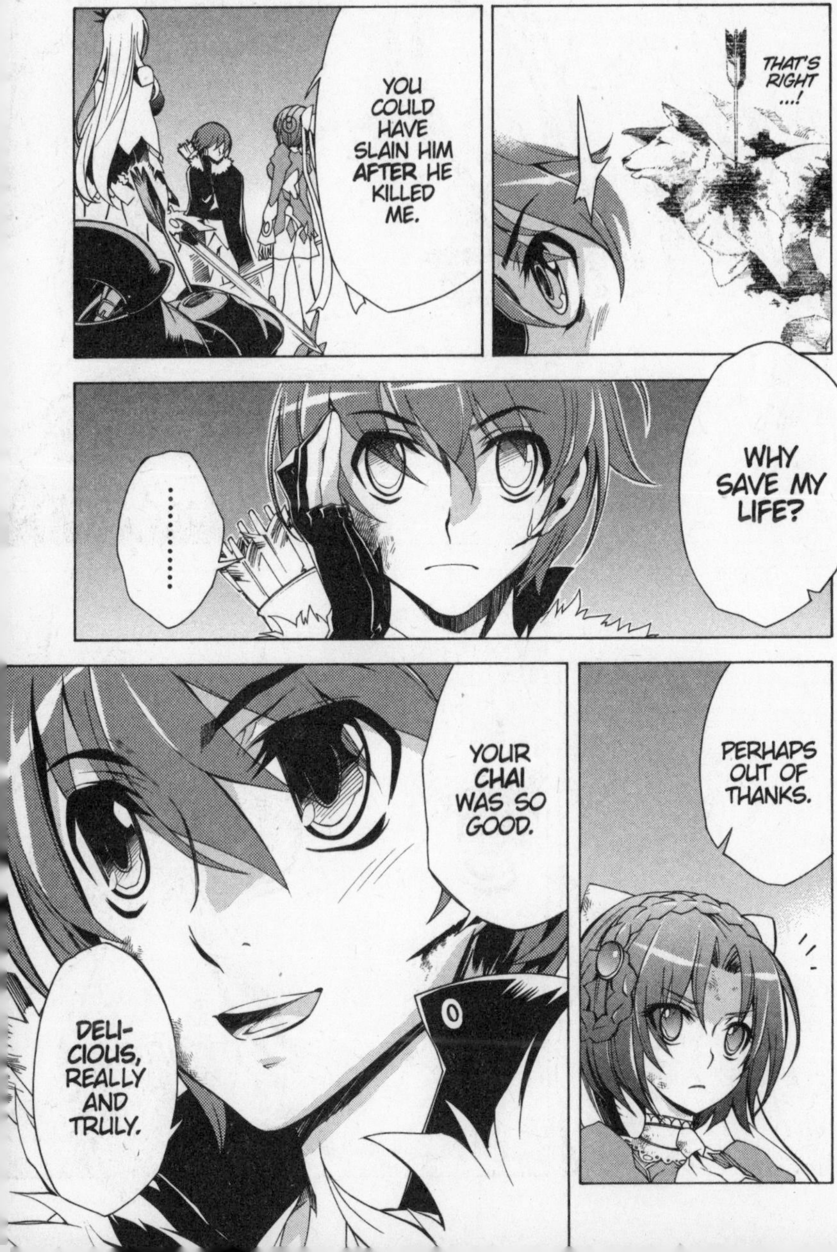
THAT'S RIGHT ...!
YOU COULD HAVE SLAIN HIM AFTER HE KILLED ME.
WHY SAVE MY LIFE?
......
PERHAPS OUT OF THANKS.
YOUR CHAI WAS SO GOOD.
DELI-CIOUS, REALLY AND TRULY.

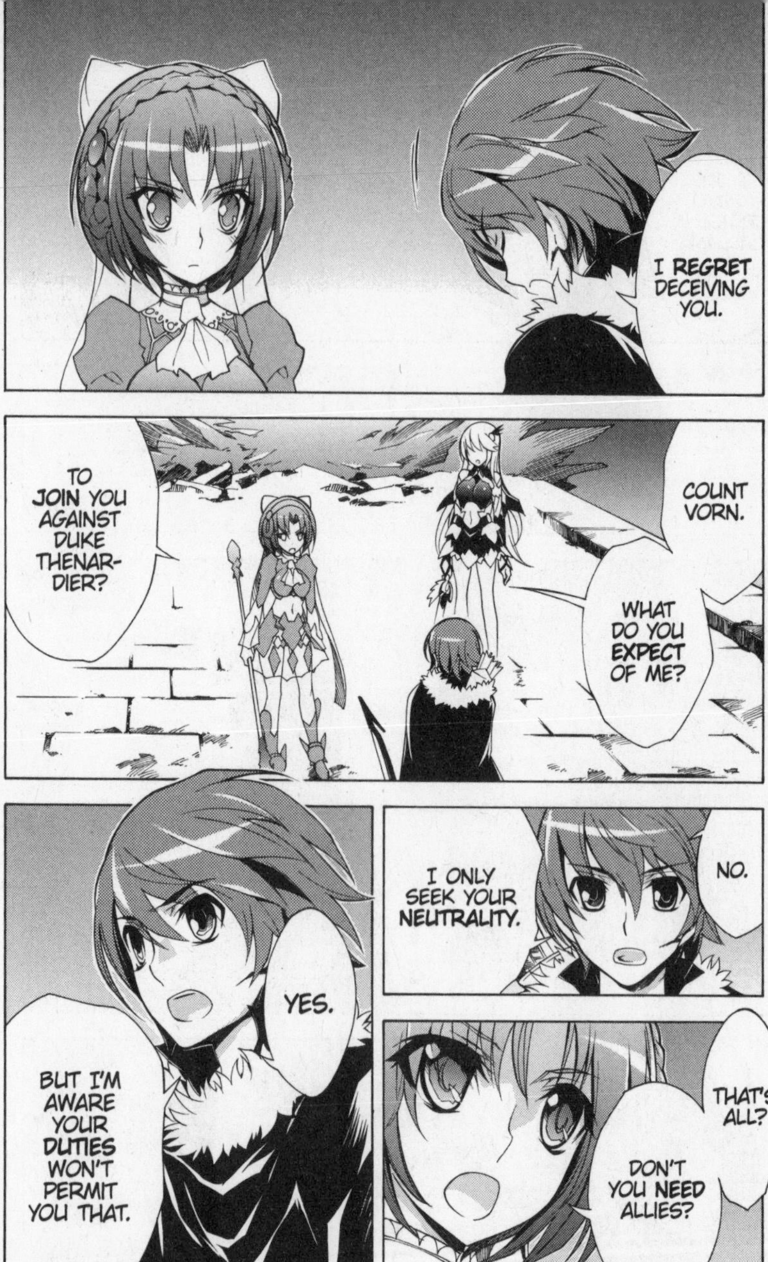
I REGRET DECEIVING YOU.
COUNT VORN.
WHAT DO YOU EXPECT OF ME?
TO JOIN YOU AGAINST DUKE THENARDIER?
NO.
I ONLY SEEK YOUR NEUTRALITY.
THAT'S ALL?
DON'T YOU NEED ALLIES?
YES.
BUT I'M AWARE YOUR DUTIES WON'T PERMIT YOU THAT.

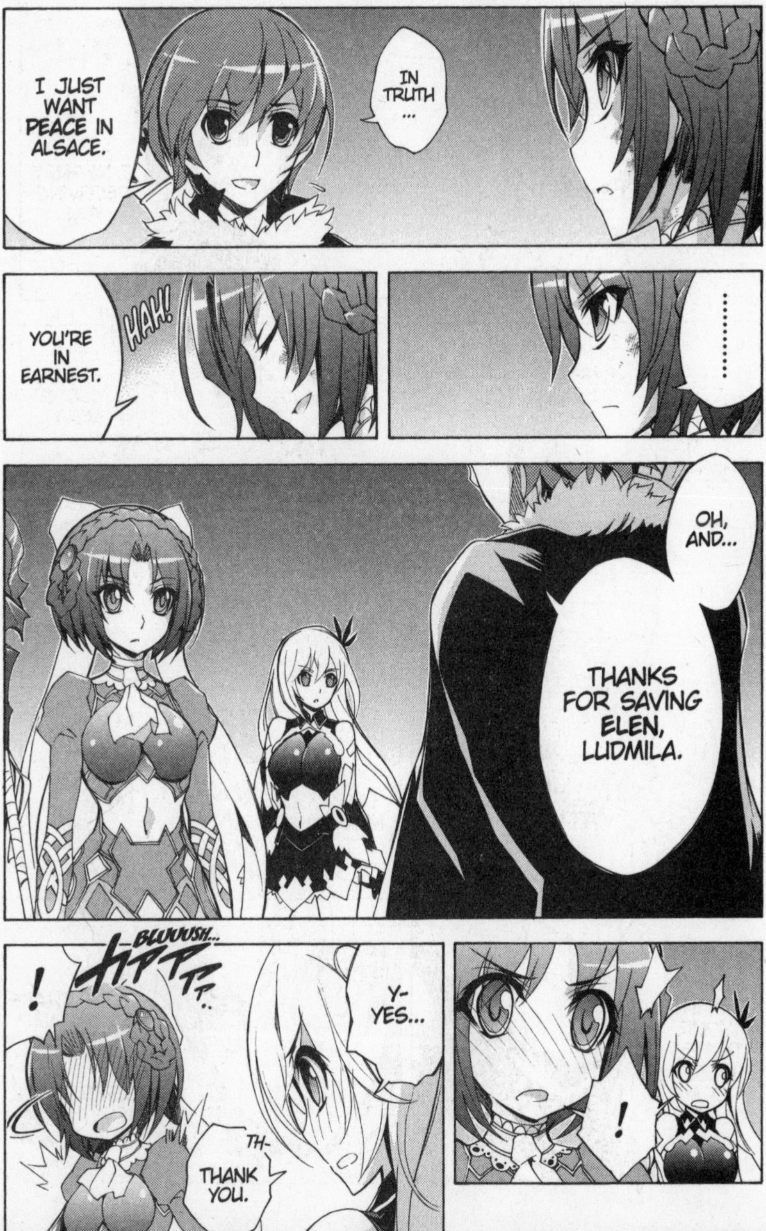
IN TRUTH ...
I JUST WANT PEACE IN ALSACE.
……
HAH!
YOU'RE IN EARNEST.
OH, AND...
THANKS FOR SAVING ELEN, LUDMILA.
!
BLUUUSH...
!
Y- YES...
TH- THANK YOU.

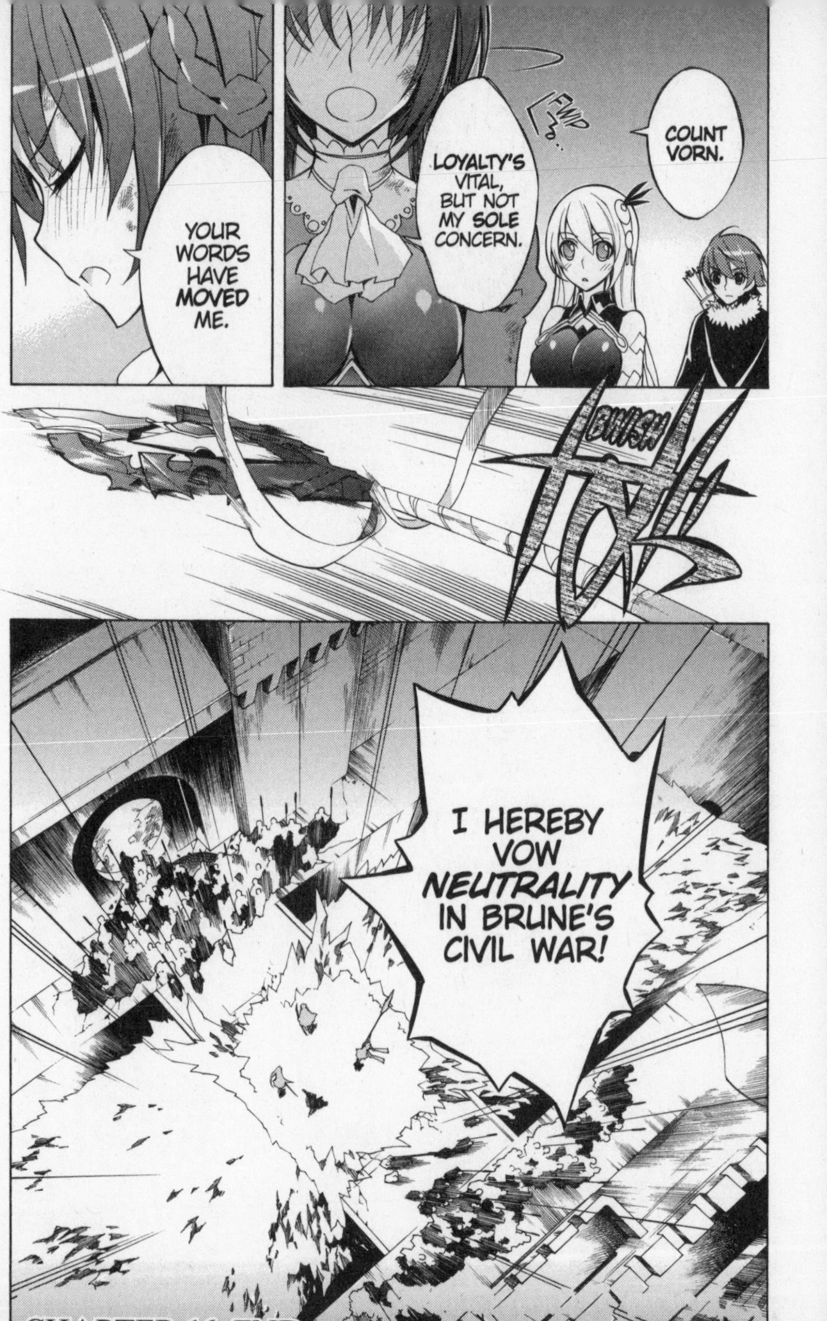
COUNT VORN.
LOYALTY'S VITAL, BUT NOT MY SOLE CONCERN.
YOUR WORDS HAVE MOVED ME.
BWISH
I HEREBY VOW NEUTRALITY IN BRUNE'S CIVIL WAR!

CHAPTER 16: END

魔弾の王と戦姫（ヴァナディース）

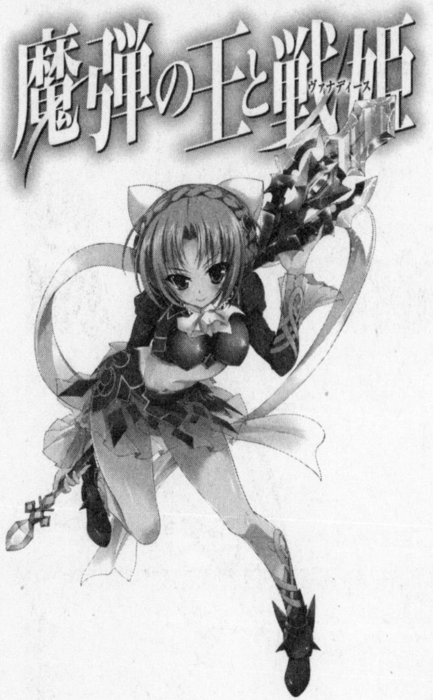

TO BE CONTINUED...

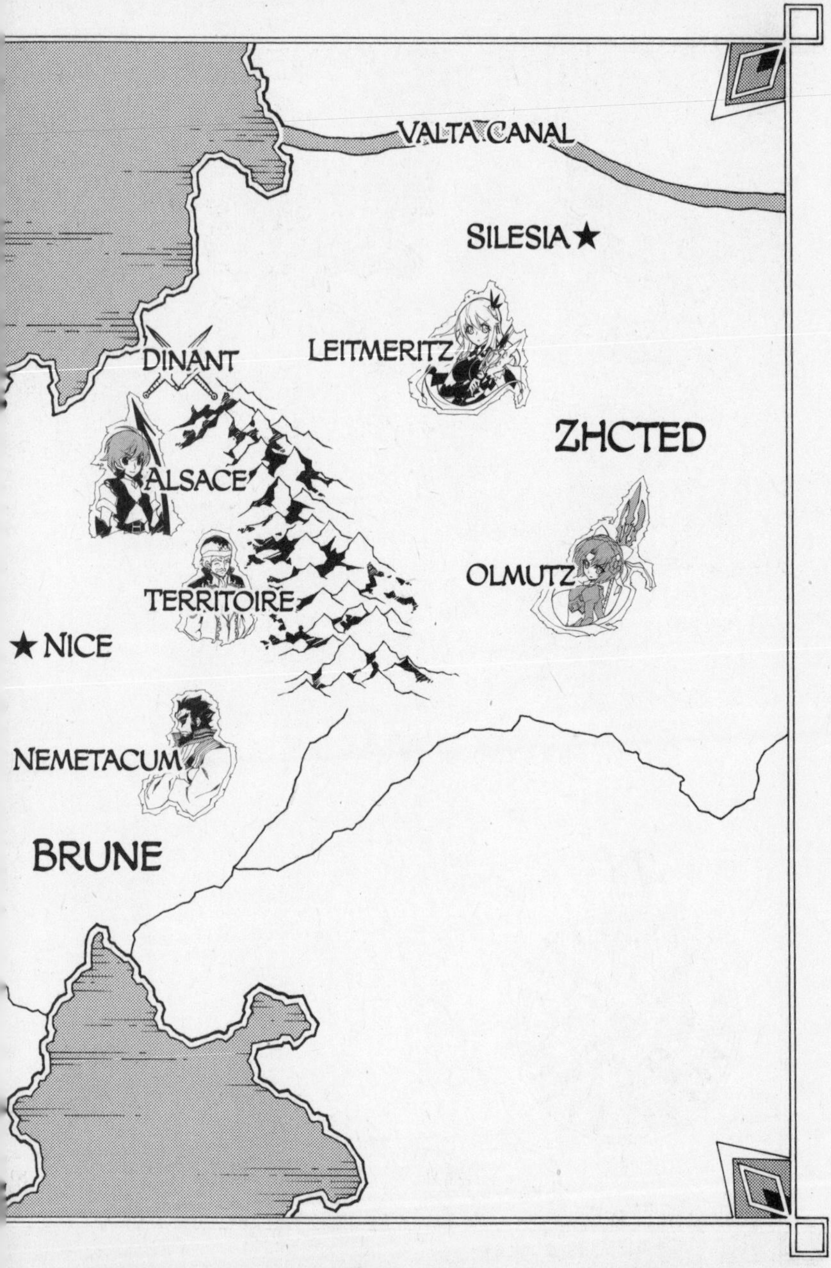
VALTA CANAL
SILESIA
LEITMERITZ
DINANT
ZHCTED
ALSACE
OLMUTZ
TERRITOIRE
NICE
NEMETACUM
BRUNE

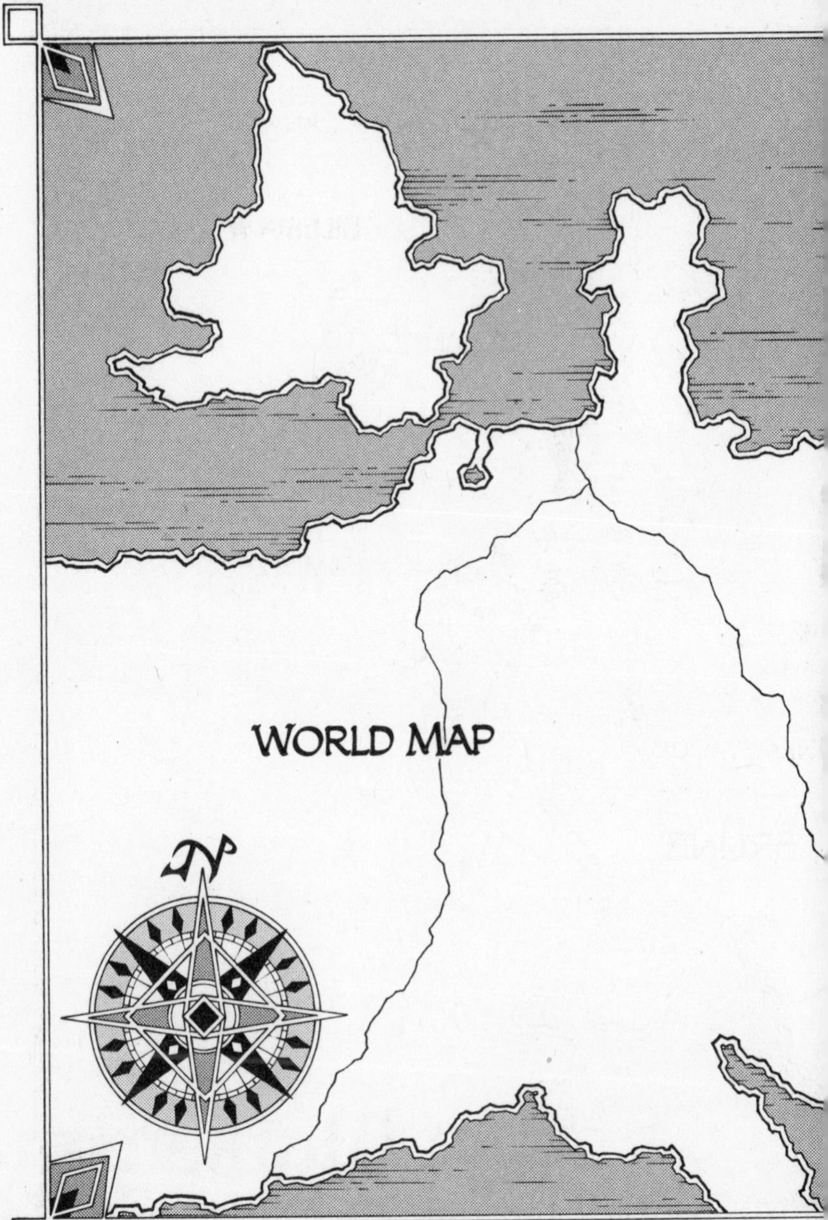
WORLD MAP
N

Lord Marksman
and Vanadis

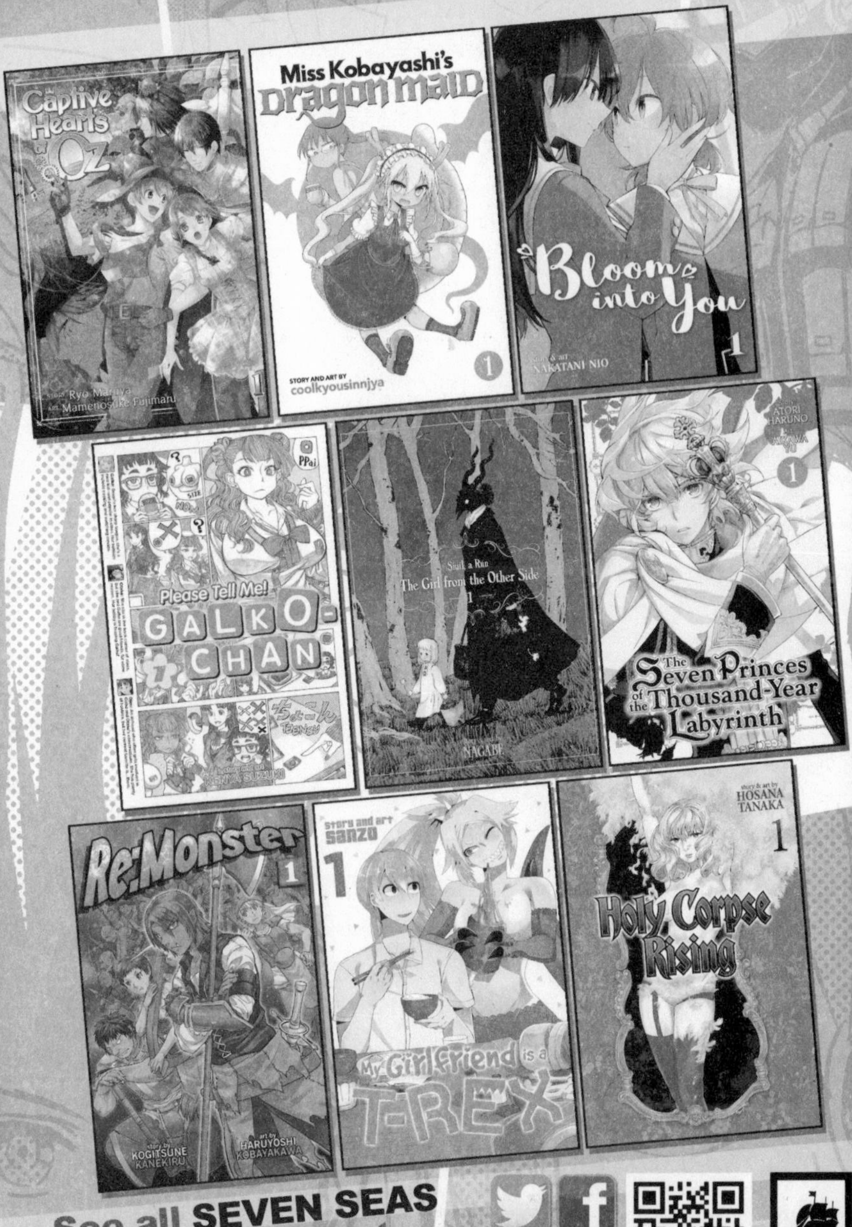
Captive Hearts of Oz
1
story Ryo Maruya
art Mamenosuke Fujimaru
Miss Kobayashi's Dragon Maid
1
STORY AND ART BY
coolkyousinnjya
Bloom into You
1
story & art
NAKATANI NIO
Please Tell Me! GALKO-CHAN
1
KENYA SUZUKI
Siúil, a Rún
The Girl from the Other Side
1
NAGABE
story
ATORI HARUNO
1
The Seven Princes of the Thousand-Year Labyrinth
Re:Monster
1
story by
KOGITSUNE KANEKIRU
art by
HARUYOSHI KOBAYAKAWA
story and art
SANZO
1
My Girlfriend is a T-REX
story & art by
HOSANA TANAKA
1
Holy Corpse Rising

SEVEN SEAS ENTERTAINMENT PRESENTS

Lord Marksman and Vanadis VOL.3

original story by **TSUKASA KAWAGUCHI** / art by **NOBUHIKO YANAI** / character design by **YOSHI☆WO**

TRANSLATION
Elina Ishikawa

ADAPTATION
Rebecca Spinner

LETTERING
James Gaubatz

COVER DESIGN
Nicky Lim

PROOFREADER
Lee Otter
Janet Houck

ASSISTANT EDITOR
Jenn Grunigen

PRODUCTION ASSISTANT
CK Russell

PRODUCTION MANAGER
Lissa Pattillo

EDITOR-IN-CHIEF
Adam Arnold

PUBLISHER
Jason DeAngelis

LORD MARKSMAN AND VANADIS VOL. 3
© Nobuhiko Yanai, Tsukasa Kawaguchi 2013
First published in Japan in 2013 by KADOKAWA CORPORATION, Tokyo.
English translation rights reserved by Seven Seas Entertainment, LLC.
under the license from KADOKAWA CORPORATION, Tokyo.

No portion of this book may be reproduced or transmitted in any form without
written permission from the copyright holders. This is a work of fiction. Names,
characters, places, and incidents are the products of the author's imagination
or are used fictitiously. Any resemblance to actual events, locales, or persons,
living or dead, is entirely coincidental.

Seven Seas books may be purchased in bulk for promotional, educational, or
business use. Please contact your local bookseller or the Macmillan Corporate
and Premium Sales Department at 1-800-221-7945, extension 5442, or by
e-mail at MacmillanSpecialMarkets@macmillan.com.

Seven Seas and the Seven Seas logo are trademarks of
Seven Seas Entertainment, LLC. All rights reserved.

ISBN: 978-1-626924-37-6

Printed in Canada

First Printing: March 2017

10 9 8 7 6 5 4 3 2 1

FOLLOW US ONLINE: **www.gomanga.com**

READING DIRECTIONS

This book reads from *right to left*, Japanese style.
If this is your first time reading manga, you start
reading from the top right panel on each page and
take it from there. If you get lost, just follow the
numbered diagram here. It may seem backwards at
first, but you'll get the hang of it! Have fun!!

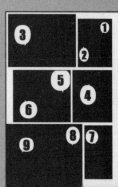